MW01258478

"In an age overflowing with
Goheen has written a book that stands out as essential for Christians today.
By focusing on the heart of the Christian faith, this accessible book offers
both clarity and practical guidance on how the church can embody a missional, counter-formative presence in our cultural moment. As I read, my
heart was stirred for Christ and my imagination ignited with fresh ways
to faithfully participate in God's mission today."

—**John Crawford**, executive pastor of formation, Redemption Tempe

"Michael Goheen's *The Core of the Christian Faith* is a rare and essential
work that masterfully weaves together missiology, theology, worldview, and
ecclesiology to equip the church for its missional calling. It challenges God's
people to bear witness to his kingdom in every sphere of life and culture,
inspiring the church to live as a faithful presence in the world God loves
and is renewing for his glory. This book's wide-ranging insights, delivered
in an engaging and memorable style, will make this my top recommenda-
tion for anyone in our church seeking to integrate their faith into every
aspect of their life."

—**David Fairchild**, lead pastor, Christ Community Church of Houston;
Texas regional director, Acts 29 Network

"In this book, Mike Goheen distills a lifetime of pastoral and academic
wisdom into a compelling vision for the church's role in God's redemptive mission. Built around a fourfold core for discipleship—the gospel,
the biblical story, the identity of a missional people, and a missionary
encounter with culture—it offers a practical and profound framework for
faithful living. A timely and Spirit-filled invitation, this work will inspire
congregations to embrace their vocation for the sake of the world."

—**Summer Montoya**, director of spiritual formation,
Redemption Church Gilbert

Praise for Michael Goheen's Writings

"A powerful presentation of what it takes for a missional church in the twenty-first century to be 'a light to the nations.' Compelling and persuasive!"

—**Gerald H. Anderson**, director emeritus, Overseas
Ministries Study Center

"A much-needed and well-crafted basic text for the biblical study of the missional church."

—**Darrell L. Guder**, Princeton Theological Seminary

"Here is the biblical depth needed for the contemporary church's reflection on and practice of its missional identity."

—**Richard Bauckham**, University of St. Andrews, Scotland (emeritus);
Ridley Hall, Cambridge

"A must-read for anyone who wants a fresh, relevant, challenging vision for the church today."

—**A. Sue Russell**, Asbury Theological Seminary

"One of the most down-to-earth, practical guidebooks I have read on how all so-called ordinary Christians can and should be playing their part in God's mission."

—**Christopher J. H. Wright**, Langham Partnership;
author of *The Mission of God*

THE CORE

OF THE

CHRISTIAN FAITH

THE CORE

OF THE

CHRISTIAN

FAITH

LIVING THE GOSPEL
FOR THE SAKE OF THE WORLD

MICHAEL W. GOHEEN

BrazosPress

a division of Baker Publishing Group
Grand Rapids, Michigan

Published by Brazos Press
a division of Baker Publishing Group
Grand Rapids, Michigan
BrazosPress.com

Printed in the United States of America

Library of Congress Cataloging-in-Publication Data
Names: Goheen, Michael W., 1955– author.
Title: The core of the Christian faith : living the gospel for the sake of the world / Michael W. Goheen.
Description: Grand Rapids, Michigan : Brazos Press, a division of Baker Publishing Group, [2025] | Includes bibliographical references.
Identifiers: LCCN 2024052070 | ISBN 9781540964793 (paperback) | ISBN 9781540968296 (casebound) | ISBN 9781493447503 (ebook) | ISBN 9781493447510 (pdf)
Subjects: LCSH: Bible—Introductions. | Missions—Theory. | Christianity and culture. | Theology, Doctrinal.
Classification: LCC BS475.3 .G64 2025 | DDC 220.6/1—dc23/eng/20250107
LC record available at https://lccn.loc.gov/2024052070

Cover design by Paula Gibson

Baker Publishing Group publications use paper produced from sustainable forestry practices and postconsumer waste whenever possible.

25   26   27   28   29   30   31   7   6   5   4   3   2   1

To Andre and Barb Van Ryk

CONTENTS

PREFACE

This book represents the fruit of a long pastoral and academic journey. I will turn seventy years old around the time that this book is published. Its content is the culmination of over forty years of pastoring and teaching aimed at forming congregations that faithfully live the gospel for the sake of the world. It is a concentrated and popular summary of what I believe to be the very core of the Christian faith that has the power, by the Spirit, to form and shape God's people for their vocation.

After wrestling with the question of which audience I should address, I decided finally to write a shorter book at a more popular level for the serious church member. Moreover, I have designed it as one component of a discipleship tool that can be used in local congregations. There are four parts—the gospel, the biblical story, missional church, and missionary encounter with culture—that make up the core of our theological education at the Missional Training Center. Accompanying this book are a series of videos and other materials that can be used together in small groups as part of the formation process in local congregations. I am thankful to Cory Willson for securing the funds for these videos. These materials can be found at www.missionworldview.com and on YouTube.

ACKNOWLEDGMENTS

There are two people that I want to single out to thank. The first is Jim Kinney, executive vice-president at Baker Publishing Group. He commissioned and edited the first book I published along with Craig Bartholomew—*The Drama of Scripture*—over twenty years ago. This is the ninth book that I have worked on together with Jim. He has been wise and patient, and I am thankful for the role he has played in my academic and publishing career. The second is Doug Loney. Doug was my academic dean many years ago at a university where we were both faculty members. Since then, Doug has played a role in editing and wordsmithing a number of my books. I wanted this book to read well at a popular level, and Doug has immersed himself in the material of this book to help me with this task. His work has been sacrificial and important. I consider both men friends and am thankful for their selfless ministry.

At this point in my career, with many more years behind me than ahead of me, I find myself reflecting often with gratitude on those who have mentored and formed me either personally or by their writing. Of those still living whose work has shaped this book, I mention Al Wolters, Tom Wright, Richard Bauckham, Norman Shepherd, Michael Williams, Chris Wright, and Jim Skillen. Their influence on this book will be evident. I often tell my students that we are all formed intellectually by trusting someone. These are some of the people I have trusted to form me. And of course, the most important place goes to my wife, Marnie, who has truly been my partner in ministry for forty-six years.

Over the past twelve years we have welcomed over 160 church leaders into our living room at Missional Training Center (Phoenix) to wrestle with the issues contained in this book. Further, we have been able to spend extended times of leadership training in Brazil, Hungary, and Chile working through many aspects of this book with gifted leaders in each of those places. Different cultural contexts bring fresh insight and wisdom. I consider it a tremendous privilege to learn from such fine, committed leaders who have so much wisdom in what is needed to nurture faithful congregations. I have been formed more by them than they have been by me. Much of what is written in this book is the fruit of interacting with and listening to them.

I am grateful for those in the body of Christ who steward their gifts and resources to serve Christ and his people faithfully. Andre and Barb Van Ryk are a couple who do this well. I am thankful for the way they bless our local congregation in Surrey, BC, and for their friendship, selfless love, and wise counsel to our family. I am honored to dedicate this book to them.

CHAPTER 1

An Opening Appeal

*The evangelical Church in the U.S. over the last five decades has failed to
form its adherents into disciples. So there is a great hollowness. All that was
needed to cause the implosion that we have seen was a sufficiently provoca-
tive stimulus. And that stimulus came.*

—James Ernest, quoted in Peter Wehner, "The Evangelical Church Is
Breaking Apart"

CULTURAL CAPTIVITY

I have many friends and students who teach children—I applaud both
their gifts and their patience!—and for them it is not unusual to deal with
tearful students in class. But for me this was new: the adult student who
sat with me and his fellow students in my living room was no child, and
yet he was weeping openly in the midst of our discussion. And others
wept with him.

The tears had come as this man—a mature, gifted, and committed
pastor—tried to express the pain and frustration of attempting to lead a
congregation that had lately become divided on many current issues, to
the extent that the health of this church was in peril. The chief area of
contention on this pastor's mind on this particular day was the political
divide: "No matter what I say," he choked out, "I am accused of unfaithfulness. Those on the right think I am a socialist. Those on the left think

1

I identify with the powerful and don't care for justice. When I attempt to affirm the genuine insights and to critique the idolatry of either side, I am attacked from *both* sides. They just can't hear me. Their commitment to ideology runs so deep I can't get through to them. I have to wonder, Is it worth it?"

During the academic years from 2020 to 2022 I met with more tearful students than I had ever before encountered in more than three decades of teaching. At the time I was teaching some seventy-five church leaders in five different cohorts, and almost every week someone would break down emotionally as they expressed the burden of ministry.

At that time, three cultural streams were flowing together in the United States where I was teaching: (1) We had been living in a pandemic with government-mandated COVID-19 restrictions that limited many cherished freedoms; (2) there had been a number of violent and even deadly confrontations between the police and Black Americans, often fueled by racism and widely reported in the media; and (3) the country was becoming more polarized as political rhetoric grew ever more radical. These developments in the life of the country were exposing some enduring and deeply held idolatries in the culture—and in the evangelical church. Division and conflict were rife even among those with a shared faith in Jesus. As the church leaders in our classes had attempted to challenge their congregations about these issues from the Word of God, they were in too many cases discovering that their parishioners' hearts and minds had been shaped by the idols of Western culture more than by the Bible. Christianity, it seemed, had become to some of their members more of a civil religion than the faith of Scripture. These leaders' attempts to shine the light of the gospel on the dark places of culture had been met with pushback, accusations, and sometimes angry departures. Pastors often found themselves the targets of everyone's anger, condemned by factions on both sides of a given issue.

COVID restrictions are behind us. Racism and its poison fruit remain. Political and ideological divisions today seem deeper and more bitter than ever, now expanding beyond politics to become competing comprehensive civil-religious stories. And other powerful idols crowd the public square and jostle for sovereignty there.

In my classes now the tears come less frequently than they did then. But the experience of those years highlighted for me the truth that suffering is the *normal* lot of faithful leaders in local congregations, *if* they take seriously their responsibility to call out cultural idolatry for what it is and to form the people of God into the new humanity by the truth of the gospel. Idols push back hard! Scripture is clear that the powers that stand behind idolatry do not easily give up their prey.

What I observed in our classes in Phoenix is a small window into the situation in which all of us as believers and leaders find ourselves, not only in the United States but everywhere in the world. It wasn't unique to that time but comes to us every year. We shouldn't be surprised: First Peter and Revelation testify vividly that this has been the experience of the church from its inception. *The powerful idolatry of our culture surrounds us.* Today the idols of autonomous freedom, identity, technology, nationalism, economic growth, consumption, hedonism, sexual freedom, political ideologies—elements embedded in our modern and postmodern humanist story—*all* pervade our culture, *all* claim our allegiance, *all* seek to betray us into unbelief.

It is nothing less than tragic when the church uncritically takes these idolatries on board. Instead of being the people of God's kingdom "shining like stars" in a dark world (Phil. 2:14–16), those in the church sometimes look just like their non-Christian neighbors. This leads many in the unbelieving world to discredit the gospel and the Christian faith. The past decade has seen a steady stream of editorials accusing the evangelical church of betraying its own faith. Some are written by thoughtful Christians expressing their pain and lament, but just as often the writers are people looking on from outside the Christian faith, who dismiss the church as hypocritical. It is no doubt true that the good that God is doing in and through the church is often forgotten. Nevertheless, there is too much painful truth that must not be ignored.

This should be a wake-up call to every Christian. It is Christ's name we bear: When our reputation is impugned it is his name dragged through the mud. Moreover, we are failing in the very role given us in the biblical story—to be what our neighbors glimpse of the new creation, of what God intends for human life. We are here, in the time and place given us by God, not for ourselves only but *for the sake of the unbelieving world.* Our accommodation to idolatrous currents and consequent cultural captivity is failure to live out the vocation God has given us.

Equally disturbing is the impact that this accommodation has had on young people raised in it. A Gallup poll conducted a few years back, revealing a general decline in church attendance in the United States, shows also that the rate of decline accelerates sharply in increasingly younger generations within the church.[1] And these young former church-goers are not leaving the church primarily because of what they perceive as conflict between the Bible and culture. (That was perhaps a greater problem a generation ago, when many young people in university, for example, felt that belief in the Bible was incompatible with science.) Today, the "disconnect" that dismays many young people is more likely to be between what they read in the Bible and what they see in the church's way of life.

Yet, of course, this is not just a story of failure! The resurrection has taken place, and God's Spirit is at work even in the darkest moments in the church's history—and there have been far darker moments than this! This cannot be only about gloom, negativity, and pessimism. I see many leaders in the church willing to humbly wrestle with Scripture and our contemporary cultural currents. They provide a glimpse into the reality that God's Spirit is very much alive. The many congregations I visit and believers I meet make it clear to me that God is very much at work in our churches. Many people not only experience the power of the new creation changing their lives but long for more of it. They recognize that to follow Christ is to align themselves in the spiritual battle between the kingdom of God and the kingdom of darkness. They often know that they need a much deeper grasp of Scripture and their cultural setting to be faithful. Moreover, much of the negativity about the church is simply unfair. The good that the church has accomplished is often ignored as its failures are highlighted.

This does not negate the fact that the departing youths see a real gap between what evangelicals say they believe and how they live. We must face the problem of our captivity to cultural idolatry.

MASSIVE CATECHESIS FAILURE

James Ernest attributes the gap between what Christians say and what they do to a "massive discipleship failure caused by massive catechesis fail-ure."[2] The evangelical church has not taken seriously its task to teach and disciple its people. Over the years we became hollow. When the powerful idolatries of our culture coalesced to exert pressure, we imploded. This is what happened during the recent convergence of COVID, strife over racist incidents, and political polarization.

We need to commit ourselves once more to formation and discipleship, to catechesis and teaching. Dallas Willard believes that "the greatest issue facing the world today . . . is whether those who . . . are identified as 'Christians' will become disciples—students, apprentices, practitioners—of Jesus Christ, steadily learning from him how to live the life of the Kingdom . . . into every corner of human existence."[3]

I send out an urgent appeal to make catechesis, formation, and discipleship a priority in our local congregations.

But what does that look like? What is needed and how is it to be done? And specifically, *what should be taught* as part of this catechesis? These are the questions that have absorbed my attention over the past decade and a half of forming leaders, especially in Arizona.

Surge School began in Phoenix as a place to disciple the laity in a nine-month program with instruction in four areas: gospel and biblical story, Western culture and spiritual practices, the mission of the church, and vocations. Early in the process of working out the Surge curriculum, I sought to learn about discipleship from the early church. That study has yielded rich insight for this book. Similarly, Missional Training Center (MTC) was founded (again, in Phoenix) to equip congregational pastors and leaders. I sought especially to profit from the wisdom of global leaders who had been wrestling with the issue of how theological education could form leaders if it took mission seriously. In devising a missional curriculum for MTC I looked to the writings of significant missiologists and non-Western leaders—especially Harvie Conn, Lesslie Newbigin, David Bosch, René Padilla, and Orlando Costas—for their insights. Seeking to understand what thematic core shapes their curricula of theological education has led me to what I articulate in this book. What core missional dynamic has didactic power through the Holy Spirit to shape God's people into a people faithful to their God-given vocation?

This book articulates what I believe to be the missional dynamic that has the formative power to motivate and empower, to equip and form those in the church—beginning with its leaders—to be faithful to the gospel and to their vocation as the new humanity, living in their particular cultural settings for the sake of the world.

THE MISSIONAL DYNAMIC

What is a missional dynamic? A *dynamic* is a motivating force that produces change and subsequently shapes the process of growth. To speak of a *missional* dynamic is to elaborate the central beliefs of God's Word that have the formative power by the Spirit to generate a missional vision and then to shape us to be a people faithful to our missional identity.

This book unfolds a missional dynamic that has four components: the gospel, the biblical story, a missional people, and a missionary encounter with culture. If we begin with the *gospel* of the kingdom revealed in Jesus the Messiah, as we must, it necessarily leads us on to understand the Bible as a cosmic *story* of restoration, with a *missional people* at its center who are called to embody the goal of redemptive history for the sake of the world, always in the context of a *missionary encounter* with their cultural setting. This fourfold missional dynamic leads us to the very core of the Christian faith. I will briefly unpack the logic of this dynamic with the use of an unfolding diagram.

The Good News of the Kingdom

We begin with the gospel. When Jesus announces the good news, it is a gospel of the kingdom. Against the backdrop of the Old Testament story, the kingdom was the climax of history when God would return in power and liberate his people and the whole creation from sin, the powers, and the curse, and restore his rule over it. This was the goal toward which the whole Old Testament story had been moving. And now the time had come. The gospel is about the kingdom of God as the end of universal history arriving in the historical events of Jesus the Messiah in the middle of history (see fig. 1.1).

Figure 1.1. **The Gospel of the Kingdom**

The Biblical Story

If we start with the good news of Jesus, we are necessarily in the middle of a grand story that encompasses the whole world. The good news Jesus announces is that the *end* of cosmic history is breaking into the *middle* (see fig. 1.2). This message sends us back to the *beginning* of the whole world: it is a story that begins with the creation of the entire world—everything! This message also sends us forward to the *end* of history: it is a story that culminates with the restoration of the entire world—everything! It is the story in which the Creator God is the author and primary actor throughout; it is *his* purpose to recover his creation that is narrated in Scripture. This is not a parochial religious story for Jews and Christians but the true story of the whole world. The gospel of the kingdom demands that we understand the Bible as one unfolding story of the work of the triune God to restore the entire world from sin and its effects for his glory—the true story of the whole world.

Figure 1.2. **The Biblical Story**

A Missional People

There is a missional trajectory to the biblical story. It moves from one people to all nations, from one geographical location to the ends of the earth. Within this trajectory God gives his people a role to play. They are to be the beginning of God's work of restoration, the new humanity, which will ultimately include people from all nations. In the period between the resurrection of Jesus and his return, God's people are sent to play this role of gathering all the nations of the earth (see fig. 1.3). At the heart of the biblical story is an invitation to become a missional people, a community called to embody God's creational purpose for the sake of all peoples.

Figure 1.3. **Missional People**

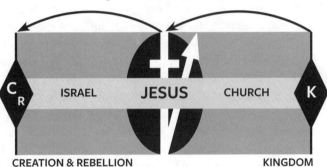

Missionary Encounter with Culture

God forms a people amid the nations that serve other gods to make known his original creational intention for human life. Israel's vocation is to embody, amid the idolatry of the pagan nations, what it means to be fully human, a nation that serves the living and true God (see fig. 1.4). As the people of God take new form in the New Testament, as a multigeographical, multiethnic people, the challenge only intensifies. Now God's people live as members of all the cultures of the world whose communal lives are shaped by idolatry. Thus, the embodiment of the missional vocation to be a preview of the kingdom will always be carried out in terms of a missionary encounter with each particular idolatrous culture of the world.

Figure 1.4. **Missionary Encounter with Culture**

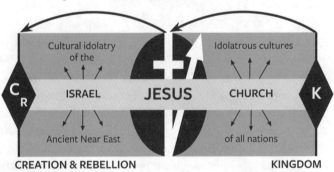

The Missional Dynamic Today

A problem today is that often each of these four aspects of the Bible's teaching has been obscured. We have too often settled for an emaciated gospel that turns the good news into a privatized, individualistic, and other-worldly message. We have too often weakened the biblical narrative by fragmenting the Bible, not allowing it to shape our whole lives. We have too often allowed the church to become a private religious body, playing the role of a vendor of religious goods and services for its members. We have too often fallen for the false pretense of a Christian or neutral secular culture. We have missed the religious idolatry of Western culture and thus become conformed to its patterns.

The gospel of the kingdom, the Bible as the true story of the world, the church as the new humanity for the sake of the world, and the missionary encounter of God's people with their culture: these are the four elements of a missional dynamic that must be recovered today to animate and guide the church into covenantal faithfulness. *This is the core of the Christian faith.*

THE CATECHESIS OF THE EARLY CHURCH

If we are to live the gospel for the sake of the world, we need a formation process that will truly equip us for our role and task. The early church understood this well. And we can learn much today from its practices of discipleship, especially from the catechetical formation process carried out to prepare new converts for baptism. What we need to observe here is how the formation process of the early church was shaped by the biblical story centered in Christ, by the missional calling of the church, and by a missionary encounter with its own (pagan, Roman) culture. The goal of catechesis was not simply to teach new converts what to believe or to give them a mere intellectual grasp of correct doctrine. The way of the early church was to renarrate the new believers' lives in order to re-form their identities and to establish new patterns of life so that their embodiment of the gospel might be attractive to others, for the sake of the world.

We cannot truly know who we are until we learn that great story that gives our own life's story its context. For those born into one narrative context and reborn by faith into another, it is essential that their new identity as followers of Christ be situated deliberately within the context of the gospel and the grand narrative of Scripture.

The pastoral purpose of early church catechesis was to "re-form pagan people, to re-socialize them, to deconstruct their old world, and reconstruct a new one."[4] This was done primarily by immersing catechumens in the story of the Bible. Beginning with Irenaeus (AD 130–202), the catechisms of the early church were focused on narrative. "The Old Testament was more than an explication and proof of the New Testament message; as the story of God's saving deeds, it was the very framework of catechesis and provided the setting for presenting Christ, the very center of that catechesis."[5] Catechesis transmitted the biblical story of salvation to form the people of God. For "the catechumen to become ready to join the Christian community, the catechist needed to replace [the pagan Roman story] by an alternative narrative, by the history of salvation as recounted in the books of the Hebrew Scriptures which culminated in the person and work of Jesus Christ and which continued in the life of the transnational church and the sufferings of the martyrs."[6]

This scriptural narrative encountered the pagan religious story that unified and formed Roman culture. The church understood well that the lives of new converts had been formed from birth by the story and cultural practices of Rome. The pagan world into which they had been born had socialized them, shaping their collective identity and way of life. That pagan story needed to be re-evaluated. Their old world needed to be deconstructed. Their lives needed to be renarrated. They needed to be re-socialized. Their identities needed to be re-formed. Their patterns of life needed to be redrawn. This could happen only by immersing them in the biblical story as the true context of their own life stories.

The pastoral purpose of the early church catechism had a missional goal: to make the catechumens an attractive community, for the sake of the world. The church's worship and discipleship practices "performed the function of re-forming those pagans who joined the church into Christians, into distinctive people who lived in a way that was recognizably in the tradition of Jesus Christ. As such these people, re-formed, would be attractive."[7]

An example of this comes from the Canons of Hippolytus, an early book of church order written by a bishop to guide church leaders. The missional purpose of catechism is explicit: new converts are to be taught so their lives "may shine with virtue, not before each other [only], but also before the Gentiles so they may imitate them and become Christians."[8] The catechism was designed to create communities that were visibly distinctive, that they might draw unbelievers to join them in following Jesus Christ.

The same kind of instruction, or process of formation in what it means to be part of the new humanity of God's calling, is needed today. We must return to the *good news* as a comprehensive and powerful message of God's kingdom centered in Jesus the Messiah. We must recover the Bible as *the one true story* of the whole world and allow it to shape our identities and our patterns of life. We must retrieve a deeper consciousness of our *missional identity* as a people called to be distinctive and attractive in every cultural setting, for the sake of the world. And finally, we must understand the religious core of the culture around us, so that we might be equipped to engage it in a *missionary encounter*.

This book is written to help lead us together along that path.

CHAPTER 2

Reading the Bible as Jesus Did

Then he [Jesus] opened their minds so they could understand the Scriptures. He told them, "This is what is written: The Messiah will suffer and rise from the dead on the third day, and repentance for the forgiveness of sins will be preached in his name to all nations, beginning at Jerusalem. You are witnesses of these things."

—Luke 24:45–48

LUKE'S TWOFOLD VANTAGE POINT

In a large room on the first floor of London's National Gallery hangs *The Ambassadors*, Hans Holbein's magnificent life-size double portrait of Jean de Dinteville and Georges de Selve.[1] The young, wealthy diplomat de Dinteville wears a sumptuous silk tunic and fur-lined coat, befitting his status as the French king's ambassador to the court of Henry VIII; his friend de Selve is more modestly (but still richly) dressed in dark clerical robes. Between the two men are shelves filled with all manner of beautifully made musical and scientific instruments. The imposing picture magnificently celebrates the achievements of the Renaissance in statesmanship, scientific and artistic research and performance, international trade, and the accumulation of knowledge, wealth, and power.

This much is certainly true of the picture.

But if we stop here, we will miss the real depth of Holbein's artistry and indeed miss the central message of his work. For we have not yet dealt with that mysterious, distorted object that he has placed immediately in front of us, seeming to hover over the mosaic floor between the feet of the two men in the picture. This odd, elongated shape is an example of *anamorphosis*: a deliberate distortion of perspective such that the object painted is revealed for what it truly is only when the viewer deliberately shifts perspective. So we must get up from the bench we've been sitting on, to look again either from a vantage point low on the left or high on the right. From this perspective, forced on us by the painter's artistry, we can see clearly that the object in the foreground is a beautifully detailed human skull, the symbol called *memento mori* ("remember that you must die"). Holbein uses this image to give context to all the grandeur he celebrates: Whatever greatness we may achieve—whether in diplomacy, learning, trade, science, or the arts—we must all, sooner or later, face the end of our mortal life and with it the end of our human achieving. However grand the political and clerical ambassadors in the picture may appear, they too, along with the humblest viewer of their portrait and even the painter himself, must at last face death.

And still Holbein is not finished with his ambassadors—nor with us. For yet another vitally important image is there within the frame, this time half-concealed at the top left corner of the painting behind a fold of the rich green brocade draperies that provide the backdrop to the scene. It is a crucifix, a vivid reminder of another, vastly different, perspective on human achievements. Though death threatens to eclipse even the greatest of human achievement, the gospel holds out to us the promise that God's world and all that fills it may ultimately find a place in the new creation. The image of Christ on the cross signifies what gives true and lasting meaning to life. All human learning and achievement will be finally judged in the light of the Christ.

Holbein's painting forces us to reconsider our perspective on the achievements of the Renaissance, since we can grasp its meaning only if we take the particular vantage point he has chosen for us. And something very similar is accomplished near the conclusion of the Gospel of Luke, where the gospel writer describes Jesus's final challenge to his disciples to *look again* at the Old Testament story, from a new perspective which will enable them to rightly read Israel's narrative: "He opened their minds so they could understand the Scriptures" (Luke 24:45). Until now, these men of Israel had read the biblical story from that nationalistic perspective that put the Jewish nation at the center of God's plan. Jesus invites them to reassess what they thought they knew, this time from a completely new point of view. And, like Holbein in his painting, Jesus offers two clues to help us read the story properly.

The first clue involves the death and resurrection of the Messiah. "This is what is written: The Messiah will suffer and rise from the dead on the third day" (Luke 24:46). The first clue is *messianic*: God's saving plan carried on through Israel will culminate in a suffering and risen Messiah. He goes on to link this to a second clue: "and repentance for the forgiveness of sins will be preached in his name to all nations beginning in Jerusalem. You are witnesses of these things" (24:47–48). The second clue is *missional*: This is how the nations will be incorporated into God's saving plan. When we view the Scriptures from the messianic and missional vantage point, we have begun at last to truly see "the big picture." Jesus teaches them (and us) how to read the Old Testament story: It may be understood properly *only* when we have aligned ourselves to see its messianic fulfillment in Christ and its missional fulfillment in the vocation of his people to witness to this good news "to all nations."

The book of Acts, Luke's second volume, closes with the same two clues. As Paul stands before King Agrippa and Festus, he defends the gospel: "I am saying nothing beyond what the prophets and Moses said would happen— that the Messiah would suffer and, as the first to rise from the dead, would bring the message of light to his own people and to the Gentiles" (Acts 26:22–23). The message is repeated: The Old Testament story culminates in the Messiah's death and resurrection and in mission to Jews and gentiles.

THE SHOCKING FULFILLMENT OF GOD'S PURPOSE

But Luke does not simply tell us about these two clues to understanding Israel's story; he uses them as the very foundation of the literary and theological structure of his own double volume (Luke-Acts). Luke's Gospel begins with his explanation to Theophilus that he is writing an orderly "account of the things that have been fulfilled among us" (Luke 1:1), then proceeds to narrate the coming of the kingdom that culminates in the death and resurrection of Jesus. And Luke is the only Gospel writer to continue the narrative past those events. He begins Acts thus: "In my former book, Theophilus, I wrote about all that Jesus *began* to do and to teach" (Acts 1:1). He then continues his orderly account of the church's mission from

Jerusalem to Rome as *things that have been fulfilled*. The risen and exalted Christ continues his ministry through his people to bring the good news to Israel and the nations.

The language of fulfillment is common in Luke. He sees the Old Testament as the record of God's single purpose, which has now reached its shocking fulfillment in Jesus and in the mission of the church. The Old Testament story is a story of restoration: God sets out on a long journey with Israel to restore the blessing of creation to his world. This story culminates in *the death and resurrection of Jesus*, by which redemption is decisively accomplished. Yet, despite the ways Israel had often interpreted the Old Testament story, it was never, in fact, *just* about Israel. God's first promise to Abraham made clear, from the beginning, that *all* the nations were in view. The story told in Scripture had always been moving toward a time when all peoples and the whole of creation would be included in God's redemptive work. And the fulfillment of this promise begins in the *mission of God's people*.

For Luke, like the Jews of the first century, the Old Testament had narrated the unfolding plan of the Creator God working out his purpose in and through his covenant with Israel. After the rebellion of humanity, this God had chosen one man and one nation to be the means by which he would restore blessing to all humanity and to the entire creation. The "Jewish" Scriptures told the story of the salvation not of Israel only but of the whole world, moving outward from one nation to *all* nations and from one place to "the ends of the earth." God's people have always had a missional role within this expanding trajectory of God's unfolding work.

The Old Testament story of God's purpose to accomplish cosmic restoration is fulfilled in the death and resurrection of Jesus: Luke makes this point no less than three times in the final chapter of his Gospel. Speaking to the two disciples traveling to Emmaus, the risen Jesus gently scolds them: "'How foolish you are, and how slow to believe all that the prophets have spoken! Did not the Messiah have to suffer these things and then enter his glory?' And beginning with Moses and all the prophets, he explained to them what was said in all the Scriptures concerning himself" (Luke 24:25–27). A little later, as he appears to his disciples, he says to them, "This is what I told you while I was still with you: Everything must be fulfilled that is written about me in the Law of Moses, the Prophets and the Psalms" (24:44). The Scriptures are being fulfilled, the restoration of all things has begun; this is Luke's startling claim concerning Jesus.

This plan of redemption always had *all nations* in view. God had promised Abraham that he would restore blessing to Abraham's descendants and then, through them, to all nations (Gen. 12:2–3). By the end of the Old Testament historical period, the Jewish people believed that the Abrahamic promise would be fulfilled through an anointed king in David's line (2 Sam. 7:11–14; Ps. 72). Thus, it was entirely fitting that first Mary and then Zechariah should announce that the promises made to Abraham and to the house of David were in their own day being fulfilled in the coming of Jesus (Luke 1:54–55, 68–75). The goal of the Old Testament story was approaching; in Jesus's life, death, and resurrection the promised blessing had arrived in Israel. But how was it to reach to *all* the nations? The astonishing fulfillment of *that* element of the Abrahamic-Davidic promise is narrated in the book of Acts.

Luke's Gospel and Acts are not simply two stories connected by chronology, first a story of Jesus and then a follow-up narrative about the early church. Rather, they tell a single story of fulfillment. Luke means to show how God's single purpose narrated in the Old Testament and worked out in the nation of Israel continues into the new era, to be fulfilled in Jesus *and* in the church of the first century AD (see fig. 2.1).

This shocking fulfillment must have startled any first-century Jew schooled in the covenant history of the Old Testament. This is why Jesus asks his disciples (at the end of Luke's Gospel) to take a very different vantage point to see rightly the picture of God's purposes painted in the Old Testament. Perhaps the clearest example of just how surprising this newly revealed picture would be is in Festus's reaction to Paul's unveiling of it (Acts 26:22–23). Festus interrupts Paul and shouts, "You are out of

Figure 2.1. God's Purpose Fulfilled

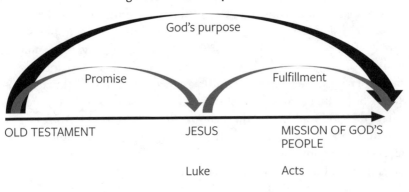

your mind, Paul! . . . Your great learning is driving you insane" (26:24). Why would this fulfillment, something we so easily take for granted, be so astonishing?

Crucifixion and resurrection on the one hand, mission on the other. None of these fit the picture of Jewish expectation that when the Messiah came, he would achieve a great victory over his enemies. Surely (they thought) God's Messiah could not suffer the humiliation of crucifixion? Crucifixion was not only a hideous means of torture and execution but also a potent sign of the victim's utter defeat and humiliation at the hands of the Roman Caesar, whereas the Jewish hope had been that when the Messiah came he would crush Rome and its ruler (Dan. 7:1–14). Luke's story of the crucifixion is an entirely new—and very shocking—view of how God's victory would come.

Likewise, the resurrection of Christ was incomprehensible to the first-century Jew (Mark 9:10). They understood "the resurrection" to be a cosmic event in which *all* would rise from death at the *end* of history. The claim that just *one* man should rise from death in the *middle* of history was inconceivable. Again, Luke tells us that the resurrection life of the new creation is being inaugurated in a puzzling way.

As for the final claim, regarding the incorporation of "the nations" into God's people, the Old Testament prophets had envisioned a pilgrimage by which all the nations would *come to* Jerusalem, there to acknowledge the glory of God and the Lord's Messiah as the world's true king. It was never imagined that there would be an outward movement of God's people *sent to* the nations to invite them into God's kingdom. Luke invites us to see a different way to understand the incorporation of the nations.

This is an example of theological anamorphosis: Jesus's first-century disciples, and all subsequent readers of Luke and Acts, are required to read the Old Testament story from the vantage point first of a crucified and risen Messiah, and second of the mission of the church to the nations. This is the place to stand if we are truly to understand the Scriptures. If we are to see clearly the core of Christian faith, we must begin by reading the Old Testament story in the light of Jesus and of the mission of the church.

THE FOURFOLD CORE OF CHRISTIAN FAITH IN LUKE-ACTS

We can discern in this messianic and missional interpretation of the Old Testament a fourfold movement: the gospel of the kingdom, the biblical story, a missional people, and a missionary encounter with culture. This constitutes the core of the Christian faith as it is laid out in Luke's narrative.

The Gospel of the Kingdom

At the thematic center of Luke's writing is the death and resurrection of Jesus the Messiah, events that are narrated as the climactic conclusion of his account of Jesus's ministry. His first book unfolds the significance of Jesus's whole work in terms of *the gospel of the kingdom*: Jesus says, "I must proclaim the good news of the kingdom of God to the other towns also, because that is why I was sent" (Luke 4:43). The coming of the kingdom defines Jesus's entire ministry from birth to ascension: Luke uses the word "kingdom" over forty times in his Gospel. The anticipated kingdom is about God's return to Israel to rule and to save. In love and power he will restore and heal his sin-cursed and broken creation. The good news Luke shares with his readers is that God's return, this restored rule and healing, is taking place already in the man Jesus—the coming of the kingdom is no longer merely a future event.

Luke's Gospel shows us how Jesus reveals the kingdom: Jesus proclaims the good news of the kingdom with his words, incarnates it in his own life, demonstrates it in his deeds, explains it in his teaching and parables, suffers for it against opposition, prays for it, and forms a community to embody it. To understand the life ministry of Jesus is to see it as the fullest possible expression of good news; in him the kingdom of God has broken into history.

The four central events of Luke-Acts—the crucifixion, resurrection, ascension, and Pentecost—are also about the coming kingdom. In the death of Jesus, God defeats all the enemies of his reign over the world; in the resurrection of Jesus, he inaugurates the kingdom in the midst of the world; and in his ascension and the giving of his Spirit, he sends the kingdom to the ends of the earth through unfolding history. To understand the Christian faith, we must start with Jesus as the turning point of world history, especially in his crucifixion and resurrection, the good news of the kingdom of God.

Unfortunately, today the notions of "kingdom" and "good news" are often separated. Instead of the big picture—that in Jesus, God has already begun to restore *all* things and to bring his kingdom to fruition here on earth—some see only the small and distorted image of a divine rescue mission whereby the souls of a few individuals are snatched out of danger and whisked away to enjoy a disembodied and ethereal afterlife. (Think of it this way: It is as if the *whole point and scope* of the D-Day landings had been reduced to the saving of Private Ryan.) Such a limited, distorted picture is simply not the gospel that Jesus proclaimed.

The Biblical Story

Luke's Gospel narrative of the coming of the kingdom does not stand alone: he embeds it from the outset in the covenant history of the Old Testament. Luke uses a variety of words to make absolutely clear he is narrating the one purpose and plan of God as it is recorded in the Old Testament and fulfilled in Jesus and in the mission of the church. A landmark study on Luke's theology is entitled *The Middle of Time*,[2] indicating that to properly understand Luke's Gospel we must read it as he intended—one part of a bigger story. Luke's Gospel stands very deliberately in a "middle place" between Israel's story in the Old Testament and the continuing story of the early church in Acts (see fig. 2.2).

If we are to rightly understand the gospel of the kingdom, we must attend to it in context, mindful of the whole canvas of the *biblical story*. The events of Jesus's life, including the climactic episodes of his death and resurrection, find their full meaning within the story the Old Testament tells. And this is a matter of some significance for the reader who truly seeks to understand what Luke is saying, for if we do not look to the biblical story to provide context for the gospel of the kingdom, it is certain

Figure 2.2. **Luke: The Middle of History**

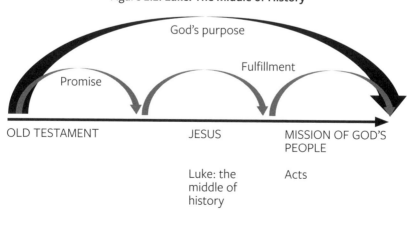

that we will look to some other story. As already hinted, a "gospel" story of individual salvation does *not* fit the Old Testament context of Luke's Gospel. "Seeing" the gospel apart from its context in the Old Testament Scriptures means *not seeing it at all*.

It is true that we will misunderstand the gospel if we do not see it within the "big picture" of the biblical story. But it is equally true, as Jesus himself makes clear, that we will misunderstand the meaning of the biblical story until we see that he is the central figure in it. The Jews of the first century *were* reading the Old Testament as one unfolding story of God's plan, and they were eagerly anticipating its conclusion in their own time. But when the Old Testament story arrived at its climactic moment in Jesus, the Jews (by and large) simply missed it, having viewed the picture from the wrong angle. Jesus makes it clear to his followers that they have a new vantage point from which to read the scriptural story. What they need is to view the picture again, from a fresh perspective, so that Jesus becomes the key to reading the whole.

A Missional People

The fulfillment of the Old Testament story is found not only in the work of Jesus (narrated in Luke) but also in the mission of the church (narrated in Acts). Jesus invites his followers to reread the Old Testament story to understand its missional direction and the missional role God's people are called to play in it. God's intention to include all nations is reaching its climax.

If we follow Luke's lead—or rather, that of Jesus as Luke records it—we see that *mission* is not a matter of mere secondary importance to the Christian faith. The story of God's work in the world is being fulfilled not only in Jesus but also in the mission of the church. When we look at the whole story from a fresh perspective, we see God working out his renewing purpose and incorporating all nations in and through the people he has chosen. The book of Acts narrates this fulfillment.

A Missionary Encounter with Culture

The story of mission in Acts finds its literary and theological center in the so-called Jerusalem Council of Acts 15. One commentator calls it Acts' "most crucial chapter . . . structurally and theologically at the very heart" of the book.[3] Indeed, the decisions made by the Council at

Jerusalem make it a turning point not only for the narrative of Acts but for the entire biblical story.

Throughout the Old Testament, the people of God had been defined chiefly by their *cultural separation* from all other peoples. They were distinct by ethnicity, defined by the geography of the homeland given them by God, and (most importantly of all) unique in being formed by the law of God. For the people of Israel from ancient times until the first century, all other cultures had been defined by pagan idolatry. To live outside of Israel and its law was to live in bondage to the cultural idolatry of the pagan nations, under sin's curse. Indeed, the primary threat to Israel's survival as a nation throughout the Old Testament had been the danger that it would succumb to the cultural idolatry of the surrounding nations.

It would seem obvious to any devout Jew of the time that, when the ending of God's great story at last arrived in history, the people of all other nations would be taken out of their pagan cultural contexts and incorporated into Israel's own God-given, Torah-shaped nation and culture. This is the very reason so many Jewish Christians assumed that all gentiles must come under the law as a prerequisite to following Christ, and it is why this was a burning issue in the New Testament. To come under the law and enter Israel was simply the only way known by first-century Jews for "the nations" to abandon their lifeless idols and come under the lordship of the true God.

But here in Acts 15 it is decided at Jerusalem that gentile followers of Jesus do *not* have to become Jewish in order to join the people of God. They may remain within their former social and political contexts and maintain their former cultural identities. This was a radical departure from the expectations established by their reading of the Old Testament. How was it possible for someone to live under the idolatrous rule of pagan gods and yet truly and faithfully follow the Messiah of Israel?

This was one of the most significant problems faced by the church in its earliest days. If the newly formed people of God were to be defined not by ethnicity, geography, cultural practice, or—most importantly of all—by adherence to the Torah, then how *were* they to be distinct from their pagan neighbors? How could they embody the true humanity apart from the law?

The questions dealt with by the early church at the Jerusalem Council are still relevant today, yet we often miss their significance, falsely assuming that our own Western culture is either Christian or "neutral" and therefore safe. But to be the new humanity in *any* culture demands a *missionary encounter with culture*. How can we live as God's distinctive people amid the idolatry of our culture?

———

To take seriously Luke's call to read the Bible with a messianic and missional lens, as Jesus himself does, requires that we ask: What is the gospel of the kingdom at the center of Luke's narrative? What is the biblical story in which God's purpose is unfolded and finally accomplished in Christ as narrated by Luke? What is the missional vocation of God's people in that story as narrated in Acts? What does a missionary encounter with our culture look like today?

PART 1

THE GOSPEL

OF THE

KINGDOM

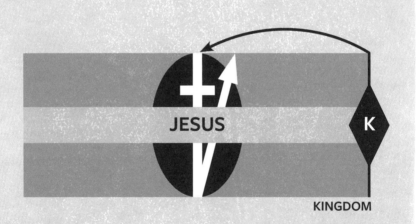

CHAPTER 3

What Is the Gospel?

After John was put in prison, Jesus went into Galilee, proclaiming the good news of God. "The time has come," he said. "The kingdom of God has come near. Repent and believe the good news! . . . Come, follow me."

—Mark 1:14–17

THE WORD "GOSPEL"

When my wife was in labor and about to give birth to our first child, everything seemed to be proceeding smoothly until, suddenly, there was a crisis. The medical team hurriedly rolled my wife's bed down the hall to surgery; another nurse curtly instructed me to go and sit in the waiting room. That wait was one of my darkest moments. What was happening? Was my wife in danger? Was there something wrong with our baby? Then, at last, yet another nurse appeared at the end of the hall, and she was pushing an incubator. She walked toward me and asked, "Are you Mr. Goheen?" When I nodded, she said, "*Good news!* Here is your baby daughter. She is healthy, and your wife is fine." I can't imagine hearing anything sweeter than those simple words: good news. And today, forty-five years later, the news is even better than I then knew.

If that nurse had lived in the first century (and spoken Greek!) she would have used the same word Jesus did when he announced good news (Mark 1:15). It was simply the common word of that day for good news. In fact, there is a story much like mine recorded in ancient Greek literature, in which an anxious husband is told the "good news" that his wife has given birth to a baby boy and the same word is used.

The modern English word "gospel" comes from the Middle English words *gōd* (good) and *spell* (news). "Gospel" or "good news" translates the New Testament Greek *euangelion*, from which we get our English words "evangelize" and "evangelical." *Euangelion* is frequently found in ancient literature to announce the good news of a military victory, political triumph, or even a good price for food in the market! *Euangelion* is the term chosen by Jesus himself and the writers of the New Testament to designate those events that form the center of cosmic history.

"GOOD NEWS" IN THE FIRST CENTURY

Jesus opens his public ministry by announcing the good news that the kingdom of God has come (Mark 1:14–15). If we are to understand just what Jesus means here—and why these words should so astonish the people who first heard them—we'll need a basic grasp of the theological, historical, and cultural background of his day. The language of *euangelion* that Jesus uses had both a Jewish and a Roman context in first-century Palestine. It was bound up with both Israel's hope for deliverance from Roman oppression and, ironically, with Caesar Augustus and his rule over the Roman Empire.

The Jewish Background

When Jesus announces to Israel the good news of the kingdom of God, he doesn't stop to offer a definition. He assumes common ground with his hearers. The Jews of the first century shared an intense longing for the coming of the kingdom. They were eagerly awaiting the historical climax of their long story when God would rescue his world from sin and rule over it again as his universal and everlasting kingdom. They were deeply immersed in the Old Testament, retelling and singing its story constantly among themselves, and it kept alive their faith and hope even as they suffered under the oppressive rule of Rome. The Old

Testament books that recorded their history nourished in them a deeper understanding of their story. The Creator God had chosen them as the means by which he would rescue his whole creation (including people from all nations) from sin and restore his cosmic rule. He had first promised blessing to Abraham and his family, and through them to the world. Later, he promised to give that blessing through an anointed king in David's line who would rule a worldwide kingdom. In the meantime, however, Israel sat in captivity under God's curse in the pagan Roman Empire . . . waiting.

It seemed to them that God's plan had run aground. How would he liberate Israel from captivity and complete his plan to restore his rule through them? Since different groups among the Jews (Zealots, Pharisees, Sadducees, Herodians, Essenes) all had their own answers to this question, it inevitably provoked conflict and tension among them. The one matter on which all agreed, however, was that God would come back to restore his rule over the world—and likely through a descendant of David. As the people of Israel read and reread the narratives from the Old Testament, their hope for the coming kingdom of God intensified.

And Israel's hope of a coming kingdom was also kept alive by reading the prophets. Perhaps the most well-known of these prophecies were the puzzling words of Daniel and the message of Isaiah 40–55. Daniel looked to a day when all the oppressive pagan empires (Rome being the last and the worst) would be destroyed and the kingdom of God established forever (Dan. 2, 7).

Isaiah also predicted the coming of such a day and spoke of its dawning as "good news" (Isa. 40:9; 41:27; 52:7; 61:1). In Isaiah 52:7–10, as Jerusalem languished in exile under the ruthless oppression of Babylon, the prophet said that there would come a herald announcing good news, "Your God reigns!" The people's servitude to their pagan masters was about to end, as their God returned to Zion as king. He would bring peace and salvation, his glory would fill the earth, he would comfort and redeem his people, he would "lay bare his holy arm," and "the ends of the earth would see the salvation" of God. This was good news indeed, and in Isaiah's vision Israel shouts for joy.

When Jesus begins his ministry in Galilee by announcing good news, *he is this messenger, this herald of Isaiah's prophecy*, come to announce the good news, "Your God reigns!" But the message is shocking to those who hear it because Jesus claims that God has indeed returned *in Jesus himself!* God has chosen this lowly human form to "lay bare his holy arm," and the ends of the earth are to see God's salvation arrive in a completely unexpected way.

Israel's misery in the first century was grounded in the reality that, although its people were living in the land God had given to Abraham, they lived there under the oppression of foreign empires (Neh. 9:36–37). They never ceased to lament pagan rule. It drove them to a deeper longing for God to come, to act in power, to end the usurpation of his authority by idolatrous pagans, and to restore his own authority over his people and the whole earth. Kingdom was just one image among many held by the Jewish people in this hope. Other images also gave glimpses of what they hoped for: a new exodus, a new covenant, a new creation, the age to come, the banquet in God's presence, the resurrection, the world reborn.

And different Jewish factions understood and expressed the hope for the kingdom in different ways. There were indeed sharp divisions among the Jews as to what it would look like, how and when it would come, who would bring it, and how they were to live until it arrived. But they shared the hope that their God would return in power, would reassert his kingly rule, and would become—manifestly—what Israel confessed him to be: King of the whole earth.

One serious problem for Jews at the time of Jesus's ministry was that their hope had become distorted by an ethnocentric hatred of "the nations." Indeed, their nationalism blinded them to the prophetic promise that, when God came to establish his kingdom, he would also gather in "the nations" under his benevolent rule.

When Jesus comes and announces the good news of the arrival of God's reign, he connects with the Jews' felt longing. But he also finds much to correct in it.

The Background of the Roman Empire

There is another dimension of the cultural background of the word "gospel." Rome had adopted strikingly similar language to describe its *own* ruler, Caesar, and his dominion over a worldwide empire. The word *"euangelion"* had been used by Rome to announce the emperor's birthday, coming of age, military victories, accession to the throne, and recovery of health. But (and this is especially important) the same word had been used to announce Caesar's inauguration of *a new era in world history*. Following a particularly dark and turbulent time in Rome's history, Octavian (later called Caesar Augustus) had re-established peace and order in the empire through a military victory. This victory was announced as "good news." He was hailed as the son of god, the savior and lord who inaugurated a rule that had brought justice and peace to Rome that would one day encompass the whole world. *This* (to Rome's faithful citizens) was the good news.

There is some debate over which of these backgrounds, the Jewish or the Roman, most shapes the biblical meaning of the gospel. But we do not have to choose. The Jewish hope for the coming of God's kingdom had always entailed the end of all foreign empires and the dethronement of all pagan gods. They had always known that when God comes to establish his rule over the whole earth, he must do so by casting down pagan rulers from their thrones. Jesus's announcement that he has come to bring the kingdom to his people is a direct challenge to Caesar, one of those pagan rulers who had blasphemously claimed divine power and authority. Jesus announces that there is no king but God, the One who truly rules over all peoples. It is Jesus who brings the good news of a new era. He alone is the Savior and Lord who will bring order, peace, and joy to the whole earth. Thus, Jesus's gospel confronts the cultural idolatry of his day head-on.

THE GOOD NEWS OF THE KINGDOM

Jesus says, "I must proclaim the good news of the kingdom of God to other towns also, because that is why I was sent" (Luke 4:43). The kingdom of God is *the* central message of the good news of Jesus. The coming of God's reign means the arrival of his renewing power to defeat the enemies of his rule and to usher in his end-time salvation, by which he has promised to restore the whole world. God's power to be unleashed at the end of history is present *now* to overcome evil and deliver people from its power, and to bring the blessings of his rule to people. That is what Israel is looking for, and what the Gospels announce. But it looks very different from what they had expected.

The presence of the kingdom of God is evident in the power of Jesus to defeat the kingdom of darkness. When he is accused by the Pharisees of partnering with Satan, Jesus responds: "But if it is by the Spirit of God that I drive out demons, then the kingdom of God has come upon you" (Matt. 12:28). The presence of the new power is evident when Jesus gives sight to the blind, makes the lame walk, heals the sick, enables the deaf to hear, forgives sinners, welcomes the poor, raises the dead, and calms the hostile seas (Luke 7:22). These are exhibits of God's restoring power to reverse all the effects of evil in the world.

Luke uses the word "salvation" to describe what God's power accomplishes in the world. Salvation has many facets, including physical (the sick are healed, 6:10; 17:19; 18:42; the dead are raised, 8:54–55), spiritual (people are liberated from demonic power, 8:36; sins are forgiven, 7:48), social (the marginalized are restored to community, 7:50; 8:48; 17:19), economic (the poor receive justice, 1:46–55; 18:7), and political (unjust rulers are displaced, 1:46–55, 71). Salvation means the breaking in of the promised life of the new creation into the present age. This salvation comes to those who believe, receive the kingdom as a gift, and enter the realm of God's rule (Luke 18:17).

Though the restoration of people to relationship with God is central to salvation, it is never the whole of salvation. Sin's malignant effects are embodied in every aspect of human life, including the cultural, political, economic, and social structures we have built. So it is that Jesus challenges the systemic evil manifest in both Israel and the Roman Empire. The kingdom brings saving power—God's power in Jesus by the Spirit—to overturn the reign of evil in the entire world.

We must not reduce the gospel of the kingdom to an impersonal "saving power," for the center of its meaning is to be found in fellowship with Jesus himself. It is not just a kingdom; it is a King who rules. This kingdom has a face and a name—and that name is Jesus. Jesus himself is the good news. He announces *his* rule, and it is as we submit to his reign in relationship with him that the saving power of the kingdom is to be found and enjoyed.

The announcement of the good news demands an urgent and immediate response. Jesus calls those who hear the gospel first to "repent and believe" and then to "follow" him (Mark 1:15–17). The call to *repent and believe* is a summons to all who hear: "Turn from all your other loyalties and embrace the presence of God's rule in me. You may not see the fullness of God's reign, but you can believe that God's healing power is present in me. Give up your old way of life and trust me for a new one." This summons is followed by the charge to *follow* Jesus. Few images express more vividly the total allegiance and absolute loyalty Jesus demands.

The announcement of the kingdom of God marks the arrival of something new in history. Though God's kingship had for centuries been proclaimed in Israel, the Jews believed that evil had an enduring grip on the world. They looked forward to that moment at the end of history when God's sovereign power would be unleashed to liberate the world from evil. Thus, to their thinking, world history was divided between "the present evil age" and "the age to come" (see fig. 3.1). Though in the present evil age the world was in bondage to sin and the "powers," a new day was coming when God himself would come back, break the power of evil, and usher in "the age to come."

Figure 3.1. **Israel's Expectation**

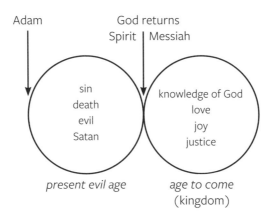

Jesus's good news was that this new day had arrived: the end-time kingdom was breaking into the middle of history *now*, in Jesus himself and in what he was doing. The power of God was at work in the world *in Jesus's own day* to save, liberate, and heal—to restore God's comprehensive rule over his creation. Yet it was also clear that evil remained powerful despite Jesus's presence. The fullness of God's promise of restoration was held back, awaiting a future day for its completion. This demanded a fundamental shift in how the Jews imagined God's restoration was to take place. It seemed that, instead of a decisive end to the present evil age with the full arrival of the promised age to come, there was to be a period in which the two ages would overlap in human history (see fig. 3.2). The kingdom of God would be present in the world, but the future consummation, the goal of history, would be postponed.

Figure 3.2. **Jesus's Message in the Gospels**

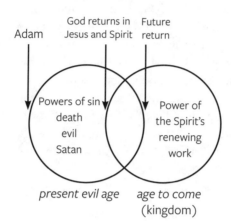

Such an unexpected coming of the kingdom! Thus, the identity of Jesus as the one who speaks these strange words is a major preoccupation in the Gospels: "Who is this?" (Luke 8:25; see also Luke 9:9; Matt. 16:13, 15). The answer is that Jesus is *God himself*, returning to his people as the prophets had promised. He is also the *Messiah* who comes to reign, save his people, defeat their foes, and restore God's temple-presence. He is the *Son of Man* who will occupy the throne given him by God the Father, from which he will rule the nations (Dan. 7:14). And he is the *Servant of the Lord* who heralds the good news of God's reign and suffers by taking upon himself the sin and curse of his people (Isa. 42, 49, 50, 53, 61).

CRUCIFIXION AND RESURRECTION

All the Gospels give considerable attention to the climactic events of the cross and resurrection. This is the center of the good news, for in these events the kingdom of God truly comes. But nothing could have been further from what the Jewish people of Jesus's day expected. The horror of the crucifixion seemed to prove that Jesus's claim to be Messiah must have been fraudulent. For Jesus was not the first to be crucified by Rome for making Messianic claims. Crucifixion was Rome's customary and brutal answer to those who challenged its authority. When Jesus was himself crucified, it seemed to Jews to obliterate his messianic claim, since it had long been their hope that Messiah would crush the rule of Rome (Dan. 7:7–14).

Neither did Jesus's resurrection make sense to the Jews (Mark 9:10). To them, "the resurrection" was to be a comprehensive event at the end of history: the whole world would be renewed on "the last day," and *all* would rise from the dead, some to life and others to death. What could it possibly mean for *one* man to rise in the *middle* of history? Thus, to most of Israel, the talk from Jesus and his followers of crucifixion and resurrection was scandalous nonsense.

But the early church proclaimed that in the scandalous event of the cross God had gained a victory over all his enemies and established his rule. They turned to the suffering servant poem of Isaiah 53 to interpret the meaning of the cross. We often abstract this song from its full theological and literary context in Isaiah 40–55 and so miss the rich way first-century Jews (and Jesus himself) would have understood his suffering. Isaiah 40–55 is first about freeing Israel from the punishment of exile. A significant image in these chapters is the new exodus: as God had once liberated Israel from its oppression under the pagan Egyptian empire, so he would do it again through an appointed servant. The Jews expected this to be accomplished in a great battle in which the Romans would be crushed.

But for Israel to be liberated from exile, the sin and subsequent covenant curse that put them there had to be dealt with. Somehow, in his suffering, the "servant" would take upon himself the role of a sin offering and pay for the sin of his people (Isa. 40:1–2) so they might be freed from bondage to the idolatrous empire (Isa. 53:10). Thus, the images of a new exodus, military victory, and sacrifice were somehow bound together in the Jewish mind. *This* was the way the kingdom was to come.

The Gospels open with John the Baptizer quoting Isaiah 40, to announce that Israel is about to be liberated from her exile (Mark 1:1–3; cf. Isa. 40:3). Jesus assumes the role of Isaiah's herald, proclaiming the good news of the coming kingdom (Mark 1:14–15; cf. Isa. 40:9–10, 52:7–10). The words of Isaiah 40–55 are at last coming to fulfillment.

With the Jewish background in mind, it is not hard to see how Isaiah 53 would function for the early church as a key to understanding the meaning of the cross, for here it was that God accomplished the new exodus, achieved a mighty victory, and took away the sins of his people by becoming a sin offering. But the *manner* of his doing so—and this must be emphasized—is utterly unexpected.

The Jews had expected a climactic military battle led by the Messiah, in which their nation would triumph over the evil bound up in the pagan empire of Rome. Through this messianic battle a new exodus—a rescue and liberation from Rome—would be achieved. Because their thinking had been so thoroughly shaped by the pervasive Old Testament emphasis on cultural idolatry, the Jews had become accustomed to seeing pagan cultures as the primary enemies of God's reign. Their nation's battle, then, would be launched against Rome and all pagan idolators. But Jesus describes a very different kind of battle, against a different sort of enemy entirely. His quarrel is not against flesh and blood in Rome, but against the satanic and demonic powers that lie *behind* the idolatry of the Roman Empire. In fact, Jesus claims, those same powers are also at work in Israel (Luke 22:53). And the deepest source of idolatry is the sinful human heart itself (Mark 7:1–23). Cultural idolatry flows from the heart, and demonic powers maintain a foothold through it because of human sin. Thus, it is not a military confrontation with Rome that is needed. Rather, it is a mighty act of God that will defeat sin at the root *as well as* achieve liberation from bondage to cultural idolatry and the spiritual powers that lie behind it.

As the Jews gathered in Jerusalem for Passover, a revolutionary spirit gripped the city with hope of a military victory over Rome and a new exodus. In this context, Jesus takes bread and wine, creating a new image that brings together the suffering servant and the Passover lamb (Luke 22:37; Isa. 53:12). As he gives his body and pours out his blood, the new exodus will be achieved, the battle will be won, and the kingdom will come. It is by the cross that he will free his people from spiritual bondage. There he will do battle against the spiritual powers, the idols of culture, and sin itself. Jesus reveals himself to be the slain Passover lamb *and* the suffering servant: a sin offering for Israel and for the world.

Here we see the connection between the good news of the kingdom (Isa. 52:7) and the cosmic significance of the cross (Isa. 52:13–53:12). God's reign over the whole earth would indeed arrive, as the Jews thought, through a messianic battle and a new exodus to rescue them from bondage to the empire. But what they could *not* see was that the battle was to be accomplished when their Messiah was humiliated in crucifixion, taking the punishment and curse of his exiled people on himself. The cross would liberate Israel from bondage and then bring freedom to *all* peoples and, finally, to the whole of creation.

Likewise, the resurrection must be understood in terms of its cosmic end-time significance. The hope of Israel had been for a new kingdom into which the dead would rise in renewed life. The resurrection they anticipated would be the climactic end point of history, ushering in the age to come, when the godly would begin to enjoy a new bodily life in the new creation and the ungodly would be delivered up to judgment. Jesus takes up this Jewish understanding of the end of history, but curiously centers Israel's hope on himself. His return from death is not simply the resuscitation of one man's body; it is nothing less than the start of the longed-for resurrection of the last day, the beginning of the age to come, the inauguration of the resurrection life of God's kingdom. Jesus is himself the firstborn of the new creation.

This is very clear at the graveside of Lazarus, where his sister Martha confesses the commonly held Jewish belief: "I know he will rise again in the resurrection at the last day" (John 11:24). Jesus corrects Martha, drawing the entire resurrection hope onto himself, asserting that the resurrection is not just an event that awaits the last day but something that *has already begun, in him*: "I am the resurrection and the life" (11:25). Anyone who believes in Jesus will begin to experience the resurrection life of God's kingdom *even now* and will be raised up on the last day (cf. John 6:35–40).

The events of the crucifixion and resurrection are presented in the Gospels not only as the culmination of Jesus's life and ministry but also as the climactic moments of the Old Testament story, which had always been moving toward the coming of God's kingdom and the renewal of all things. Shockingly, this is how the Scriptures are at last fulfilled! In his death, Jesus takes the evil of the world upon himself and so defeats all the enemies of God's reign. In his resurrection, he inaugurates the reign of God throughout the earth (see fig. 3.3).

Figure 3.3. **Post-Resurrection Understanding**

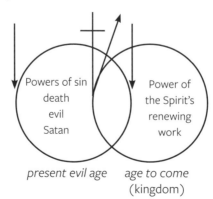

present evil age   age to come
(kingdom)

EXALTATION AND PENTECOST

Soon after Jesus's resurrection and ascension, Peter proclaims the gospel to the crowds in Jerusalem, interpreting the meaning of what they have witnessed at Pentecost. His explanation follows this outline:

1. With the coming of the Spirit, the "last days" promised by Joel have arrived (Acts 2:16–21).
2. It was Jesus himself who ushered in these last days, through his life, death, resurrection, and exaltation and through the outpouring of the Holy Spirit (2:22–35).
3. Jesus is Lord and Messiah (2:36).
4. This demands a response: If you want to participate in this life of the Spirit, this salvation of the last days, you must repent and be baptized (2:38).

Jesus's exaltation is his coronation day, when he is installed as rightful king over the whole creation and the ruler of history. The exalted Jesus shares the throne of God. The throne room of the ancient Near Eastern monarch was a common image among Jews at that time, rooted in the Old Testament prophets (Ezek. 1; Isa. 6; Dan. 7:1–14; cf. Rev. 4–5). It pictures the rule of God over universal history as he directs it toward a time when he will finally vanquish his foes. The exaltation of Jesus means he now rules history as it moves inexorably toward his victory over evil and the full establishment of his universal and everlasting kingdom. All his enemies will be defeated; every knee will bow and every tongue will confess that Jesus Christ is Lord (Ps. 110:1–2; Acts 2:34–35; Phil. 2:9–11).

Likewise, the coming of the Spirit is promised as the unleashing of God's power to renew the creation. The Old Testament prophets had foretold that in the last days, when the kingdom arrived, the Spirit would be poured out on the Messiah, on Israel, and on all peoples (Isa. 61:1–2; Ezek. 36:26–27; 37:1–14; Joel 2:28). The Spirit is the power that brings the life and salvation of the last days (Acts 2:17). Other New Testament writers give us imagery to help us see how the Spirit belongs to the future kingdom yet makes it present now. Paul uses an image from commerce: The Spirit is a "deposit," like that sum of real money given *now* to guarantee a purchase, in anticipation of the whole purchase price to be paid in the *future* (Eph. 1:14). Paul also uses an image from agriculture: The Spirit is the "firstfruits," the first part of the harvest gathered *now* in anticipation of reaping the whole harvest in the *future* (Rom. 8:23). The author of Hebrews speaks of a "foretaste," a partial but real taste of the powers of the coming age given *now*, in anticipation of the whole "meal" in the *future* (Heb. 6:4–5). All these images make the same point: The Spirit brings the life of the kingdom into history *now*, with the confident anticipation that its fullness will come in the *future*.

HALLMARKS OF THE GOOD NEWS

What then is the good news? First and foremost, the good news is *a message about Jesus* the King. God's rule is present in the person of Jesus. In his life, death, resurrection, and exaltation, and in the outpouring of the Spirit that follows, God's rule breaks into history. While the entirety of Jesus's ministry is the good news, his death and resurrection occupy the central place (Luke 24:45–46; 1 Cor. 15:3–8). It is upon these two events that the New Testament turns—as does, indeed, cosmic history itself.

To rightly understand this message about Jesus we must note five further characterizations of the good news:

1. The gospel is a message about *God*, his purpose and his action in history (Rom. 1:1–4; 15:16; 1 Pet. 4:17). The gospel both reveals and accomplishes God's plan, what God has done in and through Jesus, to bring about his purpose to restore the creation from sin and its deadly effects.

2. The gospel is a message about *the climax of the Old Testament story*, the culmination of the long history of God's redemptive deeds. The coming of the kingdom and the events of Jesus's ministry can be understood only as the fulfillment of the faith of Israel.

3. The gospel is a message about *the end time*, the last days, the goal of history present now in the world. The Old Testament had looked forward to a final day when the saving power of God would gather to its triumphant climax; Jesus proclaims, "That day is here!"

4. The gospel is a message about *a comprehensive salvation*. The new power breaking into history accomplishes the goal of the whole biblical story: the restoration of all things. The gospel is

the revelation of God's power to save, redeem, reconcile, restore, heal, and liberate a broken world and a sinful people.

5. The gospel is a message about *the work of the Spirit*. The prophets had promised the Spirit would descend in the last days. That Spirit is poured out on Jesus to usher in the kingdom (Matt. 12:28). Jesus then pours out the same Spirit on his followers, that they may experience the new life of the kingdom (Rom. 14:17).

PAST, PRESENT, AND FUTURE

The good news is about the *past*: In the life of Jesus, and especially in his death and resurrection, God's saving rule and healing reign have come. It is about the *future*: The kingdom of God will come fully one day when Jesus returns, and his restoring power will destroy all remaining resistance. But it is also about the *present*: God reigns now, and his renewing power is present now. And if we believe, repent, follow Jesus, and submit to his rule, we can be included and know something of his reconciling power even now!

CHAPTER 4

The True Context of the Gospel

Surely, if the New Testament is not proclaimed as the fulfillment of the Old, if the Gospel as proclaimed by Jesus and by Paul is not the completion of the faith of Israel, then it must inevitably be a completion and fulfillment of something which we ourselves substitute—and that most certainly means a perversion of the Christian faith.

    —G. Ernest Wright, God Who Acts: Biblical Theology as Recital

I had just finished a lecture to a broadly ecumenical group of global leaders in which I had affirmed the finality of Jesus Christ as the only mediator of salvation to the world. Sitting across from me at the luncheon that followed was a woman who was a pastor in a liberal congregationalist church in New England. She had been in the audience and was challenging me.

"The Bible does not teach that salvation comes only through Jesus," she said. "The words of Peter, 'Salvation is found in no one else, for there is no other name under heaven given to mankind by which we must be saved' (Acts 4:12) and John's testimony on the lips of Jesus, 'I am the way and the truth and the life. No one comes to the Father except through me' (John 14:6) are not making universal truth claims. Rather, both Peter and John are simply making endearing expressions of loyalty to the religious figure they've grown to love. It is rather like you claiming that you have the best wife in the world. You don't expect another husband hearing your words to arise and challenge your statement, asserting that in fact his wife is the best. Anyone listening would recognize that it is your love and loyalty to your wife that prompted your words. They would not take you to be making a truth claim about reality."

When she finished, I offered up a brief prayer for wisdom and said, "If we are to understand the words of John and Peter, we must interpret them within their original theological and cultural context." I spent the next ten minutes or so narrating the story of the Old Testament, highlighting the exclusive claims of the Jews about their Creator God and the goal of their history as one that would include the whole world. Peter and John (and Jesus) must fit into that context. One cannot lift their statements out of their Jewish story and insert them into our pluralistic Western story. Once we hear Peter's and John's words *in their own context*, then we can decide if we believe they testify to the truth or not. What we must not do is set them in a different context and reinterpret their words.

Her response remains with me to this day. She did not push back; rather, tears filled her eyes and she quickly thanked me and left. I do not know what happened with her. I never saw her again and have been curious about her response. But I remember what that encounter impressed on me: If we are to understand Jesus Christ, we *must see him in his proper context*. The gospel is the fulfillment of the Old Testament story. Any other context will change its meaning. Any story we substitute as the context for the gospel will inevitably pervert the Christian faith.

If we are to know the truth of the gospel—to understand it, to live it, and to make it known—we must know the context that makes its meaning clear. In this chapter we explore four elements of the context that establish the meaning of the gospel.

THE GOSPEL AND THE BIBLICAL STORY

The second-century church father Irenaeus presents us with a vivid and instructive example of how to guard against a misunderstanding of the good news. In his day, the truth of the gospel was under threat by Gnosticism. The Gnostic Christians, though they used New Testament language to describe their beliefs, had detached the gospel from its Old Testament context and grafted it onto a pagan story, a myth in which the cosmos was divided into good spiritual elements and evil physical elements. For the Gnostic, the essentially *good* human soul was released at death from its *evil* physical body to return to its spiritual heavenly home. Thus, when Gnostic teachers used biblical language to speak of Jesus as the mediator that brought salvation, they meant something entirely different from what the Bible says. *Because they had changed the context*, salvation had come to mean something quite different from what it meant to Jesus and his apostles. It was escape *from* this world rather than the healing *of* this world.

Irenaeus countered Gnosticism by writing and teaching a catechism that spells out the narrative of Scripture (from creation to consummation) as the true context in which to understand the good news of Jesus the Christ (see fig. 4.1).[1] He begins with a brief Christ-centered confession—called the rule of faith—that provides the lens for his reading of the biblical story.

Figure 4.1. **Gospel in Context of Biblical Story**

Creation → Fall → Israel → Jesus: **The Gospel** → Church: → Consummation
of the Kingdom Mission and
Martyrdom

A widespread problem we face today is neglect of the Old Testament and its unified storyline. This neglect allows another story to provide the context for the work of Jesus. An example of what I mean might be the following:

1. We are sinners separated from God.
2. We deserve God's righteous punishment.
3. The work of Jesus on the cross takes away our sin.
4. If we believe, we are forgiven and will be taken to heaven.

Note that I am *not* saying that these points are simply wrong. But this severely restricted and highly personalized schema (see fig. 4.2) does not give the proper narrative context by which to understand the gospel. The true story is much bigger. The "frame" that replaces it is simply too small to present the meaning of the gospel without distortion.

Figure 4.2. **Gospel in Context of Personal Salvation Story**

Individual → **Gospel** as → Forgiveness and → Heaven
Sinner under Jesus's Justification Now Future
God's Wrath Substitutionary
Atonement

Part of our problem is that we often don't read the Old Testament as *one story*. It is too often read as a patchwork of doctrines, moral guidance, predictive prophecies, and edifying tales. But in Jesus's own day, the Old Testament's character as the single, unfolding story of God's restorative work in his world was the shared assumption of all Jews. They eagerly anticipated the coming of that story's ending. Then Jesus comes among them and says that *he himself is the ending*. The good news of Jesus and the kingdom must be interpreted in the context of the scriptural story.

CREATION, REBELLION, AND RESTORATION

A second layer of context for the meaning of the gospel is the basic three-fold movement of the biblical story: creation, rebellion, and restoration. The whole of the biblical story from the promise of Genesis 3:15 on to Revelation 22 is a story of restoration against the ever-present backdrop of God's glorious purpose for the creation (Gen. 1–2) and the tragic story of human rebellion that disrupted God's plan (Gen. 3). That story unfolds in four stages through Israel, Jesus, the church, and finally the consummation. But the whole story can be comprehended under the one purpose of God: the restoration of his glorious plan for creation from the power of sin and its devastating consequences (see fig. 4.3). The gospel of the kingdom revealed in Jesus is the center point of God's restorative work. It is in the life, death, and resurrection of Jesus that God has acted fully and finally to reveal and accomplish his renewing work.

Figure 4.3. **Creation, Rebellion, Restoration**

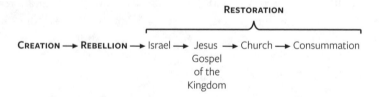

The Biblical Relationship Between Salvation and Creation

At least three implications of this creation-rebellion-restoration storyline are important if we are truly to understand the good news of the kingdom. The first is the proper relationship of salvation to creation. In our day, "salvation" is often thought of (even by devout, Bible-honoring Christians) as an escape from this world into a spiritual heaven where we will live forever. But this is certainly *not* the hope described in the New Testament! The true goal of the Christian faith is the restoration of the entire creation: The resurrection will bring us back to live as embodied creatures within a wholly renewed creation, to live as God intended in the beginning, before sin and its curse. Biblical salvation means the healing of the whole creation.

Salvation, in proper biblical context, is both restorative and comprehensive. As restorative, the work of God in the Old Testament leads precisely to the climactic historical moment when Jesus restores the creation from sin and its curse. A great many biblical images reflect God's work of *restoring* something important to its original goodness. Thus God liberates the enslaved (who were once free), cleanses the filthy (who were once clean), raises the dead (who were once alive), mends the broken (who were once whole), heals the sick (who were once healthy), saves those in peril (who were once safe), removes a curse (from those who had once been blessed), brings back *shalom* (where hostility and alienation had destroyed harmony), and reconciles the estranged (who were once in relationship). He *re*-establishes his original just rule over the unjust dominion of evil, victorious in battle over his enemies and *re*instituting an original peace. He *re*turns the homeless to their proper abode and at last *re*unites heaven and earth. Each of these images speaks of God's work to restore something good that had been lost.

Let's focus more closely on just one of those images, that of healing. You may remember the old joke in which a surgeon says, "The operation was a great success, but unfortunately the patient died." That could never be more than a dark joke, because the goal of any surgeon is to restore the sick person to health—there is no success without recovery. If God's plan is to take individuals (or perhaps just their souls) to heaven and then destroy the earth, that would indeed "take care" of sin—but it would hardly be healing.

Biblical salvation is also comprehensive. Thus, Jesus speaks of the renewal of all things (Matt. 19:28), Peter announces the restoration of all things (Acts 3:21), and Paul proclaims the reconciliation of all things (Col. 1:20). The "all things" to which each of them refers includes the entire social and cultural life of humankind. Even the nonhuman creation anxiously awaits its participation in the liberation of God's redeemed people (Rom. 8:19–22). All of creation—human and nonhuman, visible and invisible—will be restored to be, as God intended in the beginning, "very good." And this includes the social and cultural life of humankind that is the result of the task given to humankind.

The Backdrop of Creation

The second implication of the creation-rebellion-restoration context is that a robust doctrine of creation is needed if we are to understand the gospel. The creation story of Genesis 1–2 is the enduring backdrop for the whole biblical story of redemption. After all, the gospel is about liberating the creation from bondage to human rebellion and its effects so that it can once again be what God intended it to be. So, what is it that is being liberated?

Gordon Spykman speaks of an "eclipse of creation" in evangelical Christianity, which by and large skips over the doctrine of creation "in a hasty . . . shortcut to the cross." Though evangelicals may make "polemical excursions into the realm of creation to combat the evolutionist menace," they often give little thought to creation in their theology and piety.[2] We need a fuller understanding of all the elements of creation as the backdrop of the biblical story, including the goodness of creation and bodily life, wisdom and the creation order, the image of God and the creation mandate, among others. It is *this* creation that is being restored from sin and its effects.

The early chapters of Genesis describe God's marvelous plan for his creation: to fill the earth with his glory so that it might flourish. Central to his purpose is the creation of creatures in his own image to reflect his glory into the world (Gen. 1:26–28). Humankind, his image, was created to mirror God's wisdom, justice, goodness, and love into the world as they fulfilled their calling to steward the creation. As God's agents they were given the blessed vocation both of uncovering the potential God put into the creation and of caring for it (Gen. 2:15). As Abraham Kuyper has put it, "Eden is planted, but humankind will cultivate it—that is the fundamental law of creation. Which is to say: creation was fashioned by God, fashioned with life that surges and glows in its bosom, fashioned with the powers that lie dormant in its womb. Yet lying there, it displayed only half its beauty. Now, however, God crowns it with humanity. They awaken its life, arouse its powers, and with human hands bring to light the glory that lay locked in its depths."[3] The tasks of awakening life, arousing power, and unlocking glory are given to humankind so that the whole creation might increasingly reflect God's glory, bless humanity, and so thrive and flourish. The development of culture and civilization through human history originally had this splendid goal!

Men and women were created to be God's image, with a twofold priestly task: to reflect God's glory into the creation in their stewardly vocation of ruling *and* to be the creation's eyes and mouth that saw the glory of God and sounded his praise. This was the original role of humanity within the divine plan. And the gospel is about restoring the creation to its original purpose, restoring humanity to be, again, God's image.

The Backdrop of Sin

It is not just the first two chapters of Genesis (the creation) that provide the abiding background to God's story of salvation, but also the third chapter, the fall. A weak doctrine of creation can truncate the gospel, but so also can an anemic view of sin.

"We are inclined to minimize the truly alarming character of our sin,"[4] G. C. Berkouwer says, and this minimization distorts our view of the gospel. We have sometimes reduced sin to the wrong thoughts and actions of humanity and thus neglected the role of the demonic powers. We have sometimes reduced sin to the acts of individual persons and thus missed the cultural and structural dimensions of sin, as well as its impact on the nonhuman creation. And we have too often thought of sin only in terms of disobedience, ignoring the many other scriptural images that depict sin's dangerous operation.

In Ephesians, Paul reminds us of the alarming scope and power of sin as he describes the situation of the Ephesian Christians before their conversion. Then, they had been "dead in [their] transgressions and sins" because they had followed the ways "of this world" and "of the ruler of the kingdom of the air, the spirit who is now at work in those who are disobedient." They had been "gratifying the cravings of [their] sinful nature" (2:1–3). Paul describes evil as (1) the idolatrous patterns of their culture in this present evil age, (2) being animated by the spirit of satanic and demonic power, and (3) gratifying their sinful nature. Sin is thus structural and demonic as well as personal. The demonic powers and the cultural idolatry of the world are very closely associated in Ephesians 2:2, and we can see the truth of this in our own cultures. For example, demonic powers can hold us in bondage through the structural idolatry embodied in consumerism or political ideologies or racism. This view of the wide scope of evil shows our desperate need to be liberated. We must be delivered not merely from our own sinful nature but also from the demonic powers and structural evil that entrap us. A diagram representing this is shown in figure 4.4.[5] To be dead in our transgressions and sins is to be located where demonic power, structural idolatry, and our own sinful nature overlap.

Figure 4.4. **Evil as Demonic, Systemic, Personal**

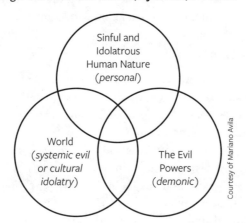

Sin is wide in its scope, touching every part of creation. It is also overwhelming in its power. Berkouwer describes sin as a "seductive power," a "deadening power," a "damning power," a "deadly force," an "active, dynamic and destructive force," a "cataclysmic and disruptive power," a "power that seeks to rule and to ruin everyone and everything," a "virulent force," and a "pernicious power."[6] I add that it is a *personified* power, as Paul speaks of sin as seizing an opportunity, producing wrong desires, springing to life, and deceiving and putting to death (Rom. 7:8–11). Indeed, sin "is a power that controls everyone and everything. . . . [It] organizes all the entities and forces God has created into rebellion against him."[7]

When we minimize the scope of sin and reduce it to the thoughts and acts of individuals, it will naturally follow that we will reduce the scope of the gospel as well. When we reduce the power of sin, then we don't recognize our need for a gospel that is even more powerful and is able to deliver us. We need a gospel of equally wide scope and power that can undo all the mischief and damage evil has done.

THE COSMIC-COMMUNAL-PERSONAL STRUCTURE OF THE CHRISTIAN FAITH

Suppose you were to take me to visit a school where you had once been a student. As you show me around, reliving old memories, we come across a long wall of class photos. We pause while you search for your particular year, until (pointing to one face among the crowd of faces) you say triumphantly, "There—that's me." It's not necessarily a sign of vanity that, when we look at something much bigger than ourselves, our first instinct is to look for our *personal* connection. We all do it. Even in a family photo, most of us see our own face before we shift focus to embrace the bigger picture. But it would be very odd indeed if we never considered the wider view and remained stuck on just our own place within the frame!

The Bible tells the grand story of God's historical journey, working in and through a covenant people to renew the whole of his sin-deformed creation. The scope of this story stretches in time from the beginning to the end, and in space across the entire cosmos. It is a big story, with a covenant community at its center. But if we remain fixated on only our own personal place in God's story, its cosmic and communal dimensions will be lost to us, and we will not in fact see the whole truth, the full picture, laid out before us. The very structure of the Christian faith is cosmic and communal as well as personal (see fig. 4.5).

The scope is *cosmic*: The Bible tells a story that begins with the creation of *all* things and ends with the judgment and renewal of the *whole* creation. And it is a *communal* story: At the center of his plan, God chooses a people and establishes a covenant with them to embody and restore his

Figure 4.5. **The Structure of Scripture**

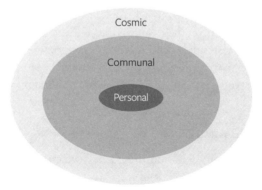

creational purpose to the world. And the story is, of course, also a *personal* one: Each and every person must find their place in this story. Those who do respond faithfully come to participate in this cosmic salvation as part of the new community, the new humanity.

It is not usually the case that Christians intend to deny the cosmic scope of the biblical story. (Who could do so, after reading Col. 1:15–18 or Rom. 8?) The problem is that often we pay it so little attention that it fades into the background. Neither do Christians routinely deny the importance of the church. (Who could do so, after reading almost anything written by Paul?) But when we mistakenly think of the church as a mere collection of saved individuals or (even more mistakenly) as a religious body that exists solely for the sake of serving those individuals, we falsify the very nature of the community at the center of the story. The cosmic dimension of the Christian faith is not mere decoration; it is the very structure of the story the Bible tells, the very shape of the Christian faith. The community Jesus called into being as the church is not merely a collection of saved individuals; it is the new humanity at the heart and center of the biblical story. Each person's salvation means that they participate in God's cosmic purpose, entering that community by faith and baptism.

The first chapter of Colossians describes the faith in precisely these terms. Paul first expounds the *cosmic* dimensions of the Christian gospel in his magnificent statement on Christ: The Son has created all things, all things hold together in him, and he is reconciling all things through the cross (1:15–20). In that context, Paul shows how the cosmic work of Christ has created a *community*: Christ himself is the head of the body, the church, and his resurrection as the firstborn from the dead is the beginning of a new humanity over which Christ has supremacy (1:18). Only then does Paul turn to the *personal* response of the Colossian believers: Once they were alienated from God, but now they have been reconciled by Christ's work. It is by faith in the gospel that they now participate in the cosmic hope held out in the gospel (1:21–23). Paul's theology consistently works out the implications of salvation from the cosmic dimension to the communal to the personal. If we miss this structure in Scripture, the true nature of the gospel will remain out of focus for us.

JESUS AND THE KINGDOM

If we are to properly understand the gospel, we must never separate the *person* of Jesus from the *kingdom* he proclaims. The good news is that

God himself in the person of Jesus returns to his creation as King, and his reign is utterly comprehensive, extending to all of time and space. Yet some Christian traditions stress the person of Jesus to the neglect of the kingdom he came to establish. In such traditions, stress is laid on the fact that each of us has a *personal* relationship with Jesus. "Mission" may well be reduced to an evangelism that is no more than an invitation to know Jesus *personally*. But if we focus again on the Gospels as they truly represent Jesus, God's all-embracing rule is present in him.

While some traditions have introduced a Jesus stripped of the kingdom, others have focused on the kingdom such that it eclipses the person of Jesus. "The kingdom," when it is the sole focus of attention, may inspire a triumphalistic crusade of social development or a program that seeks justice and peace without anchoring these things in the person and work of Jesus, in his cross, resurrection, and exaltation. Mission may be reduced to a campaign for transforming culture, changing social structures, and seeking "justice," all while downplaying the need for a personal commitment to Christ. When we separate the kingdom from Jesus himself, we are in danger of losing the Bible's own truth concerning the personal nature of the gospel.

The person of Jesus and the kingdom of God are inextricably woven together. Salvation is a personal encounter that nevertheless carries creation-wide significance. It is about knowing God intimately and participating in his broader plan for creation. That is what it means for us to be his friends (John 15:15) as well as his coworkers and covenant partners (2 Cor. 6:1). Anything less diminishes the fullness of the gospel as it is proclaimed in Scripture.

CHAPTER 5

The Whole Truth of the Gospel

The greatest need of the church today is the recovery of the full Gospel of our Lord Jesus Christ.

—René Padilla, *"Evangelism and the World,"*
in Let the Earth Hear His Voice

THE WHOLE TRUTH AND NOTHING BUT THE TRUTH

In English-speaking courtrooms the world over, witnesses pledge to tell "the truth, the whole truth, and nothing but the truth," just as they have done for more than a thousand years. The reason for the precise language of this oath is clear: Justice depends on our telling the truth of what we have witnessed, and our testimony can become twisted into falsehood if we hold back or conceal parts of the truth (failing to tell "the whole truth") or if we add to what we say something that is *not* true (failing the test of "nothing but the truth"). In this chapter we are concerned with the *whole truth* of the gospel and nothing but the truth.

When the Latin American leader René Padilla addressed the plenary gathering of global evangelicals at the landmark Lausanne Congress on World Evangelization in 1974, he said there is "no use in taking for granted that we all agree on the gospel that has been entrusted to us." He believed the gospel had been reduced in various ways as it had been co-opted by idolatrous cultural spirits, perhaps especially in the West by the spirit of individualism. He continues, "The greatest need of the church today is the *recovery of the full gospel* of our Lord Jesus Christ."[1]

CONTEMPORARY REDUCTIONS OF THE GOSPEL: *NOT "THE WHOLE TRUTH"*

By focusing on one or another *aspect* of the good news, one can end up losing the bigger picture. All reductions of the gospel carry with them the danger of minimizing its implications for our whole lives. Here we'll consider seven such reductions.

Reduction 1: The Gospel = Individual Salvation

In this reduction of the gospel, the focus is on the salvation of individuals: Each person is a sinner, and the "gospel" is about how individual people can be saved and receive the personal benefits of their salvation. Certainly, the element of truth here is clear; each of us must enter and receive the kingdom by faith and repentance. But the good news is simply much bigger, since each person is in fact summoned to participate in the (infinitely greater) work of God!

Paul shows us how to think about this. In the first chapter of Ephesians, he has a wonderful little expression: "And you also were *included in Christ* when you heard the word of truth, the gospel of your salvation" (1:13). To be "included," of course, means to become part of something bigger. And Paul has already, just a few verses earlier, offered a glimpse of the grand design in which the believers at Ephesus have been "included": God himself has "made known to us the mystery of his will according to his good pleasure, which he purposed in Christ, to be put into effect when the times reach their fulfillment—to bring unity to all things in heaven and on earth under Christ" (1:9–10). We are included in God's purpose to bring all things back together under Christ. Our inclusion comes when we hear this good news and believe (1:13–14). The cosmic map is drawn first, then we find our place on it by faith and baptism.

Reduction 2: The Gospel = The Atonement

The crucifixion is certainly a central event of the gospel (e.g., 1 Cor. 1:18; 2:2; 15:1–8). Indeed, Paul himself sometimes uses one central element of

Jesus's story, such as the crucifixion, as a kind of shorthand to signify the whole gospel. But he knows, and shows us clearly, that the cross in and of itself is not the full gospel, and we need to attend to his teaching if we are not to come away with a partial view of the truth. In fact, of the three places in which Paul summarizes the content of the gospel, he always notes the resurrection but only once mentions the cross (1 Cor. 15:3–8; Rom. 1:3–4; 2 Tim. 2:8). This is not because Paul means to downplay the significance of Jesus's death. May it never be! Rather, resurrection is the dawning of the kingdom on the basis of Christ's victory on the cross.

When the cross is the exclusive event in contemporary presentations of the gospel, the focus, again, is often that individual sinners need forgiveness and by Jesus's death may be restored to a relationship with God. While this is true—and a precious truth!—it is not the whole truth. When we perceive the "problem" to be only the sin of individuals, the resurrection will not really feature prominently in our theology. But if, in the bigger picture, the good news is about the advent of the age to come into history—with *all* its benefits, including forgiveness for sinners—the resurrection assumes its rightful significance.

To restrict the meaning of the cross only to its implications for each person is a falsifying reduction of the truth. Padilla remarks that classic theories of the atonement have "concentrated on the salvation of the individual soul but frequently disregarded God's purpose to create a new humanity." As a corrective, he urges that we "look at the cross, not merely as the source of individual salvation, but as the place wherein begins the renewal of the creation—the new heavens and the new earth that God has promised [the cosmic dimension] and that the messianic community anticipates [the communal dimension]."[2] The cross deals with the sin, the evil, and the curse in the world, and the resurrection inaugurates the new creation and the new humanity. Both are cosmic; both are communal.

Reduction 3: The Gospel = One Image of the Atonement

The gospel may also be reduced when only one image of one event in the ministry of Jesus is held up as the "good news." For example, it is common to describe the work of Christ on the cross in terms of the substitutionary atonement, which is "good news" because Jesus has indeed taken the guilt of my sin on himself so that I might be forgiven. Thus, substitutionary atonement can be presented as if it were the sum of the gospel.

The substitutionary atonement is certainly biblical, and the image is centrally important to the meaning of the cross. Like the sin offering in the Old Testament sacrificial system (Lev. 9), Jesus has taken on himself God's wrath, along with our sin and guilt. For those Christians who rightly feel that God's judgment is being soft-pedaled today, this one image of what the cross accomplishes may become the only one they see. Yet the Bible uses many images to describe the significance of the crucifixion, and all are important.

For the first three hundred years of the church's existence, the cross was primarily interpreted in terms of a military image: Jesus was seen as a victorious general who had overcome the "powers," conquering sin and death (John 12:30–33; Col. 2:15). When we see the cross in this light, it is much more difficult to reduce its significance to the saving of individual souls.

Our understanding of what the cross of Christ means is closely tied to our understanding of sin and evil. If we portray sin only in personal terms, then the substitutionary atonement is an obvious image of what the cross accomplishes. But the Bible's picture of sin is more complex. In Colossians, Paul addresses the threat of "the powers," which are "unseen forces working in the world . . . through the oppressive systems that enslaved and tyrannized human beings."[3] Demonic powers, oppressive systems, and sinful hearts: all these together hold us in bondage. For example, demonic *powers* working through the oppressive *system* of a consumer culture may enslave and tyrannize us because of our own *sinful* greed.

When we realize the full scope of the power of evil at work in our world, we see how much the death of Christ has accomplished: It defeats demonic powers, unmasks the idols of culture, roots out structural and systemic evil, and puts to death our old sinful nature. An image of a military victory conveys this well. Crucifixion as it was used by Rome was designed not merely to put its victims to death but also to humiliate them utterly and to overawe any other potential enemies of the Roman state. Roman soldiers would strip their victims naked, display them publicly, and declare victory over them. In a shocking reversal using the same imagery, Paul announces the victory of the cross. "He stripped the rulers and authorities of their armor, and displayed them contemptuously to public view, celebrating his triumph over them" (Col. 2:15 NTFE). "The cross was not the defeat of Christ at the hands of the powers; it was the defeat of the powers at the hands—yes, the bleeding hands—of Christ."[4]

The celebration of victory is an allusion to a Roman *triumphus* or victory parade. Christ "made a public spectacle of [the powers] and led them as captives in his triumphal procession" (Col. 2:15 NEB). After a general had achieved a significant military victory, there would be a parade in Rome to celebrate his feat. Riding in a chariot, he would lead his defeated enemies before the throngs to the place of their execution. Here in the humiliation of the cross Jesus leads the powers as defeated foes in his victory parade to final judgment! The cross is a victory over the powers that enslave us, and now God's people share in that victory.

We can briefly mention two more significant biblical images of the cross. In Romans 5–6 Paul speaks of Jesus as the *second Adam* or representative man who (on the cross) acts on behalf of his people to create the new humankind. The obedience of Jesus on the cross undoes the disobedience of Adam and so creates a new humanity. The cross is also often presented in terms of an act of *redemption* or a *new exodus*. "For he has rescued us from the dominion of darkness and brought us into the kingdom of the Son he loves, in whom we have redemption, the forgiveness of sins" (Col. 1:13–14). When Israel was in bondage to the oppressive idolatry of pagan Egypt, God redeemed them, rescued them, as a father might liberate his son from slavery (Exod. 6:6; 15:13; cf. Lev. 25:47–55). However, the subsequent history of Israel showed that this exodus had not truly delivered them. Though they had escaped from political captivity in Egypt, they had not escaped their religious enslavement to pagan idols. So Isaiah proclaims the promise of a *new* exodus. Once, God had made a way through the sea and had destroyed the Egyptian chariots and army in a marvelous display of his power (Isa. 43:16–17). But now, says Isaiah, God's people are to forget even this triumph from their past because their God is about to do a new thing, to bring about a new exodus that will accomplish for them what the old one could not (Isa. 43:18–19).

And Isaiah's vision of a greater exodus did indeed kindle a fire in the imagination of Israel. This was especially evident in the Passover feast, as they remembered their miraculous liberation from Egypt. Their repeated celebration of Passover taught Israel to long for God to act again in power, to liberate them from their new bondage to idolatrous Rome. And it was in just this atmosphere of urgent longing and hope that Jesus took bread and wine (symbols of revolutionary violence) at the last supper, revealing himself to be the true Passover lamb, and announced that the liberation sought by God's people was about to come—in his own death.

Paul proclaims the good news of a new exodus to the Colossians and to us. Those who receive Christ Jesus as Lord have been rescued from the dominion of darkness and brought into God's kingdom (Col. 1:13–14).

Christians have been rescued from the present evil age and liberated from slavery to the powers in order to become children of God (Gal. 1:4; 4:1–7).

What is noteworthy about these three images—Jesus's military victory, the second Adam, the new exodus—is that the individual sinner is not their focus. The canvas is larger than we thought. When we are included in Christ by faith, we enjoy the fruit of *all* that he has accomplished in his crucifixion.

There are more images of the cross in Scripture. If we are rightly to understand the good news, we must embrace each of them and allow all of them together to inform our imagination.

Reduction 4: The Gospel = A Few of Its Benefits

The good news may be distorted if we conceive of just a few of its benefits. For example, it is common to hear that "forgiveness of sins and justification by faith" *is* the gospel. Certainly, these are part of the gospel, marvelous gifts of the salvation accomplished by Christ that come to those who repent and believe. But there is more.

There are three major types of benefits that come to us in the good news.[5] The first benefits *prepare* us: These include God's calling us and creating a new heart within us, opening our hearts to receive the gospel in faith and repentance. The second type of benefits change our *status* in God's sight: These are such things as justification, forgiveness, and adoption. The third group of benefits change our *condition*: Sanctification and walking in the Spirit liberate us from the power of sin and cultural idolatry, and renew us to become fully human. The "good news" changes not only our status but also our condition. And to concentrate only on those benefits of the gospel that confer new status upon us is to dangerously narrow our understanding of what salvation means. Such a selective view of the truth may well produce a church that revels in a cheap gospel and does not take obedience and radical discipleship seriously.

The problem is exacerbated when we apply the word "grace" to the second set of benefits (those that change our status) and somehow see any stress on obedience (which changes our condition) as mere human effort that stands in opposition to God's grace. But Herman Bavinck is certainly in line with Scripture when he says that *all* the "benefits which Christ gives in His fellowship can . . . be comprehended under the one term *grace*."[6] Grace not only changes our status before God from guilty to innocent; grace also empowers us to be more and more transformed into the image of God through growing obedience. God always gives in grace what he demands. God's grace deals not only with the guilt of sin but also with sin's destructive power over our lives. "Grace" that is limited to our status but does not extend to our subsequent transformation is cheap grace.

To take this one step further, sometimes when our view of God's grace is restricted to its effect on our status before him, we begin to think of it solely in terms of benefits we receive passively. Effort of our own that we put forth may thus be considered "works" or "merit" that stand opposed to God's grace. But this is not what Scripture teaches. Paul exhorts the Philippian church "to work out [their] salvation with fear and trembling, for it is God who works in [them] to will and to act in order to fulfill his good purpose" (Phil. 2:12–13). Paul describes his own life as like that of an athlete who trains hard so he might not be disqualified (1 Cor. 9:24–27). Grace prompts effort. As Dallas Willard says, "Grace is not opposed to effort, it is opposed to earning. . . . Grace, you know, does not just have to do with forgiveness of sins alone. Many people don't know this, and that is one major result of the cutting down of the gospel to a theory of justification, which has happened in our time."[7]

Here is a summary of the problem: Grace may be reduced in our thinking to those benefits that change our *status* (justification, adoption, forgiveness), which we *receive passively*. Those benefits that change our *condition* (sanctification, obedience, holiness), in which we *actively participate*, are excluded and may even be deemed to stand *against* grace (see fig. 5.1). Indeed, this confusion has become so prominent in some evangelical preaching and praise music that we may be in danger of buying into "cheap grace." Jesus's warning is sobering at this point: "Not everyone who says to me, 'Lord, Lord,' will enter the kingdom of heaven, but only the one who does the will of my Father who is in heaven. . . . I will tell them plainly, 'I never knew you. Away from me, you evildoers!'" (Matt. 7:21–23).

Figure 5.1. **Misunderstanding Grace**

Gifts of Grace	Gifts Considered Meritorious
Change Our Status	Change Our Condition
• justification • forgiveness • adoption	• sanctification • walking in the Spirit • dying and rising with Christ
Passive Reception	Active Effort

But **all** are gifts of God's grace—God gives what he commands!

All these benefits rightly belong to the end-time kingdom, in which we are restored to our full humanity. And the very good news is that all these are ours *now*, in the present.

Reduction 5: The Gospel = A Restored Relationship with God

It is very true that a restored relationship with God is at the very center of the gospel. Human beings *have* been alienated from God by their sin and rebellion, and it *is* good news that we are being reconciled to him and restored to know, love, serve, and glorify him. This is of first importance. However central this is to the gospel, though, there is more.

In Genesis we see the newly created humankind in loving relationship with God, with one another (in a variety of relationships that will unfold in social and cultural development), and with the nonhuman creation. Too soon, all three kinds of relationship become twisted and distorted by human rebellion. The good news is that God is restoring all human life to its original creational design. The renewal promised by Jesus means not only that we can once again live faithfully in relation to God but also that we can love others in the manifold relationships we enjoy and can together care for and cultivate the creation as we were called to do from the beginning. The good news is that God is restoring all the relationships in which we are created.

Reduction 6: The Gospel = The Intermediate State

A sixth reduction of the gospel is to locate its promise of eternal life in a spiritual place apart from this world, called "heaven," which will be our ultimate eternal home. This is simply a misunderstanding of the Bible's teaching.

Often this statement of the good news of a future "heavenly" home is simply an unexamined assumption of personal piety. We imagine that when we die our souls will go to some spiritual place above, in "heaven," and that is where we will live forever. But this is simply not the teaching of the New Testament. It is much closer, in fact, to pagan Greek philosophy, or even to the Gnostic heresy against which Irenaeus fought. The hope held out in the good news is that God will restore his creation, *including the whole embodied life of human beings*, by removing sin and its cursed effects. God does not clean us up so we can go and live with him in heaven; he cleans up the world so he can come and live with us here.

To be sure, it is good news that we are "with the Lord" (in heaven) after death (2 Cor. 5:8). This has been called the *intermediate state*: we go to be with the Lord until the time of the resurrection of the body. Our trip to heaven is not one-way but a round trip! This comfort sustains our hope during times of sorrow at the loss of loved ones. We are comforted that they are *now* with the Lord, and it is better by far (Phil. 1:23; 2 Cor. 5:8). But in many funerals, shaped more by popular piety than by the Scriptures, this comfort is as far as the gospel seems to reach. It does not move beyond this interim period to consider the great hope of the resurrection itself. Our immediate comfort (that we will be with the Lord after death) must never replace our ultimate hope that we are at last to take our place in the kingdom of God, in glorified and resurrected bodies, living in this restored creation, under God's loving rule.

Reduction 7: The Gospel = Theological Doctrine

The gospel is sometimes reduced to theology—propositional statements and ideas. As all of these reductions do have elements of truth in them, it is also true that the gospel does have doctrinal content. There is in it a proclamation about historical events and what God has accomplished through them. There is content in the gospel that can be expressed in propositions. It is possible to misunderstand or twist that content and thereby preach a false gospel (Gal. 1:6–9). Nevertheless, the gospel should not be reduced to mere statements directed to our minds—even if they are "true doctrine." This kind of reduction demonstrates the influence of a culture deeply influenced by rationalism that assumes reliable truth is to be found only in ideas.

The gospel is first of all news about what God has done—in a person and in historical events—to lead his creation to its ultimate goal. The good news is also "the power of God unto salvation" (Rom. 1:16 KJV). In the Gospels the good news of the kingdom was not merely some new doctrine for Jews to add to their theology; rather, it announced that God himself was returning and acting in power in the midst of history to renew and heal his creation. God's power, it claimed, was present in the person of Jesus by the Spirit to reverse all the evil consequences of sin, against both God and neighbor.

The parable of the sower clarifies our sense of *how* the kingdom comes. The message of the kingdom is like a seed with incalculable power to bring forth the life of the kingdom: Paul calls it "the power of God" (Rom. 1:16; 1 Cor. 1:18; 2:4–5). God's renewing power makes its entrance into human history through this humble channel. This is the good news: The power of God to heal a broken world is present, first through the very presence of incarnate Jesus in history, and then through his spiritual presence as he comes to us clothed in the words of the gospel.

The good news is an announcement of the arrival of the kingdom of God in history, in the person and work of Jesus, by the power of the Spirit. The good news comes to make the blessings of his rule known (as the carol teaches us) "far as the curse is found." It is a victory over sin and a reversal of all its devastating effects. All are invited to repent and believe the good news, to enter the kingdom, to taste this salvation, to become part of the community that now shares in the fruits of Christ's work, and to participate in the new creation one day when it fully comes at the return of Jesus. Anything less than this is less than the "whole truth" of the gospel.

CHAPTER 6

Continuing in the Gospel

So then, just as you received Christ Jesus as Lord, continue to live your lives in him, rooted and built up in him, strengthened in the faith as you were taught, and overflowing with thankfulness.

—*Colossians 2:6–7*

WHAT CAN WE DO?

It was Samuel Johnson who said, "When a man knows he is to be hanged in a fortnight, it concentrates his mind wonderfully."[1] While I (thankfully) have no experience quite like what Dr. Johnson had in mind, I can say for certain that, when I was asked late on a Saturday night to preach on Romans 7, through an interpreter, to a congregation I'd never met, it "wonderfully concentrated" my own mind! It drove me into some serious late-night reading and rereading of the text, along with urgent prayer for guidance. The next morning, I tried to describe what Paul means for us to see in this chapter: that sin is the vicious and destructive enemy of humanity, a deadly power intent on capturing and enslaving us. And when one comprehends this truth about sin, the gospel of Romans' next chapter is indeed good news (Rom. 8:1–11).

A few months later, back in the classroom and lecturing on Genesis 3 and the fall of humankind, the memory of what I learned through that mind-concentrating experience came back to me vividly. In the interim I had become convinced that we tend to miss Scripture's teaching on sin in at least three ways: (1) We minimize the *seriousness* of our rebellion in God's sight, (2) we fail to see the *breadth* of evil, and (3) we underestimate its sheer *power* to destroy. As I attempted to communicate this, I noticed the eyes of one student continuing to widen with concern until at last he blurted out, "What can we do?"

What can we do? This is exactly the right question, and we will ask it only when we realize our danger and our utter helplessness in the face of this deadly enemy. The answer is, of course, that although we in ourselves can do nothing, the grace and power of Jesus Christ revealed in the gospel have the power to set us free.

If we are to take our stand in the gospel against the powerful spiritual forces, we need to understand three things. The first is the power and scope of sin: To stand firm against the enemy, we must know that enemy well. The second is the saving power and scope of the gospel: Jesus has overcome the forces of evil, and he comes to us in this message to liberate us. And finally, being liberated from sin is an ongoing process: Spiritual practices and rhythms enable us to take hold of the power of the gospel habitually and repeatedly. We will unpack these three things in this chapter.

Paul's letter to the Colossians is a good place to start. The church at Colossae knew something about the oppressive power of evil. Its members lived in a city where citizens were aware of the tyranny of "the powers" that populated and ruled the Roman Empire. For them, the question "What can we do?" was a pressing matter of life and death. Paul writes them a letter to show them what they can do.

BONDAGE TO SIN

The goal of the biblical story had always been that humanity should flourish once again, faithfully reflecting God's glorious image into the world as they steward his creation. Paul shows the church at Colossae that they themselves are part of this new humanity, destined one day to appear with Christ *in glory* (Col. 3:4). "Glory" here does *not* mean "heaven" but the honor of being restored to their original perfection as in Eden (Ps. 8:5; cf. Heb. 2:5–10). Even now, Paul says, as they put off the old and put on the new, they are being renewed in the image of their Creator (Col. 3:10).

But the Colossian church as Paul writes to it is in danger of succumbing to bondage under "the powers" that *de*humanize them. If the Colossian church was to be *re*humanized as the new humanity, it must be liberated from the powers.

What exactly are these powers? The Colossian church knew them well. They were the many "gods" who ruled and oppressed Rome's citizens and subject peoples (1 Cor. 8:5), including Venus (sex and love), Vulcan (technology), Mars (war), Mercury (commerce and wealth), Roma (the nationalistic spirit of Rome itself), Minerva (knowledge and wisdom), Jupiter (political power), and Bacchus (pleasure). The human representative of all these deities on earth was the "divine" Caesar.

For us, in our firmly secularized Western culture of the twenty-first century, it is tempting to patronize those who held such a "primitive" worldview. Hasn't science liberated us from such nonsense? Yet when rampant sexual addiction abounds, it seems the goddess of sex is not dead. When millions of lives are trivialized by addiction to social media, the god of technology still wields power. When we experience the seductive power of a consumer society that enflames us with a lust for senseless consumption, it seems that the gods of wealth and pleasure are alive and well. When we spend billions of dollars annually on arms, we betray our enslavement to the gods of war and national security. The hatred and polarization fostered by political ideologies shows us that the god of political power is still with us.

Some evangelical Christians do believe the "powers" are personal demonic entities, living somewhere between heaven and earth and doing their work by tempting individuals. This is part of the truth, certainly, but not enough to account for what Paul says about the range, scope, and influence of the powers. Other Christians (at the more liberal end of the theological spectrum) may see the powers as mere symbols of structural evil or ideology such as Nazism, apartheid, or (more recently) global capitalism. Again, though the powers reveal themselves in such forms, this characterization of them does not give us the whole picture.

What does the New Testament teach? For Paul, the powers are demonic forces enslaving people through oppressive and idolatrous systems. The power of evil is found not only in the human heart but also in idolatrous systems that we create and in the demonic powers that work in and through them.

These powers are real demonic forces at work in our world. Only a culture in bondage to religious secularism would deny this reality. No other culture in world history has done so. They have power to ensnare people by twisting the creational powers that God originally granted to humankind out of his goodness for our benefit. Sex, political power, wealth, pleasure, technology, and knowledge have power and were created good by God to bless us. But when we make idols of these creational gifts, their power is turned against us in curse and oppression. Moreover, when we shape the lives of our cultural communities around these creational powers, we build oppressive, idolatrous structures. Demonic spiritual forces thus enslave and tyrannize us through our own social structures and cultural institutions. Demonic powers working through idolatry "operate more forcefully in their *corporate, structural, or institutional effects* than any evil generated by any individual human person as such. *Evil systems* have power. Sometimes the net effect of corporate or structural evil is greater than the sum of the individuals who promote it."[2]

The Colossian church faced the power of evil embedded within the idolatrous structures of the Roman Empire. And we face similar forces today. Attempts to debunk belief in spiritual powers as myths will not liberate us. In fact, they will lead only to deeper enslavement.

LIBERATION IN THE SON

Paul has good news for the Colossian church, and for us as well. God's people do not have to remain enslaved to these dehumanizing powers. Christ has freed his people from the dominion of darkness. He has won a victory over these oppressive powers, and he is rehumanizing us in Christ to live as God intended. Paul wants the Colossians to live so that in everything it is Christ—and not the cosmic powers—who has supremacy (Col. 1:18).

The gospel is the power of God in Christ to save and restore (Rom. 1:16; 1 Cor. 1:18, 24; 2:4–5). The gospel liberates men and women from their sin, from systemic idolatry, and from the oppression of the spiritual powers. Through the gospel, the "powers of the coming age" flow *now* into the world, to restore human life and cause it to flourish as it was meant to (Heb. 6:4).

This gospel has power to free humanity from "the powers," first, because of *who* is proclaimed in it. Christ himself comes to us "clothed in the gospel."[3] In Christ "all the fullness of the Deity lives in bodily form" (Col. 2:9), and he is uniquely the very image of the invisible God (1:15). The Son is the Creator of all things (1:16), Lord over everything (1:18), the one who holds all things together (1:17), the one who is reconciling all things at the end of history (1:20). The Son originally created the powers (1:16), went on after their rebellion to defeat them at the cross (2:15), and is now head over them (2:9). One can hardly think of a more worthy and capable liberator!

This gospel has power to liberate humanity from the rebellious evil powers, second, because of *what* is proclaimed in it. The center of the gospel message is the death and resurrection of Jesus Christ. Paul gives us three striking images of the cross. The first is that the death of Jesus brings about a *new exodus*. In the Old Testament, redemption was the act of setting a slave free, and the term was often applied to the act of family members freeing their kin from bondage (Lev. 25:47–55). Redemption was mentioned for the first time in Exodus (6:6; 15:13), where God rescued Israel as his firstborn son from slavery to Egyptian idolatry. The book of Isaiah (chaps. 40–55) and later Jewish literature look forward to a new exodus, a second redemption that will once and for all liberate God's people from their slavery to idolatry. It is hardly surprising, then, that the New Testament often interprets the cross in similar terms: In the death of Jesus, a new exodus has taken place and God's people have been freed from bondage to sin, "the powers," and idolatry (Col. 1:13–14).

Paul also refers often to the cross as the center of Christ's *military victory* over his enemies: "Having disarmed the powers and authorities, he made a public spectacle of them, triumphing over them by the cross" (Col. 2:15). Here he presents the cross as if it were the triumph of a conquering general. Jesus has defeated the demonic powers and oppressive systems that hold us in bondage, as well as the sinful nature that enslaves us. They are now his captives, being led to final judgment.

Paul's final image of the cross is the *new creation* (Col. 1:19–20). In one of the New Testament's most compact and rich statements of the Son's identity, Paul proclaims that Jesus is the Creator and reconciler of all things. It is "through his blood, shed on the cross," that he restores the lost shalom of creation (1:20). Now by faith we can share in the reconciliation of all things accomplished by Christ's death (1:20–23).

The good news is also about the resurrection. Christ is also the firstborn into the new creation (Col. 1:18). In Jesus's resurrection the new creation has begun, and we can begin to share in it now. By faith we are already raised to this new life by the powerful working of the Spirit who raised Jesus from the dead (Col. 2:12; 3:1).

The cross and the resurrection cast their light over the entire creation and the whole of history. The powers, sin, systemic evil, and their grievous effects are defeated at the cross, and a new world begins in the resurrection. The cosmos, the church, and all believers share in this death and resurrection. What God has done in and for Jesus he will also do for the whole world, for his people, and for each person who believes.

ONGOING LIBERATION

Continually Receiving New Life in Christ

Our liberation from "the powers" does not happen in a moment but continues for all of life, only to be completed at Christ's return. We live in the in-between (see fig. 6.1), when the power of God's new creation has already broken into history but the destructive powers of the old age continue to exert their malignant influence.

Figure 6.1. **Living in the Overlap of Power**

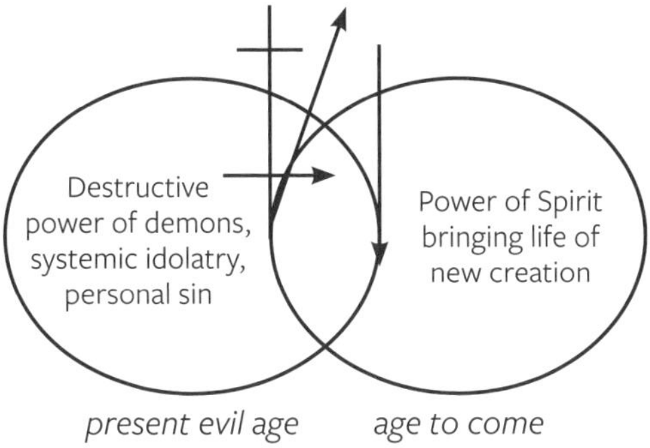

Destructive power of demons, systemic idolatry, personal sin

Power of Spirit bringing life of new creation

present evil age   *age to come*

Thus, Paul urges the Christians at Colossae to "continue to live your lives in him, rooted and built up in him, strengthened in faith as you were taught" (Col. 2:6–7). Here we arrive at the heart of the message of Colossians: Now that you are indeed *in Christ*, you have everything you need to resist the idolatrous powers, to live a life that is truly human, to be the image of God in the world. Yet *you must continue* to die to the powers of the old age and draw on the Spirit's power—the power of the new creation.

Paul uses two images to describe the way the Colossians are to continue to live in Christ. He uses an organic metaphor: They are to root their lives in him. In the same way a plant sends down roots into the soil to be nourished in its life, so believers are to be rooted in Christ to receive his life. He also uses an architectural metaphor: They are to build their lives on him. In the same way a good builder constructs an edifice on a solid foundation, so believers are to build their lives on Christ Jesus.

In these images the underlying reality is that the power of God to bring the life of the new creation has broken into history in Jesus through the working of his Spirit. Receiving this life is an intentional and continuing process.

Spiritual Disciplines

Spiritual disciplines enable us to remain constant in receiving the new life of Christ and standing fast in him. Thus, for example, Paul urges Timothy, "train yourself to be godly" (1 Tim. 4:7). Athletic preparation takes effort, self-discipline, and perseverance. And Paul understands just what he is asking of his younger colleague, since he describes himself as enduring the same kind of "strict training" (like a runner or boxer), "so that after I have preached to others, I myself will not be disqualified for the prize" (1 Cor. 9:24–27). Clearly, new life in Christ is neither automatic nor accomplished in a moment but requires sustained effort and rigorous discipline.

The renewing power of God flows into us (and through us to others) through many practices—means or "channels" of grace. The practices or means are not merely *instrumental*; they are primarily *relational*. The renewing power of God flows to us by the Spirit in communion with the living Christ, and the goal of this relationship is that we should be conformed to the image of God for the sake of the world. Christ gives us *his* life. There may be some danger even in speaking of "the gospel" rather than of Christ, lest we should miss this relational dimension. But if we understand well that Christ comes to us *clothed in* the gospel, we can speak of receiving the gospel again and again.

Be Devoted to Prayer

Just before his final greetings to the church of Colossae, Paul closes with the stirring call, "Devote yourselves to prayer, being watchful and thankful" (Col. 4:2). The word "devote" is used outside the New Testament to refer to the kind of dedication necessary for an Olympic athlete, putting training ahead of almost everything else, forgoing other enjoyable activities and exercising rigorous self-discipline. So it is for the Christian, Paul says: Nothing else must come in the way of regular prayer.

This devotion to prayer is set in the context of "watchfulness," which takes us back to Gethsemane. There, as Jesus faced the climactic moment in the cosmic battle for the creation, he understood the urgent need to pray to be faithful. He took with him Peter, James, and John, and called them to *watch* and pray so they would not fall in this climactic battle (Matt. 26:36–46; Luke 22:39–46). To "watch" here meant to open their eyes to the spiritual battle taking place, to be alert and on their guard against the power of the enemy. Then Jesus goes a little farther off to watch and pray, but when he returns to his disciples he finds them sleeping. Twice he wakens them and urges them again to watch and pray, but the third and last time he lets them sleep on. Then, as the spiritual battle reaches its climactic moment, Jesus steadfastly goes to the cross alone and there wins the battle against the evil powers. But his disciples scatter in fear and confusion. Peter even goes so far as to deny knowing Jesus.

The disciples never forgot the ignominy of that moment. They had failed to be vigilant and alert, had not remained steadfast in prayer, and thus had succumbed to the powers. They had failed their master. So it is that Peter, one of the disciples in Gethsemane, exhorts his readers, "Be sober-minded; be watchful. Your adversary the devil prowls around like a roaring lion, seeking someone to devour. Resist him, firm in your faith" (1 Pet. 5:8–9 ESV). So too Paul urges the Colossians to be vigilant against a powerful enemy that seeks to destroy them.

This kind of watchful prayer is to be saturated by thanksgiving, which is at the heart of Pauline spirituality. Gratitude brings God's work to our memory repeatedly so we might live in its light. What we thank God for, we remember, and thus we keep fresh the sense of his working in our lives.

Prayer is essential to the life of Christian faith because it is the way we receive the new life of Christ. One cannot stand firm in the gospel against the powerful winds of cultural idolatry without devotion to watchful and thankful prayer.

Daily Baptism and Prayer

Perhaps one of the most powerful spiritual practices we can learn is to pray in a manner that daily appropriates our baptismal identity. Martin Luther says that the "Christian life is nothing else than a daily baptism, begun once and continuing ever after."[4] Paul's own understanding of baptism is tied closely to his understanding of the coming of the kingdom. Baptism pictures our new identity (see fig. 6.2). By faith in the gospel, we move from the present evil age into the age to come. We *die* with Christ, sharing in his victory over the powers of the old age, and we also *rise* with Christ, sharing in his inauguration of the new creation (Rom. 6:1–14; Col. 2:11–12).

Figure 6.2. **Baptismal Identity**

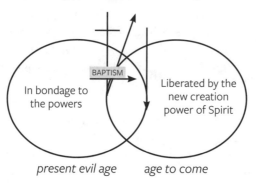

present evil age   *age to come*

The historical events of Christ's death and resurrection become part of our own story in the present, as we look back on our baptism and as the Holy Spirit works in response to our faith and prayer. Paul challenges us to live more and more into what our baptism tells us about ourselves, that we no longer belong to the old but to the new.

Baptism is a source of rich imagery in the New Testament. In baptism we are seen to share in Christ's death (drowning) and resurrection (rising) (Rom. 6:1–11). Baptism is also a picture of forgiveness and cleansing (1 Pet. 3:21), of the outpouring of the Holy Spirit (Acts 2:38–39; Titus 3:5; 1 Cor. 12:13), of being clothed with Christ (Gal. 3:26–27; Col. 3:9–10; Eph. 4:20–24), of being born into the new creation (Titus 3:5; John 3:5), and of being circumcised (as the sinful nature is cut off, Col. 2:11–12). All these images tell us who we are as God's new-creation people.

Many of the practices of the early church were designed to make these pictures come alive. Some baptismal fonts were designed in the shape of a tomb to signify death and drowning. Others were womblike to show that the baptized person would emerge as newly born into the new creation. The practice of wearing dirty clothes, removing them as one entered the waters, and being reclothed with a white robe on the other side also reinforced the imagery. In fact, it is possible that this last-mentioned practice is early enough to be behind Paul's words in Galatians 3:26–27.

Baptism does not merely picture and signify this new identity. Through prayer and the work of the Spirit, God empowers us to live increasingly into that identity (see fig. 6.3). Here are two prayers that might be used to that end:

Lord, my baptism tells me I am no longer enslaved to the old (death) but liberated to live in the new (resurrection) for the sake of your glory and for the world. Enable me to die to the old and live in the new. Drown the old humanity in me today and empower me to rise in the life of the new humanity.

Lord, enable me to take off these filthy clothes of the old age and put on the clean clothes of the age to come, for your glory and for the sake of the world. Help me to put off the filthy clothes of my culture's idolatry and dress myself in the life of Christ.

Figure 6.3. **From Old to New**

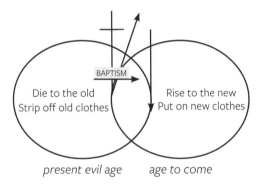

Practices of Prayer

It is helpful to make distinctions between practices, rhythms, and spheres of spiritual discipline. First are those *practices*—the "what" of discipline—that we carry out regularly to nurture our new life in Christ. Then there are the *rhythms*—the "when," whether daily, weekly, monthly, semi-annually, or annually—by which we give order to these habitual practices in our lives. And last are the *spheres* or areas of life—the "where," whether personal, marital, familial, or congregational—in which we embed our practices. Wise is the person who early on takes time to understand the various spiritual disciplines (including but not restricted to prayer), who thinks through the rhythms and spheres, and who crafts them into a rule of life.

We have primarily focused on the discipline of prayer. Though there are many kinds of prayer, I'll note just a few here to illustrate what sorts of prayers might be built into a daily rhythm to continually receive the new life of Christ's resurrection:

- Prayers of thanksgiving: At least once a week, take extended time to soak in God's goodness and grace, and express gratitude to God as the Creator (for his gifts in creation) and as Redeemer (for his gifts of salvation).
- Begin and end your day with prayer:
  - Open your day with the prayer, "O Lord, open my lips [my *heart*], and my mouth [my *life*] shall declare your praise" (Ps. 51:15). Saying and reflecting on this before getting out of bed can set a good direction for the whole day.
  - End the day with an *examen* prayer, in which you review the day, thanking the Lord for his goodness and faithfulness, confessing where you have failed, and rededicating yourself to ever-increasing faithfulness in the future.
- Prayers of transition: As you move from one activity to another throughout the day, pray for the next event coming your way. Pray for wisdom, courage, love, faithfulness, or whatever might be needed for that moment.
- Prayers of confession and renewal: Daily prayers of confession and of commitment to a renewal that grows and deepens are crucial for spiritual health. A daily pattern of confession, forgiveness, and renewal, all for the sake of our witness in the world, enables us to sink our roots deep into the soil of the gospel.
- Prayers of lament: These prayers are important, though we often neglect them. (But consider: just under half of the psalms fall into this category!) As we face pain, experience brokenness, or feel the injustice of the world, we can become angry, cynical, bitter, or apathetic if we bear that grief on our own. The pattern of lament opens a way to honestly express our raw anger or pain to God, to plead for his help, and to express our confidence and trust in his good and sovereign purposes.

Missional Orientation

We have been reflecting on how we can be formed into the new human-ity by the gospel. But we must not forget the missional direction of the biblical story. The missional vocation of God's people throughout redemp-tive history is to be the new humanity *for the sake of the world* amid the idolatrous cultures of the old humanity.

Paul always had this missional orientation in mind. In Colossians 4:3–6 (after urging devotion to prayer), he asks for prayer that the message of the gospel would be *proclaimed clearly among the nations*, even if he himself remains prisoner in a Roman jail cell. He exhorts the Colossian church to live in such a way that their wisdom is evident *toward outsiders*. They must make the most of every opportunity with their neighbors and speak in an attractive and discerning way in their responses to everyone they meet.

OUR STRATEGIC POSITION

At Waterloo, the British general Arthur Wellesley, the Duke of Wellington, knew that in facing Napoleon he was up against one of the most bril-liant military strategists in history. The course of the battle would revolve around a château called Hougoumont: Wellesley took his own position there, defending it with a large force of troops against repeated assaults by the French army. He knew the outcome of the entire battle hinged upon the English holding on to that one small piece of ground.

Prayer is the "strategic position" in the spiritual battle that we must take and *hold*. Paul exhorts the Ephesian church to stand firm against the spiritual forces of evil in the heavenly realm, putting on the whole armor of God so they might continue to stand. Then, when the armor is in place, he says, "And pray in the Spirit on all occasions with all kinds of prayers and requests. With this in mind, be alert and always keep on praying." And two more times he urges, "Pray" (Eph. 6:18–20). Victory depends on our holding the strategic position of prayer throughout the battle. The "pow-ers" seek to dislodge us, for they know prayer's importance. The Spirit is their Creator, and they are no match for his power. Prayer is the means by which the Spirit works to ensure Christ's victory. To stand firm in the spiritual battle, we must hold the strategic position of prayer.

PART 2

THE BIBLICAL STORY

CHAPTER 7

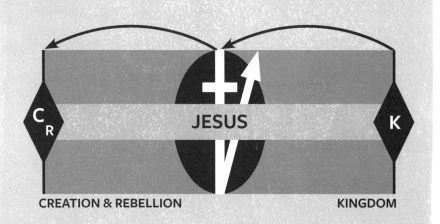

Israel's Story, Part 1

The Book of Moses

Jesus said to [his disciples], "This is what I told you while I was still with you. Everything must be fulfilled that is written about me in the Law of Moses, the Prophets and the Psalms."

—Luke 24:44

"You Christians don't seem to be aware of what you have in the Bible!" This comment was made by a prominent Hindu scholar to Lesslie Newbigin, a missionary who had spent decades in India. "You missionaries have presented the Bible to us in India as if it was simply another book of religion that gives teaching about God, salvation, morality. But the Bible is much more than that—in fact, there is nothing comparable to it in all the world's religious literature. It claims to tell the true story of the world—where it all began, where it is going, and the meaning of history in between. It purports to give the true meaning of human life as part of that story. Moreover, and even more astounding, it claims that the meaning of world history is revealed in one person: a male Jew who lived in the first century. As a Hindu I find it hard to believe that anyone could claim to know the meaning of cosmic history or would stake their life on one man. It seems preposterous. But if you are a Christian, and if you do believe that the Bible is God's Word, why would you reduce it to something less?"[1] He was genuinely perplexed.

Indeed, the Bible's claims about itself are astonishing. Can we hear how scandalous they sound to a Hindu—or even to a postmodern Western person? No other "holy book" makes such staggering assertions. The Bible begins and ends with nothing less than a view of the whole world. It demonstrates that the goal of universal history, what gives meaning to it all, has been revealed and accomplished in the life, death, and resurrection of one particular Jewish man in the middle of history. It demands that we submit our lives wholly to the vision of the world it narrates because that vision tells us what our world truly is. And, most remarkably of all, the Bible professes to narrate the story of the one true God, the Creator and Sustainer of the universe, the Lord of all history and of every nation, and the one who will bring all things to their proper fulfillment in reconciling them to himself.

The Bible tells the story of God's mighty historical deeds to restore the world to what he had always intended for it, against the backdrop of God's own work in creation and humanity's rebellion against him. The narrative runs through the history of Israel, reaching its climax in the life, death, and resurrection of Jesus, and continues through the church's mission until the consummation of all things at the end of days. It claims to be nothing less than the true story of the whole world. In the next four chapters I will briefly retell this story, observing six acts in its structure.[2] In this chapter I begin with the foundational "Book of Moses" (Mark 12:26), also known as the Pentateuch or the Law of Moses.[3]

ACT 1: GOD ESTABLISHES HIS KINGDOM–CREATION

In the opening act of the drama, we are introduced to God himself, who is not merely its primary character but also its author—and indeed the Creator of all the other actors in it, and even of the cosmic stage on which they will perform! God is introduced with two names. The first, *Elohim* (God), is the generic name for god. The second, *Yahweh* (LORD), is the personal name of God, revealed to Moses as the name by which he is to be known throughout redemptive history. Yahweh is the Lord God who redeemed Israel from Egypt and established his covenant with them (Exod.

3:13–15; 6:2–5). Moses, writing to the Jewish people many years after the events he describes, says in these opening chapters of the world's history, "The same God who liberated you from Egypt is Yahweh, the One who created the whole world."

Moses writes to a people who have just been freed from Egyptian oppression and bound in covenant to Yahweh at Sinai. As Moses writes, these mighty deeds in their recent history—the exodus and the making of a covenant between Israel and Yahweh—are given their proper historical context, stretching back to the promise God made to their forefathers Abraham, Isaac, and Jacob. But Moses takes a step further back, to show how these early promises to the patriarchs of Israel stand in the context of *universal* history. The story of Israel begins and ends with its divine author, God himself, *Elohim Yahweh*, who created the whole world. The Lord who freed Israel from Egypt is not a mere tribal deity like the gods of the nations, but the divine maker of heaven and earth.

Moses writes to a people whose views of the gods, of themselves, and of their world have for four hundred years been shaped by the pagan myths of Egypt. As he narrates the account of creation, he takes deliberate aim at these myths, seeking to reshape Israel's views of God, of humankind, and of the world, in order to equip them for what God is now calling them to do and to be. The false stories they have lived with for so many years need to be displaced by the truth.

So Moses begins with Yahweh, who is eternal: "In the beginning, God . . ." As the description of Yahweh's creating work unfolds, it becomes clear that he is utterly unlike the idol-gods of Egypt. He is the one and *only* God: everything else that exists has been created by him. His power and wisdom are revealed in the way he forms the creation by his word. His goodness and kindness shine out as he prepares a wonderful home for humanity. Yahweh stands apart from everything else in existence, as the great and incomparable Creator.

Yahweh effortlessly speaks the world into existence. The world he makes is a symphony made up of an almost infinite variety of creaturely sounds but exhibiting a marvelous and harmonious coherence. Each creature he makes is *good*, and so is the harmony of the whole. The entire cosmos echoes and re-echoes the glory of God, and evil has no part in it. The creation is also conditioned by *time*, made to develop and change, to move forward toward a goal, a *telos*, according to God's own purpose.

The rhythmic literary pattern by which God *speaks* the various elements of creation into existence and then pronounces them good is reinforced in Genesis 1 by the repetition of the formula, "and there was evening, and there was morning—the first [second, third . . .] day." But on the sixth day the pattern is disrupted as the divine King on his throne makes a momentous announcement. He is about to form a creature that will be uniquely *an image of himself*, one who will be given the task of continuing God's own work, forming and filling his kingdom so as to reflect his glory. In Egypt, Pharaoh alone was considered to be the image of god, the one with a relationship with the gods, tasked to rule on their behalf. Here Moses makes the astonishing statement that *all* people are created in God's image, that *every person* can know and partner with God, that *all* share in the task of ruling the creation, cultivating its brimming potentials to mirror the glory of God its Creator (Gen. 1:26–28).

As God completes his work of creation, he pronounces it "very good" (Gen. 1:31). The world and humanity are blessed by him, their lives woven together in a way that all may flourish and thrive (Gen. 1:22, 28). The needs of all are satisfied with the rich resources of the creation. Humans delight in their task to discover, to enjoy, to cultivate, and to care for the creation. Blessing, shalom, life, and prosperity—all these words describe the newly created world as it comes from God's hand. This is the way the world was meant to be.

ACT 2: REBELLION IN THE KINGDOM—THE FALL

The world we live in today looks very different from the delightful world of the early creation. Instead of peace, harmony, and abundance we see sickness and pain, poverty and murder, lies and hatred, selfishness and abuse, hunger and death. What could have happened?

Moses tells the second act of the world drama in these terms: God chooses a tree in the middle of the garden and commands humanity not to eat from it. This prohibition is designed as a constant reminder to humankind that their future blessing lies in loving trust, allegiance, and obedience to God. He gives them the whole of his beautiful world to enjoy freely, this one particular tree aside. This he gives them so that they might obey him freely: By heeding his command not to take what he has forbidden, they will acknowledge his lordship as Creator and their own creaturely dependence on him.

But the human creatures made in his image do not for long accept their creaturely dependence on God. They take what was forbidden, rebelling against their sovereign creator. As Moses describes it, the descent into mutiny is insidious: First the serpent merely invites doubt in the human pair, questioning God's command. "Did God really say . . . ?" But the subtle temptation to question the goodness of God's word swiftly becomes an invitation to flat unbelief: "*You will not die.*" The serpent inflames human imagination with the (false!) vision of a *fuller* life in independence from God, to be found only in disobedience to him. And so they eat.

Eating what had been forbidden was not merely some unfortunate mistake; it was (and is) a catastrophic act of mutiny. The loving relationship between God and humanity is broken (Gen. 3:8–10, 23–24), relationships among people are plagued by selfish exploitation (Gen. 3:16), their harmonious relationship with the nonhuman creation is cursed (Gen. 3:17–19), pain and sorrow begin to burden their lives (Gen. 3:16), and finally death comes to the human family (Gen. 3:19).

Genesis 4–11 tells of the disastrous tsunami of sin and curse as it surges across the whole earth. The cultural task continues (Gen. 4), but now there is exploitation, murder, and deceit. There is such wickedness that God even regrets he made humanity on the earth (Gen. 6:5–6)! The spread of sin across the earth is met with God's judgment to curb it, but that cannot cure this cancer (Gen. 6:5; 8:21). The whole sorry tale culminates in an egregious revolt at the tower of Babel, where humanity organizes itself into society, not in harmony with the Creator's design but in brazen defiance of his intention (Gen. 11). Cultural idolatry pollutes the whole human task.

And yet, amid the cacophony of evil in the early chapters of Genesis, there are a few sounds of hope. God promises to crush the evil forces that Adam's rebellion has unleashed (Gen. 3:15), and he makes a covenant with Noah and the creation, promising to preserve the world from judgment (Gen. 9). However, even this new beginning goes sideways quickly, as human rebellion increases to become universal.

As the curtain falls on act 2, we are left with the question: What will God do about the mess that humankind has made of the world?

ACT 3: THE KING CHOOSES ISRAEL–RESTORATION INITIATED

Scene 1: The King Forms a People

Genesis 12–50. Against the backdrop of seventy-two representative people groups (Gen. 10), God promises that he will make *one* man into a great nation. The nation thus chosen will be blessed by God, and it in turn will restore the blessing of creation to *all* nations: This is God's remarkable promise to Abraham (Gen. 12:1–3). It is difficult to overestimate the significance of this promise for the remainder of the biblical story. Paul even says, two thousand years later, that in this promise *God* preaches the gospel (Gal. 3:8)! God's promise is the central theme of the Pentateuch, the first five books of the Bible. But it moves beyond these books to offer a blueprint for the redemptive history of the whole world.

God promises three things to Abraham: people, land, and blessing. God will make Abraham into a great people, give them a land, and restore to Abraham's heirs the blessing of creation. Now God intends, through Abraham, to deal with the sin of Adam and reverse the curse.

However, to stop at the three gifts promised to Abraham (of people, land, and blessing) would be to miss the essential point of God's promise. His goal in giving all this to Abraham is ultimately to include *all* nations in a restoration of the whole earth. Abraham and his descendants are blessed so as to be a blessing to others (see fig. 7.1). They are intended to be a river of God's grace to the world, not a cistern for their own selfish benefit.

Figure 7.1. **Blessed to Be a Blessing**

The Abrahamic promise looks *back* to the original creation and *forward* to a new creation. Adam and Eve (a people) had been placed in a garden (given land) in which to enjoy God's creational blessing. In order to restore this very good creation, God chooses Abraham's family (a people) and gives them the land in which to enjoy God's blessing. The goal is that all humanity (a people) might enjoy the whole earth (land) and be restored to the full blessing of creation (see fig. 7.2).[4]

Figure 7.2. **Looking Back and Looking Forward**

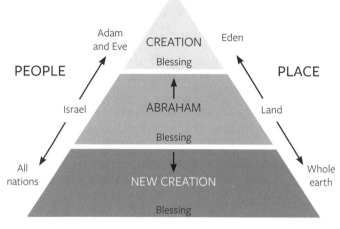

This Abrahamic promise is given powerful reinforcement with a solemn covenant, a binding agreement between two parties that could be broken only by death (Gen. 15). God promises Abraham he will be given a son (vv. 1–6), the literal beginning of that "great nation" promised earlier. Further, God promises that he will give this nation a land of its own (vv. 7–21). Then God walks alone between the split carcasses of sacrificed animals, in a covenant ceremony well-known to Abraham, a sign that whoever walks through those pieces invokes death on himself if he should fail to keep his word (Jer. 34:18–20).

This covenant promise now becomes the main thread running through the stories of the patriarchs of Israel—Abraham, Isaac, and Jacob. The promise of people, land, and blessing-to-be-a-blessing is repeated to Abraham (Gen. 18:18–19), then to Isaac (26:2–4), and at last to Jacob (28:13–15). Many barriers to the fulfillment of these promises arise: The patriarchs are impotent and their wives barren, their wives are seized for the harems of foreign kings, the patriarchal families wander the earth without a homeland, there is strife between the patriarchs and the surrounding nations, and natural disasters threaten. But in all this, God reveals himself as *El Shaddai*, God Almighty, who has the power to overcome any obstacle that would seem to prevent him from keeping his promise (Gen. 17:1; Exod. 6:2–3).

Exodus. The book of Exodus opens four hundred years later. The small clan of less than a hundred that Joseph brought to Egypt to save from famine is now an enormous people. But, far from being blessed, they have become slaves, in social, political, and economic subjection to Egypt. More important than all of this is their *religious* bondage, for they are also enslaved to the Egyptian gods under Pharaoh. They cry out to God for deliverance. Remembering his promise to the patriarchs, God protects and raises up Moses to liberate his people.

God attacks the Egyptian gods with a very focused series of plagues, by which the Egyptian deities—the Nile god, the frog god, the cow gods, the gods charged with protecting crops and livestock, and the rest—are shown to be powerless against him (Exod. 12:12). The plagues reach a climax in a strike against the chief deity of Egypt, Re the sun god (Exod. 10:21–23). "I am [Yahweh]; that is my name! I will not yield my glory to another or my praise to idols" (Isa. 42:9). God's final blow against Egyptian idols is to destroy the firstborn son of each Egyptian family. Pharaoh himself claimed to be the firstborn son of Egypt's gods, so this final act of judgment pictures a dismantling of pagan religion and the installation of Israel as the firstborn son of the true God.

God then leads his people Israel to Sinai, telling them why he has acted so powerfully on their behalf (Exod. 19:3–6). They are to be his treasured possession, chosen to bring restoration to the whole earth that belongs to him. Their vocation is found in two terms: a *priestly kingdom* and a *holy nation*. Israel is to be a kingdom that functions in a *priestly* way as they mediate God's blessing to other nations. And they can do so only by being a *holy* nation, set apart to embody God's creational purpose as the new humanity on display before the nations. They are to offer an attractive alternative to the oppressive idolatry of the surrounding cultures. God gives them the Torah to show how they are to live as the true humanity (Exod. 20–23). In contrast to the law codes of the surrounding peoples, God's law will shape his people to be a distinctively just, compassionate, and holy people before the nations (Deut. 4:6–8).

The book of Exodus ends with the making of the tabernacle, the place where God will live among his people. The structure of the tabernacle highlights the truth that God is holy. But between the instructions for the tabernacle's construction (Exod. 25–31) and the act of building it (Exod. 35–40), an odd narrative intervenes: the story of the golden calf (Exod. 32–34). It points to the difficulty faced by a sinful people living in the presence of a holy God (cf. Exod. 33:3) and comes to a resolution when God promises to live among them as a compassionate and gracious God, slow to anger, abounding in love and faithfulness, maintaining his love and forgiving wickedness (Exod. 34:6–9). Now the tabernacle can be built; now a holy God can dwell among his sinful people. The story of the tabernacle concludes with the glory of God descending on it to live amid his people Israel—the same glory that will one day cover the whole earth (Exod. 40:34–38).

Leviticus. Leviticus shows how sinful Israel may maintain a covenant relationship with their holy God, as the priests will mediate on their behalf, and sacrifices will atone for sin. As they daily distinguish between the holy and profane, and follow the social legislation given them, Israel will learn how to be a holy people in the whole of their lives, in obedience to God's command: "Be holy, because I, the LORD your God, am holy" (Lev. 19:2).

Numbers. Israel had been formed by the Lord for its task, its people liberated from Egyptian idolatry to serve God, given their vocation, given the law to shape them into the new humanity for the sake of the nations, and at last given God's own presence with them in the tabernacle. What remains is for them to receive the *land*, the stage on which to play out their assigned role. They should have reached their home quickly from their starting point in Sinai. But sadly, the story told in Numbers is that Israel is not ready for this last promise to be fulfilled: Their lives are still characterized by unbelief and disobedience (Heb. 3:18–19). Thus, they are judged by God and wander forty years in the wilderness, where the first generation dies. But the good news is that God remains faithful to his people and his promise, and he prepares the next generation to enter the land and take up their calling.

Deuteronomy. Deuteronomy records three "sermons" given by Moses to prepare Israel to enter the land. In the first, Moses reminds Israel of God's covenant faithfulness and care despite their disobedience (Deut. 1:6–4:40). In the second, Moses revisits in greater detail the law that God had given them as a covenant people (4:44–26:19). If they are to love the Lord their God in covenant faithfulness, they will shape their entire lives according to God's law. The nations are meant to see Israel as a just and holy people, an example of what human culture should look like so that they will want to know the God who shapes Israel's way of life (4:5–8). Israel is warned that pagan idolatry will be a constant threat to their witness, and thus to God's blessing on that witness. In the final sermon (chaps. 27–30), Moses holds before them two options: either faith and obedience to the Torah as the way of life, with prosperity and blessing following on, or unbelief and disobedience in the way of pagan idolatry, with death, destruction, and the curse attending. In a moving final scene Moses urges his people to choose the first path. Only along this way will they experience the life God intended in creation, and only thus will they fulfill their calling to the nations (see fig. 7.3).

Figure 7.3. **Covenant Structure**

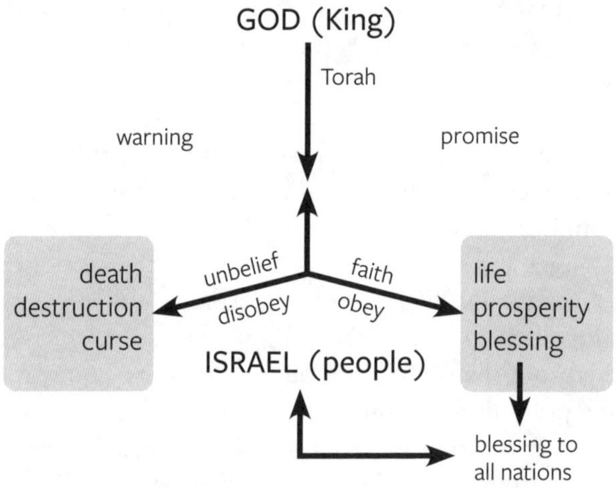

God's purpose for creation was put in jeopardy by the rebellion of the first couple. But God then chose and formed Israel to be the solution to the problem. As Israel waits on the plains of Moab, poised to enter the promised land, they are a people formed to be the beginning of the new humanity. Now they will be placed in the land amid the pagan nations to demonstrate to the nations what God intends for human life. How will they fare?

CHAPTER 8

Israel's Story, Part 2

Life in the Land

*The Old Testament ... presents universal history: it begins with the begin-
ning of time, with the creation of the world, and will end with the Last
Days. ... Everything else that happens in the world can only be conceived
as an element in this sequence; into it everything that is known about the
world ... must be fitted as an ingredient of the divine plan.*

—*Erich Auerbach,* Mimesis: The Representation
of Reality in Western Literature

Not long ago my wife and I attended a marvelous production of Shakespeare's *A Midsummer Night's Dream*. For over three hours we sat mesmer-
ized as we were immersed in a world with a forest inhabited by fairies, a
talking donkey, and magical love potions. We forgot about our own reality
for a time and allowed ourselves to be entertained and even instructed as
we entered the narrative world Shakespeare had created. At the end, after
rousing applause, we all stood up, exited the tent, and returned to the real
world. In that real world we did not furtively glance about looking for fairies or wonder whether there really is an enchanted forest. We did not try to
concoct a love potion from flowers to apply to the eyelids of sleeping victims. We knew the difference between a narrative world and the real world.

We have been telling the story of Israel. This story, likewise, narrates a world; as we read it, we enter into and immerse ourselves in its world. But there is a fundamental difference between this story told in Scripture and all others: The Bible claims to narrate the way the world really is. Its narrative world claims to be the real world.

The great German literary critic Erich Auerbach helps us to understand this. He compares the way the Old Testament and Homer's *Odyssey* represent reality. He says that the Old Testament, "far from seeking, like Homer, merely to make us forget our own reality for a few hours, . . . seeks to overcome our reality: we are to fit our own life into its world, feel ourselves to be elements in its structure of universal history." This is because the Old Testament "presents universal history: it begins with the beginning of time, with the creation of the world, and will end with the Last Days. . . . Everything else that happens in the world can only be conceived as an element in this sequence; into it everything that is known about the world . . . must be fitted as an ingredient of the divine plan." Auerbach calls this "tyrannical" because it "excludes all other claims." It claims to be "the only real world," and everything else in the world must be "subordinated to it."[1]

Auerbach, a secular Jew, has discerned something important about the Bible. As we continue to enter the story of Israel, we are not reading the parochial religious story of one small ancient nation that has only marginal historical interest. The claim is that this is the story of the Creator God, and that it truly narrates the world. If one embraces the gospel as true, one may not leave the world of the Bible for another so-called real world; it *is* the real world. We remain in its world, find meaning there, fit our lives and all else into its narrative structure and world.

We continue our telling of the Old Testament story with Israel's life in the land. In the Old Testament the books that primarily tell this story are Joshua, Judges, 1 and 2 Samuel, and 1 and 2 Kings. These books were formed into one literary unit and are meant to be read as one story.

ACT 3: THE KING CHOOSES ISRAEL—RESTORATION INITIATED (CONTINUED)

Scene 2: Life in the Land

God promised Abraham a people, a land, and a blessing, so that through him God might restore blessing to all nations and to the whole creation.

The Pentateuch tells us how God formed Israel into a nation. Now, as they cross the Jordan, God will give them the land he had promised Abraham, as a public stage on which to exhibit his creational design to the nations.

The story of Israel's life in the land is told in the historical books and focused through the lens of the covenant (see fig. 7.3 above). If Israel lives according to the law, they will experience the blessings promised in it. If, however, they break the covenant by disobeying the law, they will know the curses until they are exiled from the land (Deut. 29:25–28). In the years that follow, Israel fails in its vocation, breaks the covenant, disobeys the law, experiences the covenant curses, and is finally exiled. But the story begins with hope, with Joshua.

Joshua. Joshua succeeds Moses to lead Israel into the land of promise. Yet really it is Yahweh who is the hero of Joshua's story—it is *he* who leads Israel into the land by holding back the waters of the Jordan so they can cross (Josh. 3). And Yahweh also gives them the land, as is clear (for example) in the "battle" of Jericho and the taking of the other royal cities (Josh. 6, 10–11). It is Yahweh who divides the land among the tribes (Josh. 14), and he who keeps the promise he had made to the patriarchs: "So the LORD gave Israel all the land he had sworn to give their ancestors, and they took possession of it and settled there. . . . Not one of all the LORD's good promises to the house of Israel failed; every one was fulfilled" (Josh. 21:43–45).

The book closes with a covenant renewal ceremony in which Joshua challenges Israel to obey the law, to reject the dangerous idolatry of the nations, to hold fast to the Lord, and to serve and love him alone (Josh. 23–24). Their immediate task is to purge idolatry from the land, and Israel accepts the challenge, responding three times to Joshua: "We will serve the LORD!"

Judges. Alas, their life in the land begins badly. Israel's covenant failure appears quickly, as they fail to drive out the idolatrous nations (Judg. 1:27–36). So the Lord comes to Israel in a covenant court case, accusing them of breaking the covenant. His sentence on them is, ironically, to give them over to what they want: a life amidst the nations' "gods" (Judg. 2:1–5). This sentence is carried out in cycles (see fig. 8.1), in which Israel will fall prey to foreign gods and arouse God's anger. He will give them into the hands of the pagan nations. In their distress, Israel will cry out to God for help, and he will answer by sending a deliverer. For a short time, Israel again will experience *shalom* . . . until the whole sorry cycle inevitably begins again (Judg. 2:11–23).

Figure 8.1. **Cycle of Judges**

Six of these cycles come one after another, each featuring a new deliverer—two of them are Gideon and Samson—to save Israel from oppression (Judg. 3–16). But each cycle is worse than the last as Israel spirals ever deeper into rebellion.

Two appalling stories conclude the book, illustrating just how far Israel has fallen. The first is a story of idolatry, and the second, a story of rape that leads to war (Judg. 17–21). Far from being a distinctive people, Israel imitates the very worst of pagan idolatry. They reject the Lord and his law, doing what is right in their own eyes. Israel is in desperate need of a king to deliver it from this mess, but "in those days Israel had no king; everyone did as they saw fit" (Judg. 21:25; cf. 17:6, 18:1; 19:1). Israel's descent into covenant rebellion raises the question of what kind of deliverer Israel needs to fulfill her vocation. The cry at the end of Judges is for a king to mediate God's rule—and in the book that follows, God gives them one.

Samuel. The narrative of the book of Samuel begins with the demise of the old order of the corrupt priest Eli and his sons. God makes a new beginning with Samuel, who brings together the fragmented tribes of Israel and calls them to repentance (1 Sam. 7). Then, as Samuel gets older, Israel comes to ask for a king. The problem is not so much that they ask for a king but that they demand a leader *like the kings of other nations*: a strong, powerful military ruler whom they can trust to fight their battles (1 Sam. 8:5; 19–20). But this is not the kind of king God wants them to have, for God alone is their King, and he can (as he has proven) defeat their enemies without human help. Israel wants a king to be their champion, but God wants for them a godly king who will mediate his rule.

God does give Israel the sort of king they want, in Saul, and seeks to bend even the people's rebellious request to something good by shaping the kingship for his own covenant purposes. But Saul does not submit to God's will; his defiance grows until finally God rejects him as king. Samuel then anoints David as precisely the kind of king God wants for his people.

David rules faithfully and does what a king mediating God's rule is called to do: He defeats Israel's enemies and gives his people rest (2 Sam. 5:6–25; 7:1; 8:1–14), he enforces the law (1 Sam. 8:15–18), and he champions the temple to nurture God's presence in Israel (2 Sam. 6–7). The last concern becomes the occasion of an important promise. David, who rules on behalf of the true King, is living in a fine palace while the divine King resides in a tent. David proposes to build God's palace-temple, but God does not give his consent. Rather, God promises that *he* will establish the throne of one of David's descendants in an everlasting and worldwide kingdom (2 Sam. 7:11–16). From this point on, God's purpose to bless Israel and then all the nations is tied to *a future king descended from David* (Jer. 33:14–18; Ezek. 37:15–28).

But David's early faithfulness is followed by a longer section of narrative describing his later failures (2 Sam. 9–20). Even though David had been a faithful king, he is not the one who will usher in God's reign. That will happen as God keeps his promise to raise up a greater "Son of David" (2 Sam. 21–24).

Kings. The prosperity of Israel reached its zenith under Solomon (1 Kings 8–9), but less than three centuries later, Israel was exiled from the land. Though God had promised an everlasting covenant with his people (Gen. 17:7), they were now scattered and exiled. God had promised the land as an everlasting possession (Gen. 17:7), yet now they had lost it. God had promised to dwell in the temple forever (1 Kings 9:3), but now he had left it (Ezek. 10). God had promised a king to rule forever (2 Sam. 7:13, 16), but Israel's king was now exiled to Babylon. What had happened? In the book of Kings, Israel's demise is narrated in terms of the covenant: God's promises had not been automatic guarantees but were bound up in a covenant that each generation could forfeit by rebelling against him (see fig. 7.3 above).

The story begins well, with Solomon, who chooses the gift of wisdom by which to rule justly and who then builds the temple where God comes to dwell (1 Kings 1–9). However, in the second half of his reign, Solomon begins to rule like the pagan kings, building a powerful kingdom unjustly on the backs of his people (1 Kings 10–11). Solomon's son Rehoboam threatens more of the same, and this prompts Jeroboam to lead ten of the twelve tribes away in revolt, establishing another kingdom in the north. Only Judah and Benjamin remain.

The story that follows tells of these two kingdoms: Israel in the north and Judah in the south. Rebellious kings lead Israel into breaking their covenant with God rather than mediating God's rule (1 Kings 12–16). This double narrative is interrupted by the ministries of two prophets, Elijah and Elisha (1 Kings 17–2 Kings 8:15), who seek to stem the tide of unfaithfulness. But Israel does not listen, and the narratives of the two kingdoms resume, culminating in the scattering of the ten northern tribes in judgment under Assyrian rule. The narrative then pauses briefly to explain why Israel has been judged (2 Kings 17:7–23): They had rejected Yahweh and his law to serve other gods, following the pagan practices of their kings and refusing to listen to the prophets. Because Israel had broken the covenant, she was exiled to Assyria. The story of the southern kingdom, Judah, continues; but soon it too (led by its own rebellious kings) is overrun by the new world power, Babylon. Soon, much of the population of Judah is sent into exile in Babylon itself.

This new exile seems to signal the end of God's promise to restore creational blessing to and through Israel. He had sent Israel as a lifeguard to save the world, but its people too are now drowning. Once again, what will God do?

Prophets. A number of prophets take the stage as Israel slides further into rebellion. Initially, the prophets function as covenant enforcers, calling Israel to return to God and to its vocation (Jer. 4:1–2). But as Israel continues in her apostasy, the prophets begin to turn to the future: God will not let Israel's rebellion derail his purpose. The prophets give Israel's people hope that their covenant history is not over.

Even though he has abandoned Israel in judgment, God promises that he will return to establish his rule over a future worldwide kingdom (Isa. 2:2–5; 52:10), ushered in by a son of David who will gather, forgive, liberate, and renew Israel (Isa. 40–55; Ezek. 36–38; Jer. 33). At last, all nations will be incorporated into his kingdom and will bow before his sovereignty. This messianic King will come in power and glory as a world ruler (Zech. 9:9–13). Yet, somehow, this restoration is also puzzlingly linked to the appearance in history of a "suffering servant" (Isa. 53; cf. Luke 24:25–26).

The coming of the kingdom will, the prophets foretell, be a work of the Spirit as an end-time event (Joel 2:28–32; Isa. 42:1). God will bring judgment and salvation first to Israel and then to the nations. The Spirit will renew the covenant and write the law on Israel's hearts so that they may live faithfully (Ezek. 36:26–37; Jer. 31:31–34). Thus, God will form a faithful Israel in the last days. The nations will see and know that Yahweh alone is God, and they will join with the people of Israel to enjoy his salvation.

The prophets inspire hope in Israel: God *will* complete his purpose. He will form a people restored to creational blessing, and he will incorporate the nations into that blessing. The ending promised by the prophets is nothing less than the renewal of the entire creation (Isa. 66:22–24) when God will restore all things and make them new (Acts 3:21).

In that time, the knowledge of the glory of God will cover the earth as the waters cover the sea, and all peoples will acknowledge that Yahweh alone is God (Hab. 2:14; Isa. 11:9; 45:5–6). The words Israel used to sing in worship will become a living reality: "Praise be to his glorious name forever; may the whole earth be filled with his glory. Amen and Amen" (Ps. 72:19). Thus, Israel's hope is now set firmly on this future.

Ezra-Nehemiah. When Persia conquers Babylon, Cyrus decrees that Israel's people may return to their land. Under Zerubbabel, Ezra, and Nehemiah, Israel returns to rebuild the temple and the walls of Jerusalem, and to live in the land. Though only a small portion of the people return, their expectations are high. Moses had promised that God would restore the fortunes of Israel after exile and they would experience unparalleled prosperity (Deut. 30:1–10; Neh. 1:8–9), and the prophets had fueled this hope. But these lofty expectations were soon dashed. Israel did have its land again, but only a small portion of it, which it held only as tenant of the Persian Empire. Though there was a Davidic descendant ruling in Jerusalem, he governed only under the permission and the watchful eye of Persia. Israel had a temple, but it looked nothing like Solomon's beautiful temple, let alone like the glorious temple promised by Ezekiel. Israel was again a people, but they did not enjoy the blessings of renewal they had expected. Discouragement set in, and there began a crisis of faith among the returned exiles.

The message of Ezra-Nehemiah to a disheartened people is that Israel's return had been truly a work of God. He had sovereignly orchestrated their return, the building of the temple, the rebuilding of Jerusalem's walls, and their covenant renewal. The promise for those who had returned was that they did indeed remain part of God's ongoing plan and were called by him to perform their role faithfully. However, God's ultimate purposes were awaiting a greater fulfillment—a better leader, a better temple, a better

Jerusalem, and a better covenant renewal—to re-form Israel into the new humanity it was called to be.

Looking back and looking forward. As their subjection to the world powers continued, Israel believed their exile was continuing, even now that many were again on their own land: "We are slaves today, slaves in the land you gave our ancestors" (Neh. 9:36). The exile had been punishment for their unfaithfulness. Eventually, as they groaned beneath the cruel fist of Rome (which followed Assyria, Babylon, Persia, and Greece as their masters), Israel looked back and interpreted its history through the lens of Deuteronomy 27–30, where Moses promises blessings for faithful adherence to the Torah but warns of curses that would lead finally to exile. This, they believed, is precisely what had happened to them.

Israel's predicament under Roman rule illustrates the same tension that exists throughout the Old Testament story. On the one hand, Israel had been created to be the new humanity, formed by the Torah in the way of blessing as the beginning point of God's purpose to bless all humanity. On the other hand, Israel remained part of the old (and mutinous) humanity. The Torah could not re-form them; they had sown covenant rebellion and reaped the curse. Their ongoing exile was a living, daily reminder of their continuing participation in Adamic humanity under sin's curse.

Abraham and his family had been called to be a solution to the problem of Adam's sin and its curse. Through Abraham, creational blessing was to be restored to the world. Later, the law was given to guide Israel in the way of blessing. But in fact the law merely condemned Israel, putting it under the same curse as Adamic humanity. Israel-under-the-law was no solution. How would God keep his promise to restore blessing to the world? How would he deal with sin and its curse? How would he liberate Israel from the covenant curse so that Israel and all nations might be blessed?

Israel continued to look forward, believing that its story was not yet over. After all, the words Moses had left to the people did not end in an account of their exile (Deut. 27–29) but continued to the promise of their restoration (Deut. 30:1–10). God *would* deal with sin and the curse. God had promised to gather Israel and restore the blessing they had forfeited. God *would* have compassion and give them new hearts to turn to him, to love him with their whole hearts, to obey his law and live.

This Deuteronomic promise was elaborated years later by many prophets who spoke of the coming "new day" when God would return in power to rule and restore Israel so that blessing would flow to the nations (Isa.

19:24–25; Jer. 4:2; Zech. 8:13). He would deal with Israel's sin, liberate and save it, and rule over it. Israel, newly redeemed, would bring salvation to the nations. This was the *telos*, the ending promised to Abraham—and the ending Israel longed for.

INTERLUDE: A KINGDOM STORY WAITING FOR AN ENDING— THE INTERTESTAMENTAL PERIOD

Four hundred years lie between the end of the Old Testament story and the coming of Jesus. This is often referred to as the intertestamental period, and the historical developments of this time are quite significant for our understanding of the end of Israel's story.

The Jews believed that their whole existence was defined by the story of the Old Testament, the coherent narrative of God's work in and through Israel that awaited an ending. Moses had promised a glorious restoration (Deut. 30:1–11). Jeremiah promised a new covenant with David restoring his rule over Israel (Jer. 33). Ezekiel promised a restoration for the sake of Yahweh's holy name among the nations through his servant David and by the Spirit (Ezek. 20, 36–38). Isaiah 40–55 promised that a "servant" would come to fulfill the Abrahamic covenant and liberate Israel from exile to usher in a new creation. Daniel promised that God would destroy all the kingdoms of the world and establish his own rule through the Son of Man (Dan. 2, 7). And Daniel had furthermore also given a time frame that was to shape Jewish expectation: the foretold kingdom was to come in "seventy-sevens," which the Jews interpreted to be 490 years (Dan. 9).

These Scriptures, pored over by generations of devout Jews, sparked an expectation that was fanned into a roaring fire by the oppression of successive world empires. Israel at the end of the intertestamental period had become an inferno of kingdom expectation. As the time promised by Daniel drew near, various messianic movements arose. The time was ripe for the announcement of the coming of God's kingdom.

But under the cruelty of Rome, Israel's faith had become warped by hatred of and separation from gentiles. Their monotheism meant to them that God was their exclusive possession; their views of election and covenant spelled ethnocentric privilege; the Torah was for them a badge of God's unique favor to them alone; and the land and temple were potent symbols of their privileged status. In all this, Jewish hope for the coming of God's kingdom had become twisted into a mere longing for national restoration and vengeance on the gentiles (and also on those Jews wicked enough to compromise with them).

Within Israel at this time sprang up several different communities and sects, each of which espoused a different response to pagan rule. The Zealots were activists who advocated a holy war against their oppressors, always ready to join the Messiah to battle Rome. The Essenes were quietists who withdrew from the world and prayed for God to act. The Pharisees were separatists who established strict boundaries—such as rigidly observing the rules concerning Sabbath, circumcision, and the food laws—to keep themselves from being polluted by contact with the gentiles. They hoped that if only they were "holy" enough, God would come back.

But there was also common ground for all these otherwise disparate parties, in that all of them had misunderstood their election and forgotten their missional calling. They hated their Roman oppressors and longed for vengeance. They forgot the *telos* of their story, which promised blessing to the gentile nations, and instead gloated obsessively over God's coming judgment against their persecutors (Isa. 63:1–6; Ps. 2).

What marked Israel at this time more than anything was a burning hope that God would return, gather his people, establish a Davidic kingdom, and renew the earth. They clung to their story and longed for its promised ending. Different interpretations as to how it would end produced conflict, and even violence, among the various sects. Meanwhile, they waited.

And when Jesus came, the ending he brought with him was *so* unexpected, *so* shocking, *so* unlike anything they had looked for, that it blew away all their expectations.

CHAPTER 9

The End of the Story, Part 1

Jesus

You study the Scriptures diligently because you think that in them you have eternal life. These are the very Scriptures that testify about me, yet you refuse to come to me to have life.

—John 5:39–40

ISRAEL'S STORY AND JESUS

"The fundamental difference between the Jewish and Christian faiths," he said, "is what they see as the source of ultimate truth." The man talking with me was a distinguished rabbi and a university lecturer on Jewish history. I was young, had only recently begun to follow Christ, and really didn't grasp what he was saying to me. Only later would I realize how profound his words really were. He continued, "For the Jew, ultimately reliable truth is found in historical events which tell the story of God's work in and through the Jewish people to renew the creation. Abraham is our father, and the events of Exodus and Sinai define our identity. Truth is ultimately found in historical events and a story. By contrast, the Christian finds ultimately reliable truth in theological ideas revealed by God and contained in Scripture."

I nodded, assuming he must be right, but it took some considerable time before I came to understand that his "Jewish" view of truth was really a *scriptural* view of truth. What he called the *Christian* view of truth was really an example of how Scripture has often been forced into the mold of "truth" that has come to Western societies through pagan Greek thinking, reaching all the way back to Plato and Aristotle. In reality, both Jews and Christians should agree that ultimately reliable truth is indeed to be *found in a narrative of the mighty historical acts of God*, working in and through a people, to restore the world.

The real difference between Jews and Christians lies in which of those events they accept as key to reading the story and whether they believe that story has reached its true ending. For the Jew, the Exodus and Sinai are the key events of the Old Testament story, and the world is still waiting for its ending. For the Christian, the death and resurrection of Jesus *and* his ongoing mission in and through the church to the ends of the earth are the keys to reading the story, because in those events *the end has arrived* (Luke 24:45–49).

The memory of that conversation with the rabbi has remained vivid for me because I've come to see that a common way of reading the New Testament begins with the question, How do individuals get saved? That had certainly been my assumption when I was a young Christian, and it was the reason I couldn't hear what that rabbi was telling me. How individuals "get saved" is indeed an important question, but it is not the first question to ask when approaching the New Testament. In fact, if put first, it will lead us astray. Rather, the first and fundamental question is, How has the story told in the Old Testament reached its climax?

All Jews understood their Scriptures to be a grand, continuous historical narrative with themselves as the lead actors in it. Since nearly all the writers of the New Testament were Jews, keenly aware of their situation within God's grand story, they were intently focused on the question, How is this story going to end? Each of them—Matthew, Mark, Luke, John, Paul, and the rest—came to see that the "end" of God's story in Israel had come in their own time and in the most unexpected way imaginable. Their books are occupied with exploring precisely this shocking ending to Israel's story. In the next two chapters I want to narrate that ending as it unfolds in the last three acts of the scriptural drama, beginning with that most Jewish Gospel of all, the book of Matthew.

ACT 4: THE COMING OF THE KING–RESTORATION ACCOMPLISHED

Matthew crafts his Gospel with great care, and observing his literary design is important if we are to understand his theological message. There are three parts: (1) the prologue, setting the stage for the whole story he tells (1:1–4:16); (2) the coming of the kingdom in Jesus's life ministry (4:17–16:20); and (3) the coming of the kingdom in Jesus's death and resurrection (16:21–28:20). Matthew's intention is revealed in the strategic repetition of the phrase, "from that time on," which signals what we can expect to read in what follows. Thus, after John the Baptist is imprisoned, we read that "*from that time on* Jesus began to preach, 'Repent, for the kingdom of heaven has come near'" (4:17). And again, following Peter's declaration that he knows Jesus to be the true Messiah, we read, "*From that time on* Jesus began to explain to his disciples that he must go to Jerusalem and suffer many things . . . and that he must be killed and on the third day be raised to life" (16:21).

Prologue: What This Story Is About (Matt. 1:1-4:16)

We may be tempted to read Matthew's opening genealogy quickly, assuming it to be relatively unimportant (1:1–17). But that would be a mistake! This genealogy is Matthew's strategy to prepare us to read his account of Jesus. The genealogy is divided into three sections—from Abraham to David, from David to exile, and from exile to the Messiah—which shows Israel's story unfolding in a way that would have been familiar to his Jewish readers, the significant markers being (1) Abraham, (2) David, (3) exile, and (4) Messiah (1:17). God had made a promise to *Abraham* to undo the curse of Adam's sin and restore the blessing of creation to the world through his family (Gen. 12:2–3). This promise was to be fulfilled through one of *David*'s sons, who would rule over a worldwide kingdom (2 Sam. 7:11–14; Ps. 72:17; Jer. 33). Yet God's promise to Abraham and David had been derailed by the exile—Israel had joined Adamic humanity under the curse and needed first to be forgiven and restored before they could bring blessing to the nations. They anticipated the return of God and the coming of a Messiah who would accomplish that. Matthew's message concludes that Jesus *is* the *Messiah*, the *son of David*, and the *son of Abraham* (1:1, 18). The story Matthew is about to tell is about Jesus, the promised Messiah who will save his people from their sin so that the promises to Abraham and David may at last be fulfilled.

As Matthew prepares us to receive his Gospel in these opening chapters, three things stand out. First, this is a story about *God returning to his people* just as he promised (Isa. 40; Ezek. 40–48; Mal. 3:1). He comes to them in this baby, conceived by the Holy Spirit and born to Mary. Jesus is *Immanuel*, which means "God [is] with us" (Matt. 1:23). The story that follows is about God returning *in Jesus* to establish his rule and deliver his people. Second, Matthew emphasizes that this is a story about *rescuing Israel from exile*. The Messiah's name is Jesus ("the Lord saves") because he will save his people from their sins (Matt. 1:21). If we are thinking along with Matthew (rather than according to the assumptions of traditional Protestant theology), we will understand that this statement is about how God will liberate Israel from exile and forgive their sins in order to bring the nations into blessing, as God had promised to Abraham. Third, these early chapters are peppered with the language of *fulfillment*, stressing that the story Matthew is about to tell is the continuation and fulfillment of the whole Old Testament story. Matthew's story fulfills the promise made to Israel in Isaiah 40: that God would return and reveal his glory to all people (40:5, 10); that he would forgive and liberate Israel from their sin and exile (40:1–2); that good news of God returning to rule would be announced (40:10); that he would gather scattered Israel as a shepherd gathers his sheep (40:11); that God's return as King would be preceded by someone who announced his arrival and prepared the way (40:3–4), whom Matthew identifies as John the Baptizer (Matt. 3:3; cf. Isa. 40:3). Isaiah 40 is being fulfilled in Jesus, and Matthew will show us how it all comes about.

The Coming of the Kingdom in Jesus's Ministry (Matt. 4:17-16:20)

Israel's hope for her own restoration had been captured in the Old Testament language of God's reign, in the words of Isaiah (Isa. 40:9–10; 52:7–10) and Daniel (Dan. 2, 7). God would return to restore his rule over the world. When Jesus comes, he announces that the "day" once promised has now in fact arrived: Good news! God's rule from heaven has come. The kingdom is here. Repent and believe the good news (Matt. 4:17).

Yet it is not at all clear to most Jews of the first century that the kingdom *has* come. The world remains trapped in sin, pain, injustice, and death. Caesar still rules. Even John the Baptizer is perplexed, and he sends his disciples to ask Jesus whether he really is the long-awaited Messiah. Jesus says, "Go back and report to John what you hear and see: the blind receive their sight, the lame walk, those who have leprosy are cleansed, the deaf hear, the dead are raised, and the good news is proclaimed to the poor" (Matt. 11:4–5). Jesus's words are validated by amazing deeds that reveal the presence of God's saving power (Matt. 4:17, 23–25; 8:1–17, 23–34; 9:1–8) to bring an end to sickness and pain, to demonic power, to hunger, to natural disasters, to death, and to oppression. The saving power of God's kingdom *has* come (Matt. 12:28).

Yet surprisingly, Jesus also makes clear in his teaching that the kingdom has *not yet fully come* (Matt. 7:21; 19:28). The coming of the kingdom is also a *future* event, when he will completely eradicate all evil, all the effects of sin, and all opposition to his rule. Though the saving power of God's reign is already here in Jesus even while the powers of the old age remain, the kingdom has *not yet* arrived in its fullness (see fig. 9.1).

Figure 9.1. **Coming of the Kingdom in the Gospels**

The "kingdom" that Jesus announces thus does not fit the Jewish expectation, and soon opposition to him springs up among the Jewish leaders (Matt. 9). Careful attention to food laws, tithing, Sabbath-keeping, and ceremonial cleansing were all strategies the Pharisees had enforced to keep Israel clean from pagan pollution while they remained under the control of foreign powers. But Jesus eats with all the wrong people, forgives sinners on his own authority, heals on the Sabbath, and refuses to keep their fasting regimen. Jesus challenges the cultural symbols that reinforce hatred, separation, and a thirst for vengeance. Animosity toward Jesus increases, until at last he speaks sternly to his detractors of judgment and woe to come for those who oppose him (Matt. 23–25).

Jesus's announcement of the kingdom calls for repentance and faith; his command is "follow me" (Matt. 4:18–22; 9:9). For first-century Jews, the arrival of the kingdom means the gathering of Israel, and Jesus does begin to gather the "lost sheep" of Israel (Matt. 15:24) with a view to one day incorporating the nations (Matt. 8:10–12). He tells this gathered community that they are "the light of the world" and the "city on a hill" promised to Isaiah (Isa. 2:2–5; 51:4; 60:3; Matt. 5:14–16). They are the beginning of the new humanity of the end time. But also gathered into this community are "sinners": the lost, the poor and the sick, the prostitutes, and the tax collectors (Matt. 9:9–13)—those who (according to the Jewish leaders) would *not* inherit God's kingdom.

Jesus teaches the community he gathers how to live as citizens in the kingdom. Matthew strategically places five teaching sections throughout his gospel (Matt. 5–7, 10, 13, 18, 23–25). The way Jesus forms his disciples is in stark opposition to the hatred, separation, and vengeance that motivated the Jewish guardians of the law. Suffering love, Jesus says and shows, is the way the kingdom comes. If Jesus's followers live as he instructs, they will be the light that Israel was meant to be (Matt. 5–7). The community that follows Jesus must obey him as Lord, embracing a discipleship of total commitment, following him in the way of the cross.

Jesus's teaching often takes the form of parables with a very specific intent: to address the mistaken notions of the kingdom that were then widespread within Israel. Thus, the parable of the sower teaches that the kingdom will *not* come with irresistible power (Matt. 13:1–23). The parable of the weeds teaches that God's judgment will *not* fall immediately (13:24–30, 36–43), nor will it come in a blaze of military glory. Instead, the kingdom will begin small and grow gradually, like yeast or a mustard seed (Matt. 13:31–33).

Jesus reveals that the final coming of the kingdom is to be delayed, which creates a time to gather in the lost sheep of Israel, with a view to incorporating the gentiles at a later stage. The community of disciples is summoned to join Jesus in his mission, like fishermen sent to fish for people (Matt. 4:19), or harvesters sent into the field to gather crops (9:35–38), or shepherds sent to gather sheep (10:6). He sends out twelve disciples to do what they have seen him doing: announcing the kingdom and demonstrating its arrival with deeds (Matt. 10:1–8). The twelve represent the twelve tribes, the beginning of the new Israel.

The unusual ministry of Jesus sparks the question, Who is Jesus? (Matt. 16:13–20), and the answer is not a simple one. He is the Messiah who fulfills the promise of the Old Testament, the Son of God who represents Israel in his role of King, and the Son of Man, who shares the throne with God (Dan. 7:13–14). Even more, he shares a special unity and identity with the Father. He is Immanuel, *God himself* returning to save Israel.

The Coming of the Kingdom in Jesus's Death and Resurrection (Matt. 16:21-28:20)

Jesus secures the victory of the kingdom in his crucifixion. As Jesus challenges the structural evil of Israel's own life, and as the hostility of Israel's leaders grows, Matthew turns his kingdom narrative toward the cross (16:24). Jesus's seemingly outrageous behavior in the temple (disrupting the trade in animals for sacrifice) finally pushes them over the edge. He is arrested and convicted (in a wholly unjust and unlawful "trial"), then sentenced by Pilate (under pressure from the Jews) to die on a cross.

Shockingly, it is this event that becomes the mightiest redemptive act of God! It is hard for us today to comprehend just how horrifying and loathsome the crucifixion was for the first-century person. But it was designed to humiliate, torture, and finally kill the victim. It was a public event designed to strike fear into the heart of anyone who dared defy the Roman Empire. No first-century Roman or Jew, it seemed, could ever come to believe that *this* could be an act of God.

Yet Matthew joins the rest of the New Testament in his testimony that the death of Jesus is indeed the *mightiest* of God's acts. Together with the resurrection, the crucifixion is the turning point of world history. The cross is the culmination of his kingdom narrative: the ultimate victory of God's reign over all opposition; a substitutionary sacrifice in which the suffering servant takes the curse of the law on himself to redeem Israel so that the blessing of Abraham might go to the nations; a paradoxical act in which we see wisdom in foolishness, power in weakness, glory in shame, victory in defeat, justice in injustice, and ultimate meaning in a seemingly random act of cruelty. This climactic moment of redemptive history was—and still is—shocking! But at the time, the crucifixion seemed especially to vindicate the Jews in their rejection of Jesus's messianic claims.

Jesus inaugurates the kingdom in his resurrection. And yet the early church, *primarily made up of Jews*, affirmed the scandalous confession that the cross was the victory of God's kingdom. How could they? Because he was alive from the dead (Matt. 28:1–8). But what did this mean? The resurrection of Jesus was just as incomprehensible to Jews (cf. Mark 9:10) and gentiles as the crucifixion had been.

In Jewish thought, resurrection was to be a cosmic, end-time event signaling the ultimate renewal of the whole cosmos, in which God's people would participate by their own bodily resurrection. What could be the meaning of just one man rising from the dead in the middle of history? The first Christians understood it as the evidence that God's kingdom had been inaugurated, that Jesus was the firstborn from the dead, the author of resurrection life itself. All his people, and at last the entire creation, would one day share in his resurrection.

Together, the cross and the resurrection constitute the center of world history (see fig. 9.2). At the cross God defeats all the enemies of his creation and effectively ends the tyranny of the old age. In the resurrection God inaugurates a new age in which the entire cosmos and the whole life of humankind is renewed.

Figure 9.2. **Cross and Resurrection as Hinge of Cosmic History**

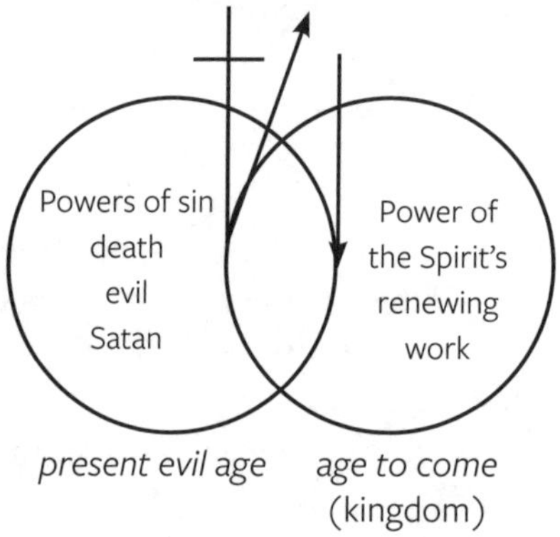

Powers of sin
death
evil
Satan

Power of
the Spirit's
renewing
work

present evil age   *age to come*
(kingdom)

Jesus sends his disciple-community to all nations. Matthew ends his story with the sending of gathered Israel to the nations (Matt. 28:18–20). He had opened his narrative by connecting it to the Old Testament (1:1–17); he now closes it by showing how the story is to continue (see fig. 9.3). In Jesus, God has returned to Israel to save them from their sins. He had begun to gather the lost sheep of Israel (15:24), involving them in his own mission to Israel (9:35–10:42), and now he is sending them to the nations to continue what he began, incorporating the nations into the salvation God has accomplished for Israel (see fig. 9.4).

Figure 9.3. **Locating Matthew's Story**

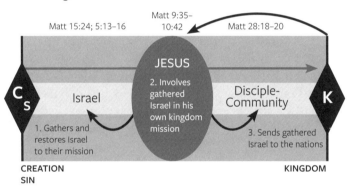

Figure 9.4. **Mission of Jesus and Gathered Israel**

Matthew 28:18–20 began to be called the "Great Commission" comparatively late in church history, and this label has often obscured its explosive climactic role in Matthew's Gospel. Matthew tells the story of the confrontation between Jesus's messianic claims and the Jews' violent rejection of those claims. Animosity builds throughout the book, and by the end, the question is urgent: Who is right? Interestingly, unlike the other Gospel writers, Matthew does not make the resurrection the climactic point of his gospel but hurries us on to the last scenes in Galilee (28:7, 10; cf. 26:32). There, Jesus says to his assembled disciples, "All authority on heaven and on earth has been given to me" (28:18). Those disciples—in fact all first-century Jews reading Matthew's Gospel—would have recognized these familiar words from Daniel (7:13–14). The risen Jesus claims to be the Son of Man who shares the throne of God and rules with all authority and an everlasting dominion. This is what makes it the climactic moment of Matthew's Gospel: Jesus is vindicated.

The breathtaking scope of Jesus's authority is stressed with Matthew's repetition of the word "all." *All* authority is given to Jesus; *all* the nations are to acknowledge his authority; *all* his commands are to be obeyed; *all* the days yet to come in history will be filled with Jesus's own presence as he brings the mighty work of God to completion. And Jesus will exercise his authority by sending restored Israel to continue the work of gathering— which will now expand to embrace all nations, for the gentiles too are to be baptized into this community and taught to become disciples.

But what is a disciple? Matthew has carefully built a profile of a disciple throughout this book. The disciple makes the kingdom the all-encompassing priority of their life (Matt. 6:33; 7:21–24; 13:44–46) and obeys Jesus as Lord. (Matthew never allows the disciples to call Jesus *Rabbi*, only *Lord*—except when Judas greets Jesus in 26:49!) The disciple fulfills the law, does the Father's will, bears fruit, practices justice and righteousness, and shows mercy and compassion. The disciple follows Jesus, aligning their whole life with Jesus's own, becoming a living part in the kingdom mission of Jesus. The people of God are no longer one nation among others but now take on this new form of a disciple-community whose members will eventually be drawn from many nations (see fig. 9.4 above).

This community is sent to gather in more members from Israel *and* the nations, making them into disciples in the power of the risen Christ. The Son of Man rules world history with all authority and power, but (astonishingly) it is through this humble mission of an otherwise insignificant community that he chooses to summon the world to submit to his glorious reign.

The curtain falls on act 4 with the anticipation that God's salvation accomplished in Christ will now include all nations. But how will this take place? What is our role?

CHAPTER 10

The End of the Story, Part 2

Mission and Consummation

The Bible sets out before us a vision of cosmic history from the creation of the world to its consummation, of the nations which make up the one human family, and—of course—of the one nation chosen to be the bearer of the meaning of history for the sake of all, and of one man called to be the bearer of that meaning for the nation. . . . The Bible is universal history.

—Lesslie Newbigin, The Gospel in a Pluralist Society

The question took me by surprise. "Why have you come over here to push your religious propaganda on us?" I was lecturing in a university in the Crimea shortly after the fall of Communism. The class was made up of about two hundred law students, the vast majority of whom were atheists. The title of my lecture was "Communism, Capitalism, and Christianity: Three Visions for Public Life." A young man who had feigned a lack of interest until now, suddenly raised his hand and asked the question.

My answer was long—especially when it had to be given through a Russian translator—but it generated interest and lively discussion. I responded that during my time in Ukraine I had observed many signs of the failure of the Communist story. I had also seen evidence of a turn to Western capitalism to fill the vacuum. But this story, too, would collapse one day, leaving behind shattered dreams and broken lives. I believed that there was only one story that would ultimately endure—the story told in the Bible. The secular humanist story in both its communist and capitalist forms seeks to relegate religion to the private and "spiritual" realm. But the Bible refuses to be categorized as "religious" in that narrow and degraded sense: It claims to be public truth for all people and all times. I referred to the prophecies of Daniel 2 and 7, which look to a day when the kingdom of God will fill the earth, when *all* other dominions and empires—including the capitalist West—will finally fall.

I asked the young man to consider hearing the Bible on its own terms: "The Bible asserts that it is the truth for all of life. I am not bringing religious propaganda, but offering what I believe to be the best narrative context there could be for law and for every other aspect of public life. You are free, of course, to reject its claim. But at least hear what the Bible professes for itself. And if you do not believe the biblical story to be true, you still need to face the question, Which story will shape your life and career? The stakes are high. Your parents and grandparents gave their allegiance to Communism, and the cost has been enormous."

I finished with a question: "If you do not believe the biblical story to be true, which one do you believe is true?" He answered in a voice tinged with regret, "I don't know. I am only twenty-one." "Fair enough," I responded, "but it's an issue you cannot avoid. Your life and the public life of your nation will be shaped by some story. I commend the story told in the Bible." He listened with keener interest after that, and the whole encounter breathed fresh life into the class discussion. As far as I know, no one left that room convinced by what I had been saying. But at least they had begun to ask questions and to frame issues in a new way.

We have narrated the story of Israel. Jesus tells us that the fulfillment of that story has come, first, in his death and resurrection, and second, in the ongoing mission of the church (Luke 24:45–49). In the last chapter we saw how the restoration of the world promised in the Old Testament has been accomplished through Jesus the King. In this chapter we will see how this good news includes peoples from all nations and, finally, how the story will end.

ACT 5: MAKING KNOWN THE NEWS OF THE KING—THE MISSION OF THE CHURCH

Jesus inaugurates a new era of salvation. The kingdom banquet is ready to be enjoyed, but more people must first be gathered to the table. An unexpected era opens up, in which the exalted Christ continues to gather Israel and all nations by the Spirit in and through the church. Though Matthew does not continue his narrative beyond Jesus's words of sending, Luke does; and from that continuation in Acts we take up the story again.

Scene 1: From Jerusalem to Rome

Luke opens his sequel with these words, "In my former book [the Gospel of Luke], Theophilus, I wrote about all that Jesus *began* to do and to teach," implying that this second volume will tell what Jesus *continues* to do and teach (Acts 1:1). We stand in historical continuity with the early church and so are swept up into this mission. The story they began is ours to continue.

As the story opens, the *risen* Christ appears to his disciples. There is talk of the *kingdom* and the *Spirit* (Acts 1:3–5), and all this—resurrection, kingdom, Spirit—leads the disciples (formed as they have been by the long years of prophetic hope) to the conclusion that the end has at last arrived. They ask the obvious question: "Lord, are you at this time going to restore the kingdom to Israel?" (1:6). Jesus answers yes—but in a way that is totally unexpected. His kingdom will come as the disciple-community receives the power of the Holy Spirit and becomes a witnessing community in Jerusalem, in Judea and Samaria, and to the ends of the earth (1:7–8). That's not how any Jew would have expected the kingdom to be restored to Israel and the nations gathered in!

Then Jesus ascends to the right hand of God and shares his throne. The throne of God was a well-known image of that place from which God ruled the nations and all of history (Ezek. 1; Isa. 6; Dan. 7). As the slain Lamb—and *not* as the vindictive Lion of Jewish hope (Rev. 5:5–6)—Jesus begins his sovereign work of ruling, judging, and saving, moving history toward its appointed goal (Rev. 6–22).

The exalted Christ pours out his Spirit at Pentecost. The prophets had promised that in the last days the Spirit would be given to the Messiah (Isa. 42:1), to Israel (Ezek. 37:14), and to all people (Joel 2:28–32). Here the Spirit (given first to Jesus) is now given to Israel, whose people gather from the margins of the empire. The Spirit comes as the powerful presence of God, and the accompanying strange phenomena raise the question among the onlookers: *What is happening?* Peter answers that God is fulfilling Joel's prophecy that the Spirit would be "poured out in the last days" (Acts

2:14–36). These "last days" have arrived by the life, death, resurrection, and exaltation of Jesus of Nazareth. And now Christ has sent the Spirit upon Israel (2:33–36). From this point onward, in fact, the Spirit will become the primary actor in the book of Acts, bringing good news to the ends of the earth. He is the powerful presence of the risen Christ to implement the work of Jesus and gather first Jews and then gentiles into the end-time salvation that has been accomplished.

Peter concludes his sermon by inviting his hearers to repent and be baptized. About three thousand Jews respond and are gathered into the end-time Israel. Luke then describes this early community, offering us a model for what the people of God now look like (Acts 2:42–47). For us, this description seems rather normal. But for the first-century observers of all this, the very form of God's people was changing.

Luke describes this new witnessing community as focusing its gathered life on those channels by which the exalted Christ brought to them the life of the kingdom through the Spirit: the apostles' teaching, fellowship, the breaking of bread, and prayer. Their life was characterized by power, generosity, justice, mercy, joy, and praise, both as they gathered and as they scattered throughout Jerusalem. They enjoyed the favor of all people. As this attractive life of the kingdom became more evident, the exalted Lord added to their number. Luke shows that the life and power of the Spirit of Christ indwelling the believing community radiate the light of the kingdom and draws people from darkness.

The story of the church's witness continues in Jerusalem, where Israel is "gathered" (Acts 3:1–6:7). It then reaches outward to Judea and Samaria, bringing in Jews and gentile God-fearers (6:8–11:18), and eventually moves through the provinces of the empire to Rome itself, gathering gentiles (11:19–28:31), just as Jesus himself promised (1:8). In each major section of Acts, we read, "So the word of God spread" or something similar (6:7; 12:24; 19:20). It is the power of Christ present in the word of God, embodied in the lives of the community, and explained in their speech that spreads to Jew and gentile from Jerusalem to Rome.

The first stage of the Spirit's witness is through the apostolic community in Jerusalem, in the gathering of Israel (Acts 3:1–6:7). Israel must be first gathered and restored before gentiles can come in. Peter and John continue the mission of Jesus as they heal a man crippled from birth (3:1–10), and then proclaim the good news (3:11–26). But the words and deeds of these two disciples immediately bring hostility, and the church turns to prayer, asking for boldness and power (3:23–4:31). The reprisals of the jealous Jewish leaders escalate from verbal abuse to floggings. But human opposition cannot stop the spread of the gospel because it is the work of God's Spirit.

While we hear much of the witness of the apostles, it is the attractive life of the community that authenticates the truth of the good news (Acts 4:32–35; 6:1–7). The powerful verbal testimony to the resurrection of the Lord Jesus (4:33) is authenticated by a communal life of generosity and justice (4:32, 34–35).

The gospel spreads from Jerusalem into the provinces of Judea and Samaria, incorporating not only Jews but also God-fearing gentiles (Acts 6:8–12:24). Witness moves beyond the apostles to include other leaders, especially Stephen and Philip. Stephen's witness brings further opposition, and eventually he becomes the first martyr (chap. 7). When persecution breaks out against the church in Jerusalem, many believers flee the city, but as they scatter, they preach the word wherever they go, spontaneously telling the good news to their friends and neighbors (8:4).

The most important event arising from the persecution of the early Christians is the conversion and call of Saul of Tarsus (Acts 9:1–30), who had led a campaign against the young church. On the road to Damascus, a blinding light strikes Saul and a voice demands, "Saul, why do you persecute me?" He asks, "Who are you, Lord?" and hears in response, "I am Jesus, whom you are persecuting" (9:4–5). From that moment, Saul becomes a follower of Jesus. Better known by his Roman name, Paul, he will now play the strategic role of leading God's people into the next stage of redemptive history to gather "the nations" into the covenant family of Israel.

Something new begins to take place in Antioch, where Jews and gentiles come together to form for the first time a community with a non-Jewish identity (Acts 11:19–21). No longer identifiable as either Jew or gentile, for the first time this mixed group of believers is called "Christian," identified not by their ethnicity but by the one whom they follow. Thus, Antioch begins a new chapter in redemptive history. Saul and Barnabas are chosen and sent to preach the gospel in other cities of the Roman Empire to establish more such gentile communities (13:1–3). For the first time we see a planned effort to take the gospel to establish witnessing communities in places where it has not yet been heard.

Paul becomes the central human witness from now on. His work includes planting new witnessing communities and then building them up to radiate the light of the gospel. He (with various companions) makes three journeys to plant and build up churches in Asia Minor, Greece, and Macedonia. His practice is to go first to the Jews, but when they reject him, he turns to the gentiles.

As God's people increasingly take on a gentile identity, it raises large questions and concerns among Jewish leaders in the young church about the long history of Jewish identity as the people of God. Thus, some Jewish Christians from Jerusalem travel to Galatia, attempting to convince gentile Christians that they must come under the rule of Torah and become Jewish if they are to be part of God's covenant people. But Paul fires off an angry letter to the Galatian churches, urging them to remain true to the gospel: It is faith in Christ that now marks off God's people, not Jewish ethnicity or culture. The struggle between the Jewish troublers and those who embrace Paul's teaching builds, until a council is held in Jerusalem to settle the matter. This council concludes that gentile believers may maintain their own cultural identity and be admitted to the company of God's people as equal members (Acts 15).

This is a crucial moment in redemptive history. God's people are no longer defined by the Torah or by ethnicity or national identity; they can be God's people living as the true humanity within *any* cultural context. But this produces another dilemma: How may God's people live as the new humanity amid cultures that serve other gods? The answer is that the mission of God's people requires a missionary encounter, by which Christians embrace the good of every culture while rejecting the reigning idolatry of each.

With the matter of gentile inclusion settled, Paul begins his second journey, during which he establishes churches in each region's important cities (churches to which he will later write letters): Philippi, Thessalonica, Corinth, and Ephesus (Acts 15:36–18:22). Paul then returns to Jerusalem, where he is arrested by the Romans. The remainder of Acts shows Paul in various judicial hearings as he is moved in stages from Jerusalem to Rome. Yet even these trials (in both senses of the word!) afford Paul opportunities to proclaim the good news to gentile rulers (9:15–16). During his time in Rome, he writes letters to the churches in Philippi, Ephesus, and Colossae to nourish their life. And there Luke abruptly concludes his story. While Paul is in Rome, under house arrest, boldly preaching about the kingdom of God and the Lord Jesus Christ, the story simply . . . ends. The sudden ending is a literary device designed by Luke to invite his readers to take up their own roles in what is clearly an *unfinished* story. And so, you and I are invited—urged—to become a part of this story, to follow Jesus and continue his kingdom mission on the way to the new creation.

Scene 2: To the Ends of the Earth

Thus far in the biblical story, we have followed an overarching plot that includes Israel, Jesus, and the early church. And all three are significant for us, since *we* are now called to take our place in the story and continue the mission of Israel, of Jesus, and of the early church.

First, we are called to continue the mission of Israel to be a light to the nations. God promised to make Abraham a great nation through whom he would restore the blessing of creation to all nations (Gen. 12:1–3): He was blessed to *be* a blessing. The nation that descended from Abraham was to be the new humanity, to embody God's original creational intention for human life for the sake of the nations (Exod. 19:3–6). Israel was summoned to embody God's purpose of restoration, the goal of the story, as wide as creation itself. As Israel was obedient to this calling, it would be a light to the world. The attractiveness of its life would draw nations to God. Today, Israel's mission has become our mission as the global church of Jesus Christ scattered throughout the world (Gal. 3:7–9; 1 Pet. 2:9–12).

Second, we are called to continue the mission of Jesus to make known the kingdom. Though Israel largely failed in its calling, Jesus did not. He fulfilled God's purposes for Israel, gathering a community of his followers and charging them to continue what he began (John 20:21). We are part of that community, called to continue Jesus's mission.

Jesus's mission centered on the coming of God's kingdom, the restoration of God's rule over all human life. We continue as witnesses to this comprehensive salvation. Jesus embodied the kingdom in his life, announced it in his words, and demonstrated it in his deeds. He welcomed the poor and marginalized, formed a community, and taught them how to live as a faithful kingdom people. He suffered as he challenged the idolatrous culture of his time that opposed him and his people. And he prayed for the eventual coming of the kingdom in its fullness. All of this shapes our mission today as we follow Jesus. But our own cultural situation is quite different from that of first-century Palestine. Jesus did not give us a rigid model of mission to imitate mindlessly but rather invites us to continue his mission, doing what he did in creative and imaginative ways amid new and different cultural contexts.

Finally, we are called to continue the mission of the early church to bear faithful witness to Jesus. The early church was charged to witness to the good news of Jesus everywhere—in life, word, and deed—among all peoples, until the end (Matt. 24:14). With the coming of the Spirit, the church both enjoyed and embodied a foretaste of the salvation of the kingdom. The ultimate kingdom "banquet" awaits a future time, yet those who follow Christ have begun already to taste it. As the church enjoys this foretaste, it *becomes* a foretaste—or, if you like, a preview—of what the future kingdom will look like.

Think of a movie trailer, made up of snippets of actual footage from a coming attraction. This trailer is designed to create interest in an audience for the film before it is released. The church is similarly to be a kind of "trailer" for the kingdom: real footage of the life of the kingdom today, designed to interest and attract others to the "main feature" when at last it comes.

The early church communities in Jerusalem and Antioch established healthy patterns of communal life, devoting themselves to God's means of grace in order to build up their new life in Christ. As a result, these communities became attractive previews of the kingdom, drawing people to Christ. Beyond this local witness, the Antioch church also sent Paul and Barnabas to places where there were no witnessing communities. Thus, the church was then (and should be now) characterized by its zeal for witness, nearby and far away.

Though the notion of "witness" gives meaning to this era of God's story, it can easily be misinterpreted. "Christian witness" may be reduced to mere evangelism or cross-cultural missions. Though these are important elements of our witness to Christ, they are not the whole of it. When we grasp that the salvation of the kingdom restores *all* of human life, we begin to see that our witness to God's kingdom must be as wide as life itself! We witness to what it means to be truly human as God intended. And though we may suffer as we encounter other equally comprehensive and competing religious stories that seek to shape our culture, we must witness to Christ's claim to lordship over every inch and every moment of human experience.

ACT 6: THE RETURN OF THE KING—RESTORATION COMPLETED

When God set out on the long historical journey to renew his creation from sin and its effects, his purpose was to restore what he had once created *very good*. The Bible tells this story of God's journey. In the last chapters of Revelation, God reaches his destination: a renewed heaven and earth, entirely cleansed of evil. The Holy City, God's heavenly dwelling place, the "new Jerusalem," descends from heaven to earth. Heaven and earth are united, and God's world is healed from sin and its effects. A loud voice from God's throne proclaims: "God's dwelling place is now among the people, and he will dwell with them. They will be his people, and God himself will be with them and be their God. 'He will wipe every tear from their eyes. There will be no more death' or mourning or crying or pain, for the old order of things has passed away" (Rev. 21:3–4).

At the last, God and humanity are reconciled. Relationships among human beings are healed. Love and justice reign. The whole of human life is purified. Even the nonhuman creation shares in this liberation from its former slavery to the curse. Here is the stunning goal and destiny of the true story of the whole world: a renewed creation—healed, liberated, and restored.

Three major events usher in the restoration of creation and the arrival of God's kingdom in its fullness: (1) Jesus returns, (2) the dead are raised bodily (some to share in the life of the new creation and others to final wrath), and (3) the world comes before Christ to be judged.

Revelation 21–22 is a vision of a creation completely restored to its original goodness. We do not have a picture of Christians suddenly transported out of this world to live a spiritual existence in heaven forever. Instead, salvation is the *restoration* of God's creation: a (re)new(ed) earth. The redeemed of God live in resurrected bodies within a creation newly liberated from the effects of sin (Matt. 19:28; Acts 3:21; Eph. 1:9–10; Col. 1:19–20). Just as nothing in creation remained untouched by sin after Adam's fall, so nothing in creation can remain untouched by God's restoration in Christ. The blessing of the creation is to be fully restored (Gen. 1:22, 28; Rev. 22:7, 14).

But not all will share in this new creation. Sadly, some people are shut out (Rev. 21:27; 22:15) and perish (Rev. 20:11–15) along with Satan (v. 10) and the cultural idolatry of Rome (19:20–21). But those who remain faithful to Christ, refusing the idolatry of their culture, enter the renewed creation: Eden and Jerusalem restored. John ends his book with Jesus's words, "Look, I am coming soon!" (22:7, 12, 20). He exhorts his readers to stand firm in the faith and warns those who remain outside the kingdom to enter while they may. For Jesus is coming soon. All who follow Jesus echo John's response: "Amen. Come, Lord Jesus."

CHAPTER 11

The Urgency of Reading
the Bible as One Story

*The narrative unity of Scripture is no minor matter: a fragmented Bible
may actually produce theologically orthodox, morally upright, warmly pious
idol worshipers!*

—Craig G. Bartholomew and Michael W. Goheen,
The Drama of Scripture

Jeremy Olimb tells the story of his family's visit to a water park in Denver
and their experience on the lazy river ride, where they rented a family-sized
tube and began their leisurely float trip. It was not until they reached the
exit point that the tremendous power of this "lazy river" became evident.
As his youngest son jumped off the tube into the water, he was immediately
swept off his feet to disappear under the surface. Jeremy's oldest son, and
then his wife, tried to help the young one, but the powerful currents proved
too much for them as well—they too were in danger. Jeremy set his own
feet firmly at the bottom of the "river" and, while attempting to hold his
balance, struggled to rescue his family. After a few frightening minutes,
all were able to get to shore—shocked by just how powerful the current
had proven to be.

Jeremy likens that experience to the church, living amid the powerful idolatrous currents of modern Western culture. As in the lazy river, these cultural currents are invisible and yet forceful and relentless as they carry us with them. We may not even notice them—until we try to stand against them. Only then will we realize how much power is opposing us, and how difficult it is not to be swept along.[1]

One safeguard against our being carried away by these idolatrous currents is to understand the Bible as one story and allow it to shape our lives. "If this biblical story is not the one that really controls our thinking," says Lesslie Newbigin, "then inevitably *we shall be swept into the story that the world tells about itself.* We shall become increasingly indistinguishable from the pagan world of which we are a part."[2]

HUMAN LIFE IS SHAPED BY SOME STORY

The Bible tells a single, gradually unfolding story of God's restoration of the whole creation and human life from the corrupting power of sin. This does not deny that there are many and various genres of literature in Scripture, including poetry, law, ethical teaching, wisdom, prayers, letters, and doctrine. Yet all these nonnarrative elements are embedded within the larger, primary *narrative* structure of the Bible.

Recovering our sense of this overall narrative shape is important, though not easy. The Western habit of mind, building on the scientific revolution and the Enlightenment, is to dissect and atomize whatever we see in order to understand it, and the Bible has not escaped this kind of treatment. Thus, many today view the Bible as fragments that may be suitable for devotions, sermons, theology, and morality, but remain merely fragments. But the Scriptures insistently tell one coherent story. If we lose this sense of what the Bible is, our lives will inevitably be shaped by some *other* story.

We can illustrate how narrative works in the following example:[3] Consider the simple statement, "It is going to rain." The meaning of the words here is clear enough, but we cannot truly understand their *significance* without some broader narrative context, some story that renders the words meaningful. Each of the three stories below could give this observation about the rain some meaning.

First, it may be that for six months we have been meticulously planning an extended family reunion and outdoor picnic to be held on *this* particular Saturday. Now, suddenly, the person who has been in charge of all those preparations groans (after watching the weather forecast) and says to her husband, "It is going to rain." This is very bad news indeed! Or perhaps a farmer who has been struggling against drought for months and is now facing the prospect of losing all his crops—maybe even the farm itself—hears his wife joyfully shouting out the latest weather report: "It is going to rain!" This is clearly the best of news for that weary farmer. Or, to choose an example from Scripture itself, consider the prophet Elijah's announcement of a drought as God's judgment on Israel, when he said that it would not rain again in the land until he received word from the Lord. Following his victorious encounter with the prophets of Baal on Mount Carmel, Elijah announces, "It is going to rain" (2 Kings 17–18). In context, this means that (1) God's judgment has ended, (2) Yahweh is God and Baal is not, and (3) Elijah is indeed a true prophet of God. One simple statement can mean many different things, depending on the narrative context that surrounds it.

It is like that with our own lives. How we understand each aspect of our lives depends on what we believe to be the true story of the world. When I taught a university course on worldview, I would sometimes begin by asking, "Why would you take on so much debt to get a university degree? What is the purpose of your higher education?" Several answers are possible. If the Western story (driven by economic idolatry) is true, the primary purpose of an education is to acquire the necessary qualifications and skills to secure a well-paying job. At the cultural level, the same worldview suggests that the purpose of education is to enable each person to be an economically productive member of society. As an example, the Canadian province of British Columbia states that the purpose of education is "to acquire the knowledge, skills, and attitudes needed to contribute to . . . a prosperous and sustainable economy."[4] However, if the *biblical* story is true, there ought to be a different reason: Education allows us to gain insight into God's world, to equip us to glorify God and serve our neighbors across the whole spectrum of human life. (This will include, of course, formation for a vocation to make a living.) The point is, *some* story will give meaning and shape to one's university education, and, indeed, to every other aspect of one's life—marriage and family, leisure and work, art and technology, language and architecture.

By "story" here I do not mean a fictive narrative put together to provide meaning for our otherwise meaningless lives. In this context, "story" means *an interpretation of real history* that gives the meaning and context of human life, telling us where the world has come from, where it is going, and what our own role is within it.

Story, then, allows us to talk about *the way the world really is*, giving a true account of how God has created the world. Since God created it, the world does have a beginning. But it was not created to be changeless. From the beginning, the change and development that we call history has been an essential element of the world God created. Human beings were given the task of developing the creation culturally and socially to move it from a garden to a city. God's ongoing redemptive work moves along the grain of that developing, historical nature of the world. So the biblical story has a goal, which is to establish the city of God. To speak of a story is not simply to employ a useful metaphor. Rather, story describes the way the world actually is by virtue of the way God created it and the way he works out his redemptive purpose in it.

A story gives meaning to life by placing humanity within a narrative that has a direction and a goal. A story also reveals what the world is really like. We all understand the experience of "living inside" a story, figuratively, when we read a novel, watch a movie, or attend a play. In each of these cases we enter, by imagination, the narrative world of that story. The Bible too narrates a world, and we are told a lot about that world as we immerse ourselves in the biblical story. But the fundamental difference between this story and all others is that the Bible tells us about the world *as it really is*.

BIBLICAL AUTHORITY IS NARRATIVE

The second reason it is critical to recover the Bible as one story is that it is the only way we can authentically subject ourselves to its divine authority. The Bible's very structure is narrative, and we can properly understand its authority only if we read it as it truly is. We confess that the Bible is the Word of God that carries divine authority to shape our lives. The problem is that, though many Christians might believe this to be true, they sometimes work it out in a way that goes against the nature of Scripture itself! Some find the "authority" of the Bible in timeless theological or moral principles, which they attempt to squeeze out of the narrative to apply in the "real" world. Others choose devotional nuggets plucked out of the story to encourage us for life in the "real" world. Still others compile a list of scattered promises and commands (pried loose from their narrative context) to direct their lives in the "real" world. But none of these ways of reading Scripture respects the kind of book that God has given us.

Imagine that the script of a long-lost Shakespeare play is somehow discovered.[5] Although the play originally had six acts, only a little more than five have been found—the first four acts, the first scene of act 5, and act 6. The majority of act 5 is missing. The play is given to Shakespearean scholars and actors who are asked to work together to perform the rest of act 5 that is missing. They immerse themselves in the world of the partial script that has been recovered. They soak in the first four acts, the first part of act 5, and then the ending in act 6. They live into the trajectory and story-world of the earlier acts. They then improvise the unscripted part of the fifth act, allowing their performance to be moved by the impetus of the plot and shaped by the narrative world of Shakespeare's story as they have come to understand it. In this way their performance moves the play toward the conclusion offered by the author in act 6.

Something like this may help us to understand how biblical authority works today. The biblical drama of redemption unfolds in the six "acts" of creation, rebellion, Israel, Jesus, the church, and consummation. We must immerse ourselves in the biblical story, inhabit its world completely. We must also come to know the author of the story. In fact, the divine playwright has given the gift of his own Spirit to us, the "actors," so that we may understand, read, and perform his script. Now, given the trajectory of the story as it has been told to this point, given the world that the story has opened up, and knowing that we have been entrusted to perform the continuation of act 5 *of that story*—the mission of the early church—how should we live today? How can we play our part in God's unfolding story? How can we align our lives with its purpose and goal? How can we continue to live faithfully in its world?

The actors in the play improvise, which demands both innovation and consistency. Consistency means that our lives will be shaped by the narrative world and the trajectory of the biblical plot. We must pore over and immerse ourselves in those earlier acts to understand them so that we may move along the grain of the story's essential narrative impetus. Yet we must not forget innovation. Faithfulness means carrying on in that trajectory while living creatively in a new redemptive-historical era wherever God leads us.

To understand biblical authority, we must truly find our place in the story. Only in this way can the Bible's authority be known authentically.

Losing sight of the Bible's narrative unity greatly erodes its authority and its power.

Scripture gives us not just the true story of the world; it also equips us with a "toolbox" that we need in order to live in that story. The Bible contains many kinds of literature, each working in its own way to lead us to Christ and draw us into the biblical story. The historical books of the Old Testament reveal God's unfolding covenant purpose and invite us to align ourselves with it. The law shapes God's people as a holy nation living according to God's creation order within the ancient Near Eastern context for the sake of the surrounding nations. The prophetic books call God's people to covenant faithfulness through repentance and the promise of a future hope. The poetry of the Psalms nourishes God's people for a faithful response to him through imagination and song. The wisdom literature enables us to understand the wisdom of God's creation order so we can conform ourselves to it. The Gospels witness to and proclaim that the whole Old Testament story has been fulfilled in Jesus and the coming of the kingdom, and they summon us to believe and follow him. The epistles work out the implications of the good news in the specific missional contexts of the young churches. Each of these literary tools in its own way equips God's people to live more faithfully in the biblical story.

THE MISSIONAL ROLE OF GOD'S PEOPLE IN THE STORY

A third reason to read the Bible as one story is that it enables us to understand our identity as God's people, setting out the role we are called to play in the story as a missional people who participate as God's covenant partners in his redemptive mission.

God is the primary actor in the biblical story. The Bible narrates his long historical journey toward the renewal of the creation. God begins with one man, family, and nation, promising to restore creational blessing to them. But the story moves from this *one* people to *all* the peoples on the earth, from the *one* place they live to the *ends of the earth*. The question is, What role are we, as part of God's people now, called to play in this journey toward that destination?

Adam's failure to be what God intended for humanity is remedied by the election of one man, Abraham, to start anew. The new humanity begun in Abraham is to be the starting point of what the Adamic humanity failed to be. God does not reject the other nations but chooses Abraham precisely *for their sake* (Gen. 12:2–3). Israel is restored to the blessing God intended in creation in order to become the rallying point where *all* nations might be blessed.

God meets Israel at Sinai after he liberates it from pagan Egyptian idolatry (Exod. 19:3–6). He summons the nation to be a display-people, demonstrating to the world what true humanity looks like. The story of the Old Testament following Exodus narrates how faithful—or not—Israel's people are to this call. Their continuing failure moves God to provide a king who will enable them to be the new humanity they were called to be. And he promises that one in David's line will finally achieve that goal (2 Sam. 7:11–16; Ps. 72:17). God will one day form a faithful new humanity in Israel, into which all nations may be grafted. An anointed king descended from David will establish a worldwide kingdom within which Israel *and all nations* will be blessed.

Jesus comes as that King, to gather and restore Israel. His death secures victory over the evil of the present evil age, the idolatry that continually seduced Israel and drew it away from its calling. His resurrection inaugurates the age to come, and the gift of his Spirit gives this life to his people, equipping them to live out their calling, to do what they were summoned to do from the beginning—to be the first members of the new humanity amid the nations.

The resurrected Christ summons this newly gathered Israel and says to them, "As the Father has sent me, I am sending you" (John 20:21). This nucleus of gathered and renewed Israel is sent to continue the mission of Jesus to the ends of the earth, gathering all nations into the new humanity. This time between the resurrection of Christ and his return is characterized by the mission of the church in every culture of the world. To miss this is to misunderstand fundamentally where we are in the biblical story.

If—and only if—we follow the trajectory of this story closely, and if we immerse ourselves in the missional identity of God's people in the story, then we come to understand the role we have been assigned. Mission is not just one more task of God's people; it defines us. We are sent as witnesses to the good news that God is restoring his rule again over human life.

> The Spirit thrusts God's people into worldwide mission.
> He impels young and old, men and women,
> to go next door and far away
> into science and art, media and marketplace
> with the good news of God's grace. . . .

Following the apostles, the church is sent—
sent with the gospel of the kingdom. . . .
In a world estranged from God,
where millions face confusing choices,
this mission is central to our being. . . .

The rule of Jesus the Christ covers the whole world.
To follow this Lord is to serve him everywhere, without fitting in,
as light in the darkness, as salt in a spoiling world.[6]

Mission is central to who we are in Christ. We will recover our true missional identity only if we reclaim Scripture as one story and take up the role we have been called to play in it.

THE BIBLICAL STORY GUARDS US FROM CULTURAL IDOLATRY

There is a final reason that reading the Bible as one story is especially important. Since our missional role is *to be* the new humanity and *to embody* God's creational purpose for human life, we must not "be conformed to this world" (Rom. 12:2). Paul has in mind conformity to human culture as it has been shaped by the idolatry of the present evil age. Only by seeing the Bible as one story can we equip ourselves to resist the idolatrous spirits that shape our culture.

All cultures—and this certainly includes the culture of the modern West—have been shaped by religious faith commitments that stand in tension with the gospel. Core religious assumptions have been formed over many years, and they find expression in the institutions, customs, practices, and habits of our culture. That formative story is pressed upon us from birth, through marketing, technology, education, language, and entertainment.

The gospel calls us to live *counter*culturally—to live in a way that challenges the idolatry of our culture. But at the same time we are called to embody the gospel *within* our culture. And there is the rub! How can we live as participants in our culture and at the same time challenge its pervasive idolatry? How can we be a collaborative community that shares in the cultural task, but also a contrastive community that rejects the idolatry that is shaping its development? *We must continually rehearse the biblical narrative* among the people of God so that it confronts the coercive power of all rival stories.

In this context, N. T. Wright speaks of *subversion*. We are to "tell this [the biblical] story as clearly as possible, and to allow it to subvert other ways of telling the story of the world."[7]

Lesslie Newbigin employs the notion of a *missionary encounter*. He believed that by the mid-twentieth century, the Western church was in an "advanced case of syncretism."[8] Contemporary Western culture tells "two quite different stories" as the "real story" of the world: the humanist story and the story that is told in the Bible.[9] A missionary encounter is a clash of these foundation stories. It occurs when the church indwells the all-embracing claims of the biblical story while living amid the equally comprehensive claims of the dominant cultural narrative. Newbigin charges that the Western church has too often allowed the biblical story to be absorbed into (what it assumes is) a more comprehensive Western story.

Richard Bauckham makes the same point with the language of *resistance*. He argues that the only way the church can resist being co-opted into the very powerful narrative of economic globalization and individualistic consumerism is by countering that narrative with the biblical one. He asks, "What do we really need in order to recognize and to resist this new metanarrative of globalization?" His answer: The biblical story must be recovered as a metanarrative of equal scope and explanatory power. By "metanarrative," Bauckham means "an attempt to tell a single story about the whole of human history in order to attribute a single and integrated meaning to the whole."[10] The only effective resistance is to affirm the Bible in its canonical unity.

The following illustrations, used by Brian Berger in his members' class at Redemption Church in Gilbert, Arizona, make this point vividly. He draws a circle on the board and then asks prospective members what American Christians pursue as the ultimate goal of human life. What does it mean to "win" and "succeed" in American culture? What kinds of things bring satisfaction and meaning to our lives? What is the chief end of human life? Almost immediately he gets some version of the answer that indicates material prosperity or financial success (see fig. 11.1). He probes deeper: Why do we want money? The answers: For financial security and retirement; for big, impressive houses; for nice vacations; for newer and better technology; for good entertainment; for a nice car; for brand-name clothes; for toys like boats, motorcycles, and cottages; and so on.

Figure 11.1. **Goal of Human Life in the United States**

What does success look like?

- Material prosperity
- Financial security
- Big, impressive home
- Nice vacations
- New, better technology
- Good entertainment
- Really nice car
- Toys—boats, motorcycles, etc.

Berger then observes that he gets the same answers each time the class is taught. What accounts for this? Movies. Ads. Influential people like parents, bosses, teachers, friends. TV shows. Social media. News. Popular music.

He points out that these pursuits and goals are not as universal as we may think. This is not the list that would have been given at other points in history, or even given today in other parts of the world. Many Hindus, for example, see such pursuits as childish. Where does this notion of success come from? In fact, it is because we all live in the same culture with the same worldview, customs, and patterns. We swim in this cultural water. We are unaware of its influence, and it is forming all of us, all the time. This worldview and way of life that we inhabit is the product of a long historical story that has shaped our culture. Berger represents this cultural story with an arrow (see fig. 11.2).

Figure 11.2. **American Cultural Story**

He then asks what *we* believe as Christians. The class typically offers various answers: God is triune; Jesus died on the cross and rose from the dead; we are saved by faith in Jesus; we are to love our neighbors; we are to be just and merciful; and so on. He writes each on the board, circling them to give each the appearance of a ping-pong ball (see fig. 11.3).

Figure 11.3. **Christian Beliefs**

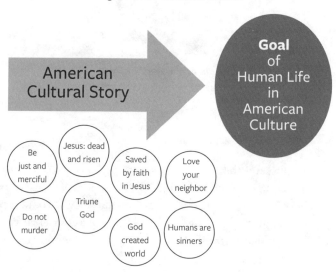

Finally, he graphically illustrates the problem that follows when the Christian faith is reduced to a number of various beliefs, distinct doctrinal truths, and moral demands. They are like ping-pong balls that are thrown into the swift and powerful current of the Western story, having little power to withstand the currents that move us *toward the goals of human life defined by our culture* (see fig. 11.4). By themselves, considered as so many free-floating theological tenets and ethical imperatives—even though they are true—our Christian beliefs are all too often unable to withstand the powerful, idolatrous cultural currents that surround us. Christians are carried along toward the same way of life as our unbelieving neighbors.

What is needed is a grand story that offers a more compelling *alternative* vision of what "success" or "winning" really looks like—what it means to be truly human. Only the Bible offers such a story.

An Australian sociologist who makes no claim to be Christian asks rhetorically why the church in the West is in serious decline. He answers: "The

Figure 11.4. **The Powerful Current of the Cultural Story**

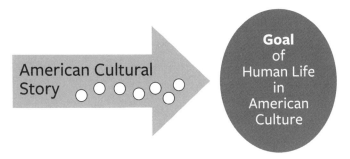

waning of Christianity as practised in the West is easy to explain. The Christian churches have comprehensively failed in their one central task—to retell their foundation story in a way that might speak to the times."[11] He recommends that the church, to regain relevance in contemporary life, should tailor the biblical narrative to fit the "broader" story of the West. *But he is wrong.* What is truly needed is the exact opposite: We in the church must faithfully retell the biblical story as the true story of our world, with authority to speak to all the issues of our day. We need to rehearse this story in our preaching, teaching, discipleship, sacraments, and worship—the whole life and ministry of the local congregation—so that the people of God may be equipped as faithful disciples to stand firm in the gospel.

Our lives *will* be shaped by some grand story. The question is, *which one*?

PART 3

GOD'S
MISSIONAL
PEOPLE

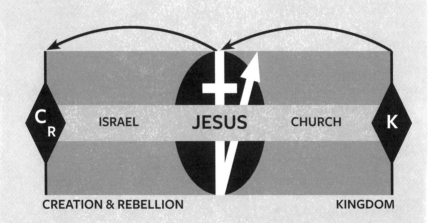

CREATION & REBELLION   KINGDOM

CHAPTER 12

The Missional Vocation
of God's People

Imagine all the people
Living life in peace.
—*John Lennon, "Imagine"*

I imagine most readers will recognize the words above from the title song of John Lennon's famous second solo album. Still his most widely recognized tune (as it has been since its release), "Imagine" was, in part, Lennon's personal protest against the war in Vietnam (then still dragging on after a decade of American involvement). It was also perhaps his response to the many social controversies and violent confrontations that had marked the late 1960s and early 1970s, as a youth-centered countercultural movement began to coalesce against the racism, sexism, political oppression, and poverty that they saw as a blight on modern life. Lennon wrote the song, with some influence from his partner Yoko Ono, just a few weeks after the May Day protests of 1971, when twenty-five thousand demonstrators marched on Washington to demand an end to the war. The police response to their protest was swift and brutal, and almost half of them were arrested—the largest mass arrest in US history.

In his song, Lennon invites us to imagine a world of peace, unity, and brotherhood, where there is no more war or hunger or poverty. Borders, greed, religion (or, rather, religious bigotry and intolerance, as he made clear in a subsequent interview), and personal property are all swept away to make room for this better future. He believed that "if you can imagine the possibility, then it can be true." Ono added that this song offers a "complete vision" of global unity and "will start to unfold as you believe in it."[1]

But the song itself moves from imagining the future to inviting its hearers to become part of that future, to embody it in the present and invite others into it. "You may say I'm a dreamer / but I'm not the only one. / I hope someday you'll join us, / and the world will be as one." The new "peace-and-love" countercultural movement of the 1970s hippie culture was already forming as a social expression of this vision—as Lennon and Ono say, they're "not the only ones." They saw themselves as joining with many others to form a community that would embody this vision of the future in the here-and-now of their own day. And they invited their hearers—us—to come and join them so that together we might make real the goal of global unity and peace. "It will start to unfold as you believe in it."

Of course, we know what happened to this movement. Idealistic hippies became materialistic yuppies, and the dream faded. It is perhaps enough to observe that today Yoko Ono (who, with Lennon, had dreamed of a future with "no possessions") now has a net worth in excess of $700 million.[2] Just imagine.

The peace-and-love movement of the 1970s may have faded into history, but John Lennon's song did get at least two things right. First, he saw that we all long for a future world of peace, justice, and harmony, a world without greed, poverty, hunger, hatred, violence, and discrimination. And second, he urged that, for this hope to stay alive, it must become visible in a community whose lives anticipate that future by embodying it in the present: "I hope someday you'll join us, and the world will live as one." This is precisely the role of the church in the biblical story—to embody the future world of the new creation *in the present*, with the invitation to "come and join us."

One substantial difference between Lennon's vision and the Bible's is that the latter has indeed already been embodied, revealed, and accomplished— once and for all, concretely, in this present world—in the life, death, and resurrection of Jesus the Son of God. He has also given his Spirit to his followers so that the future world of blessing is not simply confined to the

130

imagination; it is a present, living reality and a vital power that has already broken into history, and it will one day be revealed fully and completely.

The church is the new humanity in Christ, a community that has already received this new life of peace and human flourishing by the Spirit for the sake of the world, and it will one day inherit it in its fullness. As we live into this present-and-yet-coming kingdom, we invite others to come and join us. This is the role of God's people in the biblical story.

MISSIONAL TRAJECTORY, MISSIONAL VOCATION, AND FULFILLMENT

The Bible narrates God's work in history to restore his creation, and this story unfolds in a consistent pattern from the particular to the universal, from the one to the many, from one nation to all nations, from one place to the ends of the earth.

Three central themes in this narrative deserve our close attention (see fig. 12.1).[3] First, God's purpose for his creation is *blessing*. He chooses Abraham and his family and promises them blessing, with the ultimate goal of incorporating all the families of the earth into that blessing. Second, God's purpose for all people is that they should come to *know* him as the true God. God begins this by revealing himself to Israel as the living God, intending through them to reveal himself to all nations. And third, God's purpose is that the world should live under his *rule* of wisdom, love, justice, and peace. God establishes Zion as the locus of his rule over the nation of Israel (mediated by David) with the ultimate goal of expanding his kingdom to the ends of the earth.

Figure 12.1. **Missional Trajectory**

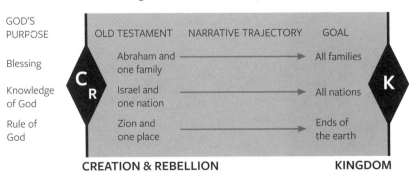

131

It is within this narrative arc that we find the *missional vocation* of God's people, their role within the overarching mission of God. God's people are called to embody in their lives the blessing of God amid the curse of the nations, the knowledge of God amid the idolatry of the nations, and the reign of God amid the oppressive rule of pagan gods. All of this they do *for the sake of all the nations*. God's ultimate purpose is that all nations to the ends of the earth might join with God's people and be restored to the blessing, knowledge, and just rule of God.

The story of Israel was oriented toward the future: God's ultimate goals were promises awaiting fulfillment (see fig. 12.2). The Old Testament describes a future in which all nations, and the whole creation itself, will share in God's restoration. In the New Testament these promises are shown to be fulfilled in two "installments." The first of these is Jesus himself, who (especially through his death and resurrection) accomplishes God's plan. Jesus (1) mediates blessing to all the families of the earth as the descendant of Abraham, (2) mediates the knowledge of God to all nations as the one who takes upon himself Israel's vocation, and (3) extends his reign now to the ends of the earth as Israel's promised king (a descendant of David).

Figure 12.2. **Missional Vocation**

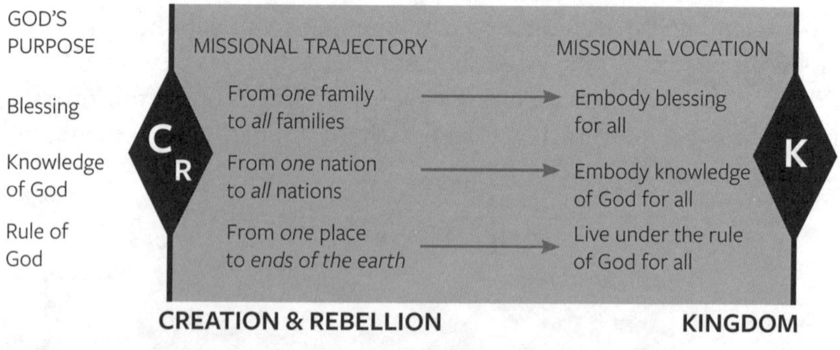

GOD'S PURPOSE	MISSIONAL TRAJECTORY	MISSIONAL VOCATION
Blessing	From *one* family to *all* families	Embody blessing for all
Knowledge of God	From *one* nation to *all* nations	Embody knowledge of God for all
Rule of God	From *one* place to *ends of the earth*	Live under the rule of God for all

CREATION & REBELLION   **KINGDOM**

The second installment of the fulfillment of God's promises rests in the mission of the church (see fig. 12.3). God's people are gathered, restored, and sent by Jesus to embody the blessing, the knowledge, and the rule of God, and by their words and actions to make these known to all nations, to the ends of the earth.

Figure 12.3. **Fulfillment in Jesus and Mission**

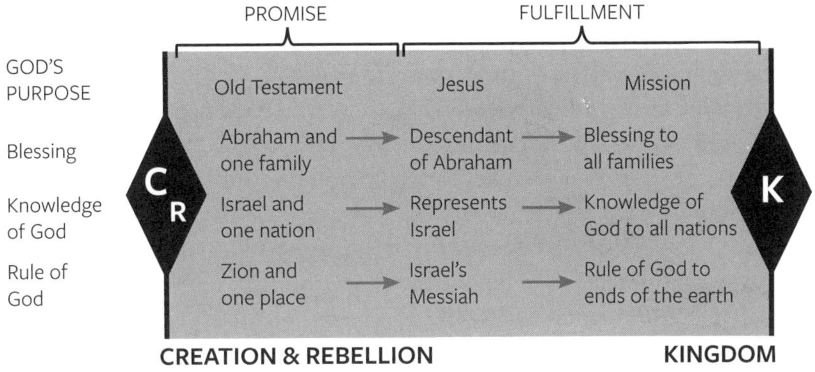

Let's trace these three missional trajectories, beginning with the dissemination of God's *blessing*.

The Family of Abraham and Blessing

The LORD had said to Abram, "Go from your country, your people and your father's household to the land I will show you. I will make you into a great nation, and I will bless you; I will make your name great, and you will be a blessing. I will bless those who bless you, and whoever curses you I will curse; and all peoples [families] on earth will be blessed through you." (Gen. 12:1–3)

Blessing is a rich biblical notion that defines God's purpose for his world. To be blessed is to flourish and thrive in the abundance of life as it was meant to be. It is a gift of God's generosity bestowed on us by his powerful word that we might experience the fullness of life in the whole of our bodily lives as God intended. Blessing comes not simply as good things passed from one to another but in our receiving these good things in communion with God the Giver. The blessing of God on our lives is intended to overflow in our response of blessing. We bless God in praise and thanksgiving, and we bless others with what we've been given. Blessing means living rightly with God, with other people around us, and even with the nonhuman creation in which our lives flourish. Blessing describes the way things were meant to be.

God's blessing works its way outward from one family to all the families of the earth. The biblical story begins with a creation that is blessed (Gen.

1:22, 28) and ends with blessing restored to the whole world (Rev. 22:14). The first eleven chapters of Genesis form the essential backdrop to this theme, since they are concerned with all nations and the whole earth. They narrate a story of tremendous loss, as the blessing of creation is replaced by the curse of the fall (Gen. 1:22, 28; 3:14,17; 4:11; 5:29; 9:25). But then Genesis 12 narrows the focus from the universal to the local. The blessing of God that had been lost to the whole human family is to be restored through his choice of one particular man and his offspring. The nations are not forgotten: God's restoration of blessing begins with Abraham but will at last embrace all the people of the earth.

God tells Abraham that he will bless him *so that* all peoples on earth will be blessed through him. *One* is blessed to bring blessing to *all*; this defines the missional vocation of God's people. They are to receive and embody blessing not for themselves alone but for the sake of the whole creation.

God reiterates his promise to Abraham (Gen. 18:18) and then says that it will be realized as Abraham directs his children and his household after him to keep the way of the Lord, by doing what is right and just (Gen. 18:19). This is the way of a blessed life: As Abraham's family embody the blessing of God, God will draw the nations into that same life of blessing.

Throughout Israel's history the people reminded themselves of this high calling in their worship. "May God be gracious to us and bless us . . . so that your ways may be known on earth, your salvation among the nations" (Ps. 67:1–2). Each time they failed and fell into the idolatry of the nations, the prophets called them back to their vocation. Jeremiah challenged them to rid themselves of idols and return to the path of truth, justice, and righteousness (compare Jer. 4:2 to Gen. 18:19), promising that then *the nations would be blessed* (Jer. 4:2). Though in Zechariah's time Israel had deserted her vocation and increasingly experienced the curse as part of the old humanity, the prophet delivered God's promise that he would remove the curse and make them *a blessing to the nations* (Zech. 8:13; cf. Isa. 19:24–25).

God had always intended for humanity to enjoy the blessing of creation (Gen. 1:22, 28). But as they turn from him, they bring on themselves the curse (Gen. 3–11). This dynamic is made clear in the covenant God makes with Israel (see fig. 12.4). He gives them the law to define what a life of blessing looks like. If they keep God's law, they will enjoy blessing. If they do not, they join those of Adam's descendants estranged from God and living under the curse.

Figure 12.4. **Blessing and Curse**

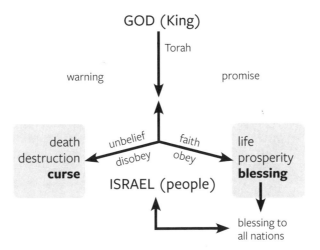

Ultimately, Israel breaks covenant and ends up under the curse in exile (Deut. 28:15–68; 29:25–28). The question is how Israel can be liberated from that curse, be restored to blessing, and so fulfill its calling to bless the nations.

Paul tells us that Jesus, as a descendant of Abraham, represents Israel and takes its curse on himself (liberating Israel from it), "in order that the blessing given to Abraham might come to the Gentiles through Jesus Christ" (Gal. 3:14). God had announced "the gospel in advance to Abraham: 'All nations will be blessed through you.'" And now, because of God's liberation of Israel from the curse, all who trust in Jesus can be blessed along with Abraham's family (Gal. 3:8–9).

The book of Matthew connects the Abrahamic promise to its fulfillment in both Jesus and in the mission of God's people. Matthew's Gospel intentionally begins with *Abraham* and ends with *all nations*. The opening genealogy (Matt. 1:1–17) narrates a story in four episodes: (1) God promised blessing to *Abraham* (Matt. 1:2–6; cf. Gen. 12:2–3); (2) that promised blessing would come through a king in *David's* line (Matt. 1:7–11; cf. Ps. 72:17); (3) the problem was that Israel was under the curse in *exile* (Matt. 1:12–16); and (4) the story of Matthew is how that story is fulfilled in the Messiah, Jesus (Matt. 1:18).

Yet the fulfillment of God's promised blessing to all peoples does not end with the Messiah's work. The book of Matthew ends with the sending *outward* of gathered and restored Israel to "all nations" (Matt. 28:18–20). God's people are empowered to embody blessing, and the time has come to deliver it to all the families of humankind. In Matthew's Gospel, the fulfillment of the Abrahamic story and the dissemination of God's blessing is found in Jesus and in the church's mission.

The Nation of Israel and the Knowledge of the True God

Then Moses went up to God, and the LORD called to him from the mountain and said, "This is what you are to say to the descendants of Jacob and what you are to tell the people of Israel: 'You yourselves have seen what I did to Egypt, and how I carried you on eagles' wings and brought you to myself. Now if you obey me fully and keep my covenant, then out of all nations you will be my treasured possession. Although the whole earth is mine, you will be for me a kingdom of priests and a holy nation.' These are the words you are to speak to the Israelites." (Exod. 19:3–6)

The biblical story begins with humanity living in communion with God in Eden but losing it in Adam's sin, and the story ends with the restored knowledge of the glory of God covering the earth. Between the beginning and end of the grand history, the knowledge of God works outward from one nation to all the nations of the earth.

God chooses Israel as his "treasured possession," one nation through whom he will make himself known to all nations as the true and living God (Exod. 19:3–6; Deut. 7:6). This will take place as Israel becomes the focus of God's saving *and judging* actions in history. God's dealings with Israel through their historical journey will play out on the global stage. All nations are meant to see who God is by what he does.

The exodus is the foundational event of Israel's history, where God displays his power in a mighty act of redemption to liberate Israel from the gods of Egypt and from bondage to the Egyptians (Exod. 12:12). God acts to redeem Israel because he pities them in their misery, and because of his covenant promise to the patriarchs (2:23–25). But he also demonstrates his power explicitly so that his name is proclaimed through the whole earth (9:16). God's mighty act of deliverance for Israel (the particular) is done so that the nations of the earth might know he alone is God (the universal). This is a continuing theme throughout the Old Testament story, and the key to Israel's own interpretation of history (Dan. 9:15).

God acts in *Israel* so that he might reveal his glory to *the nations*. He dries up the waters of the Jordan River, allowing Israel to pass into the promised land, "so that all the peoples of the earth might know that the hand of the LORD is powerful and so that you might always fear the LORD your God" (Josh. 4:24). Israel prays that God might be gracious to them so that his "ways may be known upon earth, [his] salvation among all nations" (Ps. 67:1–3). Nehemiah narrates the story of Israel and says that God's redemptive action is to make a name for himself among the nations (Neh. 9:10).

What does it mean to know the Lord? Solomon's prayer at the dedication of the temple is helpful. He prays for the foreigner who has come from a distant land "because of your great name and your mighty hand and outstretched arm." He asks the Lord to hear him "so that all the peoples of the earth may know your name and fear you, as do your own people Israel" (2 Chron. 6:32–33). To know God is to acknowledge the Lord as the true God, to see who he is by what he has done—the one and only God amid the false gods of the nations, the Creator of heaven and earth, Ruler of history, the God who judges and saves.

But Solomon's prayer for the stranger who comes to Israel goes further, as he asks that such a one should not merely know the Lord, but also "fear" Him. True *knowledge* of God demands a faithful *response*. In the Old Testament, "the fear of the Lord" is shorthand for a full covenant response, devoting all of life to God. Such "fear" is the first lesson of wisdom; it means walking in obedience, loving and serving God with one's whole heart (Prov. 4:23; Deut. 10:12–13). The "fear of the Lord" is the faithful covenant response *of Israel* to the mighty deeds of God on its behalf. But Solomon prays that the nations too might fear the Lord "as do your own people Israel" (cf. Josh. 4:24). This is Israel's *missional vocation* before the nations. Israel's people are to know God, to model "the fear of the Lord" in their trust, allegiance, obedience, and love. They are to be a picture of what God's saving power can do for a nation living faithfully before the living God.

Immediately after its liberation from Egyptian idolatry, Israel's calling before God is spelled out in three terms: as his treasured possession, a priestly kingdom, and a holy nation (Exod. 19:3–6). God chose Israel as his own treasured possession because the whole earth belongs to him. His election of Israel was the beginning of his recovery of the whole world. They were also to be a priestly kingdom. Just as a priest mediates the knowledge of God to those who gather for worship (Num. 6:22–27), a priestly kingdom mediates that knowledge to the surrounding nations. And, as "priests" in this sense, they were called to be a holy nation living according to God's design for human life (Deut. 4:5–8). This threefold identity defines Israel as God's "chosen," and the remainder of the Old Testament narrates how well its people fulfill their calling.

The answer, sadly, is that Israel does not do well. Its story ends in exile precisely because the people failed to know and *fear* their Lord. Yet God does not abandon his faithless people. The word of the Lord comes to them in their exile through the prophet Isaiah (Isa. 40–55), promising that the glory of the Lord will be revealed for all people to see (40:1–5).

How will God's glory be revealed? He will perform yet another mighty act of salvation on behalf of Israel, and all nations will see what he does. The Lord will "bare his holy arm in the sight of all the nations, and all the ends of the earth will see the salvation of our God" (Isa. 52:7–10). This mighty act of God is portrayed as a second exodus in which God will accomplish what the first exodus did not: He will make his great name and power known to the nations by a mighty act of liberation (43:16–19). Israel will be witnesses to his deliverance (43:9–13; 44:6–8). "The nations" who serve idols will both see the work of God and hear Israel's witness to it, and they will at last acknowledge that there is no God apart from the Lord. They too, along with Israel, will turn to the Lord and be saved by him (45:20–25).

At the center of these chapters in Isaiah is the constant stress on the unique glory of God. "There is no God apart from me. . . . I am God and there is no other" (45:21–22). And God will act for Israel "so that from the rising of the sun to the place of its setting people may know . . . I am the LORD" (45:4–6). God's deliverance affects His people locally, but the ultimate effect is universal.

These chapters in Isaiah (40–55) became for the early church the most important chapters in the Old Testament by which to make sense of the strange fulfillment of Israel's story in Jesus and in the church's own mission. They saw that God had returned in glory *in Jesus* and had accomplished a new exodus on behalf of Israel in his death and resurrection, removing the curse of sin and death and leading them into the new life of his kingdom. Now God, in Jesus, sends Israel (represented in the Twelve) to the nations to be witnesses of this mighty saving act (Acts 1:8). "Turn to me and be saved, all you ends of the earth, for I am God, and there is no

other" (Isa. 45:22). The early church understands that the time has come
for people from all nations to hear of the mightiest of God's acts in Jesus,
and to acknowledge that the Lord is God. The book of Acts narrates this
fulfillment of the story.

Zion and the Kingdom of God

May he rule from sea to sea and from the River to the ends of the earth.
(Ps. 72:8)

The third missional theme is that the reign of God will be established
in one place and then expand to the ends of the earth. The biblical story
begins with God portrayed as the Great King over the whole of creation
and ends with the restoration of God's reign over the world. In between,
God's renewing work to restore his rule moves from one specific locus
(Jerusalem) to the ends of the earth.

The theologically rich notion of "Zion," pervasive in the Psalms and
prophets, offers us a window onto this missional theme, and four aspects
of it are helpful here. First, God establishes his throne and rule in Zion.
The psalmist calls Mount Zion "the city of the Great King," where "God
chooses to reign" and the Lord himself will dwell forever (Ps. 48:2, 6;
1 Kings 8:16; 9:3). On the one hand, Zion is held to be a specific geographical location, the city of Jerusalem, where heaven and earth meet,
where the Creator God has established his rule. On the other hand, the
biblical writers acknowledge that God's reign is not and cannot be confined to a temple in Israel or anywhere else (1 Kings 8:27), for Yahweh is
no mere local deity: "The Lord reigns, let the nations tremble. . . . Great is
the LORD in Zion; he is exalted over all the nations" (Ps. 99:1–2). Though
Zion is the locus of God's reign, his rule is universal.

Second, Zion includes the inhabitants of Jerusalem who live under the
rule of the Lord by obeying his decrees (Isa. 62:11–12). Third, God's rule
in Zion is mediated through a human king. The Lord has chosen Zion as
his dwelling place and there sits enthroned, but he has sworn an oath to
David that one of his descendants will sit on *his* throne forever and ever
(Ps. 132:11–14). (The psalmist here refers to the promise God had made to
David, that he would establish the throne of David's dynasty forever; see
2 Sam. 7:11–16.) And a final characteristic of Zion is that God will establish
his rule there by defeating all the enemies that have opposed him. Over
against the kings of the earth that rise against the Lord and his anointed,

God says, "I have installed my king on Zion, my holy mountain. . . . I will make the nations your inheritance, the ends of the earth your possession'" (Ps. 2:6–8). This is the biblical Zion: *God's people Israel living under God's victorious rule in Jerusalem as they submit to God's anointed king.*

But the Old Testament story makes clear that God's reign in Zion is not destined to remain confined to this one geographical location; it is to spread "to the ends of the earth." This phrase is found throughout the psalms and prophets to show the universal extent of God's rule in and through his anointed king. The psalmist prays for Israel's king: "May he have dominion from sea to sea, and from the River to the ends of the earth" (Ps. 72:8; cf. Ps. 2:8). The prophets look to a day when the rule of a future king in David's line "will reach to the ends of the earth" (Mic. 5:4; cf. Zech. 9:10).

The book of Isaiah is particularly important here. One major integrating theme of Isaiah is the establishment of God's sovereign rule on Mount Zion. The book of Isaiah unfolds in three parts. In the first section (chaps. 1–39), the city of Jerusalem, called to be faithful to God, has instead become a prostitute (1:21). Her people are not living as Zion, not submitting to the rule of the Lord. They are warned that if they continue in their idolatry, injustice, and false worship, they will be exiled—though Isaiah also promises that God will one day restore them, to be again a faithful city. This first section of Isaiah ends with the image of Israel in exile. The second section looks to a time (several centuries later) when Israel is in exile (chaps. 40–55). Isaiah projects his message into that exilic future, promising that a day is coming when Israel's sin will be paid for, when God will return in glory to Zion and establish his rule to the ends of the earth (52:7–10). All of this will be accomplished in a second exodus by a suffering—and yet exalted—servant. In the third section of the book (chaps. 56–66), Israel is indeed gathered and restored to Zion under the rule of God. All the enemies of God's rule have been defeated, the nations are now incorporated into Zion, and even the whole creation is included in blessing. Zion, the place of God's reign, has become the new creation. God has established his rule in Zion to extend over the whole earth.

The missional vocation of Israel is defined by this narrative: They are to *live in submission to the rule of God* as a faithful city for the sake of the nations. When they betray their allegiance, like a prostitute, they will be exiled under God's judgment. But they will at last be gathered again and restored to their original calling to live under God's reign, and "the nations" too will be included within that kingdom.

When Jesus comes, he is the promised Son of David who announces that the reign of God has arrived (Matt. 1:1; Mark 1:14–15). Jesus is *both* God returning to reign *and* the human anointed king through whom God reigns. He gathers the lost sheep of Israel (Matt. 15:24) into a flock to whom the kingdom is given (Luke 12:32). In his death, Jesus overcomes all the enemies opposed to his rule and is installed on Mount Zion as ruler (Rev. 14:1; cf. Ps. 2:6). In his resurrection, he inaugurates the universal reign of God. In his exaltation, he shares God's throne to rule history and bring the whole world in subjection to his rule (Rev. 4–5). He sends his peoples to the ends of the earth to witness to the good news that God reigns (Acts 1:8; 28:31). We who follow Jesus are thus citizens of Zion, the new Jerusalem, a people living under the victorious rule of God (Heb. 12:22; Gal. 4:26). All peoples of the earth are summoned to enter his gracious and benevolent kingdom and join the people of God under his rule. It is in this mission that God's long-promised purpose to establish his rule to the ends of the earth is fulfilled.

THE MISSION OF THE CHURCH

The missional vocation of the church must be understood in terms of these themes within the biblical story. "Mission" is not first either *speaking* or *doing* or even *going* (although it includes all three). It is essentially a matter of *being*; mission is what the church *is*. The church is to embody blessing, to know and fear God, and to live under the reign of God. This is the original purpose of humanity in creation now being recovered in God's redemptive work. Our lives are to be attractive as we live out God's creational design for human life to show what being truly human looks like.

This life is to be lived in a way that puts God's name on display before the nations. Since we live within the social context of the old humanity with its idols, our lives must show the contrast between serving the living God and serving other gods. And this new life is not for our benefit alone but is also for the sake of "the nations," the old humanity, still serving false gods, among whom we live. God does his redemptive work first *in* his people but does not stop there; he works also *through* his people to reach "the nations."

This has always been the shared missional calling of God's people throughout the biblical story, from Israel to the church. But the mission of the church after the work of Christ differs from that of Old Testament Israel in that "the end of the story has arrived." God's purpose to incorporate the nations into his blessing, his knowledge, and his rule is no longer something just to be anticipated; it has come. Thus, the church is now *enabled* to fulfill its vocation because of the work of Christ and the presence of the Spirit: we are now *sent* to the nations, for God's people no longer exist as a national, ethnic, geographical community but are now an international, multiethnic, nongeographical community. And there is a more *intentional* dimension to the missional vocation of God's people, since mission now includes deliberate and purposeful speaking, acting, and going.

Like John Lennon we imagine a better world, but ours is that particular world revealed to us in the biblical story of the creation and the new creation. It is a world of blessing in which the knowledge of the glory of God fills the earth under the reign of God. It was first revealed in God's pattern of life laid out for Israel but at last supremely revealed and accomplished in Jesus Christ. It is a world still waiting to be revealed in its fullness, but also now present in history in the Spirit. It is a world that we are called to embody here and now, amid the brokenness of our culture's idols, for the sake of others. So we offer the invitation: Come and join us.

CHAPTER 13

A Missional People Today, Part 1

Scattered Life

Is it not an illusion that constantly fogs our thinking about the Church that we think of it as something which exists manifestly on Sunday, is in a kind of state of suspended animation from Monday to Saturday? The truth of course is that the Church exists in its prime reality from Monday to Saturday, in all its members, dispersed throughout the fields and homes and offices and factories, bearing the royal priesthood of Christ into every corner of His world. On the Lord's Day it is withdrawn into itself to renew its being in the Lord Himself.

—Lesslie Newbigin, "Bible Studies: Four Talks on 1 Peter"

For most of her life Chan Yang lived in North Korea, where government propaganda ceaselessly portrayed its own nation as both powerful and prosperous. Television showed image after image of fully stocked department and grocery stores, even though nothing in those stores was really for sale. The government showcased its army carrying out meticulously choreographed military parades and exercises, presenting itself as a fearsome world power. And since no *counter*story was ever allowed to be told, Chan Yang, like many North Koreans, simply believed and inhabited the story she was told.

Then some daring South Koreans committed themselves to subverting the fake story of the North. They began to smuggle in thumb drives, CDs, cell phones, and other media to expose the people of North Korea to a very different story, to break the spell of the false narrative simply by revealing the truth. Chan Yang heard this new, subversive story. She saw video and heard sound recordings of people living ordinary lives in South Korea— who were all much better off than she was—and gradually she came to realize that the story she had always been told about her own country, its leaders, and its people was a lie. She says: "What we learned wasn't true. I had been fooled. I wanted to be free." The new story she heard kindled in her a strong desire for a new way of life, so at last she defected with her family to become part of a new community in South Korea.[1]

The story of Chan Yang's experience gives us a glimpse into the missional calling of God's people in contemporary Western culture. We are bombarded by *in-formation*—consider just what that word truly means! Every day we are pressured to conform to the false belief that the humanistic and consumer narrative is the way (the *right* way, the *only* way) to be fully human and to enjoy true life. This information comes from movies, schools, governments, coworkers, advertising, popular culture, social media—indeed, from every corner of our culture. There seems to be no alternative story, and so it all appears to be plausible.

Our humanist story is but one of the many stories of the old humanity that hold us in bondage by their idolatry. The only way that this powerful Western story can ever be challenged and the people under its sway liberated is if we tell and live a different, subversive counterstory that shows the true means of achieving a richer and fuller life. The spell of the dominant cultural myth will be broken only if this other story is told *and lived out* by a community of real people—as Chan Yang herself would tell you.

The people of God are formed by him to be the new humanity, a community living within the biblical story, in the way God intended for human life in creation. The contrast between the life of the new humanity and that of the old unmasks the reigning cultural story as a lie. The church lives to be the true and new humanity, a showcase to the world of where true blessing and life can be found. We are called to live in such a way that folks outside the Christian faith will exclaim, like Chan Yang, "What I was learning isn't true. I've been fooled. I want to be free. I want to be part of this new humanity."

How can we be this kind of people today?

A BIBLICAL MODEL IN ACTS

The book of Acts offers a New Testament model of what the church should look like. The Old Testament people of God had, since the time of Moses, been identified by their formation as a national and cultural community living under Torah. But with the coming of Christ, the outpouring of the Spirit, and the sending of Israel to the nations, the old *form* of God's people had changed, and it was no longer clear what new form they should take. This was new territory, a new chapter in redemptive history. Luke narrates the shocking fulfillment of how the (gentile) nations were being drawn into God's family by way of mission and how that changed the form of God's people. The churches in Jerusalem and Antioch are briefly described by Luke as prototypes of this new form (Acts 2:42–47; 11:19–30; 13:1–3).

Luke describes the *gathered life* of the Jerusalem church. They are devoted to four things: the apostles' teaching, fellowship, the Lord's Supper, and prayer (Acts 2:42). The word "devoted" here is strong: It connotes the single-minded and rigorous commitment of an Olympic athlete to his training. These four things are the channels through which the Spirit gives to the church the resurrection life of the new creation (see fig. 13.1). Christ is present and his life is received. It is an ongoing, communal process.

Figure 13.1. **Channels of New Creation Life**

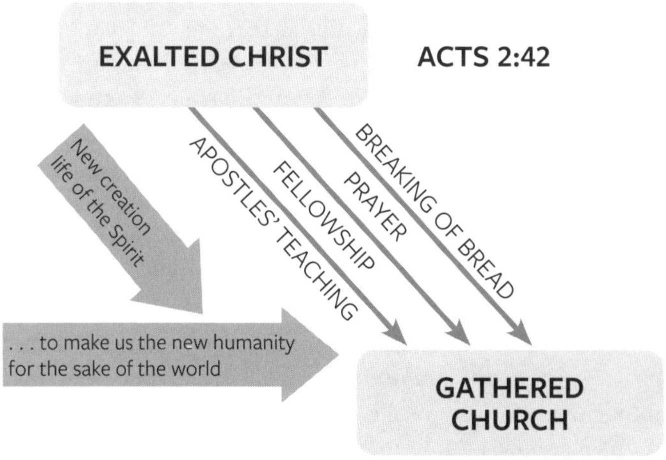

Luke then describes their *scattered life* amid the public life of Jerusalem. Meeting Christ through these channels forms the church into an attractive community that embodies a foretaste, a preview, of the life of the kingdom to their Jerusalem neighbors (Acts 2:43–47). Their communal life in the city is marked by power, generosity, justice, unity, joy, and praise, such that they enjoy the favor of all people. Luke describes the result: "And the Lord added to their number daily those who were being saved" (2:47).

However, though it is growing and prospering, the church in Jerusalem is soon scattered by persecution (Acts 8:1). And as they go out from the place of their beginning, the Jerusalem Christians make the gospel known in new places. They mostly spread the word among Jews, but some tell the good news of the Lord Jesus to gentiles, a good number of whom believe and turn to the Lord (11:19–21). A church forms in Antioch. Like the Jerusalem church, this community is committed to the Word of God and prayer (11:26; 13:2–3), and their lives—especially their radical generosity—offer an attractive alternative to the surrounding cultural norms. Again, a great number of their neighbors see the fruit of faith in their lives and come to believe the gospel (11:27–30).

But there are differences between the Antioch and Jerusalem churches. In Antioch, the believers are not all Jewish. The church is a new community made up of people from *many* ethnic backgrounds (Acts 13:1). To the outsider, the only thing that seems to bind them together is Christ, and so they are labeled, perhaps derisively, Christians (11:26). They also take the next step in mission; they recognize that the way God is making known the good news is through communities who live it, do it, and speak it. They look beyond Antioch and see that there are many parts of the Roman Empire that do not have such a witnessing community. Under the moving of the Spirit, they set aside Paul and Barnabas and send them off to establish churches in these parts (13:1–3).

In these two descriptions we note three things about the church. Most important, the primary witness to Jesus is a community whose lives have been changed. It is because of this life change that their words bearing witness to Jesus as the *source* of that life carry weight. This is beautifully set forth in a description of the Jerusalem church: Luke records that God's grace is powerfully at work among them, shaping their communal life to reflect radical generosity and unity, and concern for the poor (Acts 4:32, 34). Sandwiched between these two descriptions of the church's life, we read: "With great power the apostles continued to testify to the resurrection of the Lord Jesus" (4:33). The verbal witness to the gospel is powerful because it is substantiated by a communal life that demonstrates God's powerful work in them.

The second thing to note is that the church looks outward from its own place to places and peoples still lacking a witness to the gospel. The Antioch church is intentional in planning to send someone to establish a witnessing presence in parts of the empire where there has been none. The remainder of Acts narrates the missionary travels of Paul, whom they send. Thus, the church is living, speaking, and doing the work of the gospel, but also sending it farther abroad.

The final observation is that this kind of life can be sustained only if there is a vital, gathered community where the risen Christ meets his people in power and, through the Spirit, gives them the resurrection life of the new creation. The church's mission is not a matter merely of planned strategic action to reach unbelievers (although we can't *exclude* this intentional dimension). It is first a matter of *being* the new humanity, a community of life amid a culture of death, a people of blessing amid the curse of idolatry. And the only way that we can be formed into that kind of attractive people is through the missional means of grace God has given his people—through praise, fellowship, Scripture, prayer, and sharing the Lord's Supper.

The shape of the church can be likened to an ellipse, which has two focal points (see fig. 13.2). The first is the *gathered* life of the church, where God's people meet to celebrate and nurture the new life that they have in Christ by the Spirit. God's saving power is known and experienced here in this gathered life, and then it overflows in witness and service to the world. Thus the second focal point is the *scattered* life, where we witness to God's saving power in life, word, and deed onward to the ends of the earth. If either of these focal points is neglected—as is too often the case—it has fatal consequences for the church's vocation. If we should lose the vital inner life of the church, we cut ourselves off from the very springs that nurture resurrection life for witness. But if we should lose a vigorous witness in the world, we risk turning the church into an introverted, self-absorbed community that has forgotten its true calling. In this chapter and the next, we will briefly sketch these two modes of the church's being: inner and outer, gathered and scattered. In this chapter we begin with the scattered life of the church in its various forms of witness.

The job of the church is to point *backward* to what humanity was created to be and to point *forward* to what humanity will one day be in the new creation. But ultimately, we point to Christ as the one who has embodied all of this, who has accomplished it in his death and resurrection, and who now gives it to us today by the Spirit. Luke employs the word "witness" to describe this pointing, which takes place in our living, our vocations, our speaking, our doing, and our sending.

Figure 13.2. **The Church as Ellipse**

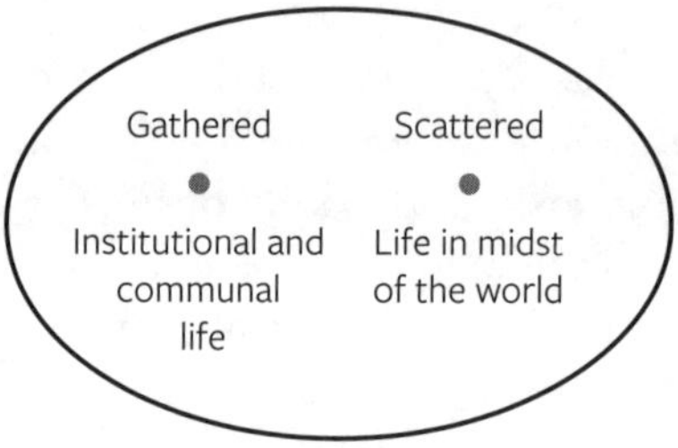

Gathered	Scattered
●	●
Institutional and communal life	Life in midst of the world

LIVING

We point to new life in Christ with our lives. The fundamental calling of God's people is to live distinctively amid the idolatrous ways of life of our culture that characterize the present evil age, the old humanity. Throughout the biblical story God shows his people what distinctive living looks like by, for example, giving the Torah to Israel or Paul's teaching in his letters to the young churches. God instructs his people in how to be fully human in their particular context, for it is only as our lives are truly distinctive over against the idolatrous currents of our culture that others will be drawn to the gospel. Friedrich Nietzsche, a mortal enemy of the Christian faith, comments, "They would have to sing better songs for me to learn to have faith in their Redeemer: and his disciples would have to look more redeemed."[2]

What would it take for us as a Christian community to "look more redeemed" in the presence of our twenty-first-century neighbors? Here are a few suggestions for reflection (some of which I will return to in later chapters).

The Christian church should be a community

- that demonstrates self-control and marital fidelity (in a world saturated by sex)
- that conforms to God's creational order for gender and sexuality (in a world that worships autonomous freedom in these matters)

- that embraces male and female together as integral to the image of God (in a world of patriarchalism and feminism)
- that is committed, boldly and humbly, to *truth* (in a world of relativism and pluralism)
- that lives in God's presence (in a secular and naturalistic world)
- of contentment and generosity (in a world of insatiable desire and greed)
- of thankfulness (in a world of corrosive dissatisfaction and envy)
- of sacrificial, self-giving love (in a culture of self-absorption, narcissism, and entitlement)
- of integrity, wholeness, and character (in a culture of false appearance and manufactured image)
- of mercy and justice (in a world of economic and ecological injustice)
- oriented to the poor and marginalized (in a world that panders to the rich and powerful)
- whose words are gracious and true (in a world of cynical lying and trivial, malicious communication)
- of wisdom (in a world of confusion and proliferating information)
- committed to the important issues of our globe (in a culture of selfish apathy)
- of purpose (in a culture that perpetually seeks amusement)
- of joy (in a world dominated by a frantic and hedonistic pursuit of pleasure)
- of patience and self-control (in a world of instant gratification)
- of mutual accountability (in a world of fiercely guarded and competitive autonomy)
- whose commitment to Christ includes public life (in a world where religion is considered a merely private concern)
- that loves, blesses, and welcomes all those who stand in opposition to the gospel (in a world of division and hostility)
- of forgiveness and kindness (in a world of conflict, hatred, and anger)
- that refuses the economic and political options of the left *and* right (in a world divided by idolatrous ideology)

149

- of unity and commitment to Christ (in a world of competing ideologies)
- of racial equality and love (in a world stained by systemic racism)
- of stewardship (in a world of waste)
- whose members love their national neighbor and the foreigner (in a world of nationalism and idolatrous forms of patriotism)

This kind of distinctive life must be evident both as the people of God live together in community (gathered) and as they live in their various callings throughout the week (scattered). The church must condemn and work against racism within the public life of culture—*and* eliminate racial inequality from its own life. The church must struggle for economic justice and care for the poor in society—*and* must embody the same justice, generosity, and compassion toward its own poor. The church must stand publicly against the hostility and division produced by idolatrous political ideologies—*and* must find ways for its own members to live in unity, peace, and healthy disagreement with one another. The church must oppose the wastefulness and ecological injustice of the surrounding consumer society—*and* must live together as good stewards of the scarce resources of our globe. The church must refuse to submit to the privatization of religion in public life—*and* in their meeting together must worship, preach, confess sin, practice the Lord's Supper, and pray in ways that express the gospel as public truth.

VOCATION

We point to new life in Christ in our vocations. Our lives must bear witness to the gospel not just when we are gathered but also as we are scattered in the public life of culture. It is in the ordinary work of believers in business and politics, office and factory, service industries and education, farming and information technology that "the primary witness to the sovereignty of Christ must be given."[3] Unfortunately, this challenge has not been taken on board by many congregations. Even though most Christians are godly and well-meaning believers, in their day-to-day activities their public lives are often shaped by the idolatrous humanist story of Western culture. This is the fruit of a disastrous dichotomy between the secular and sacred.

The sacred-secular dichotomy has crippled the church in its mission. With the rise of modern humanism as the dominant public faith, the Christian faith has largely been relegated to the private sphere. We allow the humanist story to dictate to us which activities, professions, and social spheres are sacred—that is, related to God and under the authority of Scripture—and which are secular—cut off from God and no longer shaped by the gospel (see fig. 13.3).

Figure 13.3. **Sacred-Secular Dualism**

SACRED-SECULAR DUALISM	
SACRED	**SECULAR**
Activities	
prayer worship	sports voting
Professions	
minister missionary	journalist politician
Social Spheres	
church family	university business

The Bible teaches us that all of human life belongs to God. Abraham Kuyper put it famously: "There is not a square inch of the whole domain of human existence over which Christ, who is sovereign Lord over *all*, does not cry: 'Mine!'"[4] C. S. Lewis amplified this claim: "There is no neutral ground in the universe: every square inch, every split second, is claimed by God and *counterclaimed by Satan*."[5] Lewis rightly insists that God's just claim on all of human life is fiercely contested by Satan; there is no naked or empty public square. The "secular" is not neutral space but is under the domination of "the powers." For the Christian to retreat to some "sacred" realm is to abandon much of human life to those powers.

N. T. Wright reminds us, "It is the Christian claim that every square inch of the world, every split second of time, belongs to Jesus, *by right of the creation and by right of redeeming love*."[6] The Bible rejects the dualism that seeks to separate any part of human life from God and his authority. God created humankind to cultivate and care for the creation and to create a culture that mirrors God's glory. This grand original purpose was thwarted by our first parents, who chose to cling to a spurious authority of their own making, believing Satan's lie that they "could be as gods," and so plunged the world into rebellion. The cultural calling of humankind continued, but culture was (after Eden) increasingly pursued in service to *other* gods. Babel is the archetype of misdirected human vocation. However, God is still at work in his world to restore his creational purpose, and the people of God offer proleptic glimpses of a humanity brought back to their original, creational purpose in the kingdom of God.

Our vocations are a primary witness to the sovereignty of God because they challenge the public-private and sacred-secular dichotomies that seek to distance much of God's creation from his authority. Faithfully living out our vocations makes clear the public and comprehensive nature of God's sovereignty amid a culture that serves other gods. We align ourselves with God's kingdom in the battle for all human life. When Christians are faithful in their vocations, they are "planting the flag in hostile soil . . . worshiping Jesus in the place where other forces, other gods, hold sway."[7]

When we speak of "witness" in our vocations, we are not speaking simply about evangelizing our coworkers or having high ethical standards in our work. Though these are certainly important, faithful vocational witness is concerned for something more. We are called to live out God's creational design for our own area of vocation, to challenge the cultural gods that seek to deform that design. Imagine the believer who works in business and seeks to love her neighbor by providing goods or services for a *fair* profit, though she is part of a business culture that prizes maximum profit above all else. Or consider the PhD student who studies to gain insight into the order of God's world in light of Scripture, though he works amid the postmodern idols of the university that reject God's order and reduce "truth" to human construction and power plays. Or what about the believer working in government who genuinely desires to pursue public justice in a political landscape where choices have largely been reduced to two humanist options, neither of which has a full vision of public justice?

In each of these areas the challenge for the believer is to ask three fundamental questions: (1) What is the creational intention and purpose of my area of work? (2) How has cultural idolatry twisted it? (3) What paths are open to me to expand and deepen areas of the creational intent in these spheres while challenging and minimizing the idolatry that twists them? For example, the creational intent of business is to steward God's resources in a way that loves our neighbor by providing goods or services to them for a reasonable profit. But our modern Western culture is deeply shaped by the economic idolatry that makes economic growth, production, and consumption the chief ends of human life. In such a culture, the goal of business is no longer about love of neighbor, but solely about maximizing profit. How might believers in business move their enterprises more toward love and stewardship?

This raises the question of the *goal* of faithfulness in vocation. Some want to reduce it to transformation: Our goal is to transform culture to be more just and fair. Certainly, we would love to see that and are thankful when God uses our small efforts to achieve a social order that reflects God's purpose just a little more faithfully. However, when we look at the New Testament, we recognize that the far more likely outcome of such faithfulness is suffering. When we challenge "the powers," they push back hard. Our goal needs to be to please the Lord and to offer in our vocations a wise and faithful witness to the sovereignty of Jesus Christ. And we must be willing to face suffering if such faithfulness requires it.

To be faithful in this way will require that congregations nourish the life of Christ in worship, discipleship, the reading and study of Scripture, sharing the sacraments, and more. Too often, the outward look from our gathered life is lacking and the nurture of faith is reduced to the personal. We sing songs about individual salvation, hear sermons that offer personal application, confess sins concerned with personal ethics, and partake of the Lord's Supper for our own personal spirituality. We need to equip believers *for their vocations* just as much as for their "private" lives of faith. As church leaders become attuned to this task, they will design worship to nourish believers, cultivate discipleship, provide support, and shape congregational structures that will form believers for their vocations. And we need groups of believers of similar vocations willing to meet and struggle together to understand what true faithfulness looks like in their particular area of working life. And we will also need to sink our roots more deeply into the resurrected life of Jesus (Col. 2:7).

SPEAKING

We point to new life in Christ with our speaking. Using our words, which identify the source of our new life, we need to speak of God's mighty act of redemption in Jesus, what he has done, what he is doing, and what he will do. He *has* inaugurated the new creation in the cross and resurrection. He *will* complete the work of new creation when he returns to renew all things. He *is* giving us a foretaste and experience of this resurrection life by the Spirit.

The good news we proclaim is as wide as creation. Our task is not just to "get people saved" but also to make the good news known amid every imaginable issue and circumstance in life. Our friends and neighbors must hear *good news*! The gospel is connected to every part of human experience and is relevant to the lives and needs of each person. Our words of witness should flow organically in informal conversation about the real issues of life, the commonplace as well as the lofty.

What are the deepest longings of our neighbors' hearts? They might be personal longings: yearning for healed relationships or freedom from addiction, for seeing their children flourish or answering questions of identity. They might be concerned with the fundamental issues of life: questions about God or salvation, about the meaning of life or the source of true happiness. They might be concerned about global issues: longing for justice and peace, for the hungry to be fed or for victims of sexual trafficking to be freed. The good news has something to say to all these things.

It is clear we can witness in this way only if we are deeply and graciously present in the lives of our friends and neighbors. We need to love them—to build relationships and cultivate an untiring, genuine interest in people's lives, sharing (as we are permitted) their joys, sorrows, aspirations, fears, needs, pain. We must listen humbly, carefully, with a nonanxious presence, with sympathy and solidarity. Witness may begin with nonthreatening questions and continue with *real* listening. What are you struggling with? What kind of world would you like to live in? How do you think the world will be freed from its problems?

Our friends and neighbors must ultimately also hear the call to repentance. Our witness in words should be *relevant* but also *challenging*. The gospel does offer good news about new life, but it calls people to forsake their old ways of life. It calls for a costly, radical commitment to Jesus. It invites people to find a new and liberating way of life following Jesus. It calls them to become part of the new humanity, with a commitment to align their lives with God's own mission. To present a "gospel" that makes no demands of its disciples and does not enlist them in mission gives a false view of the Christian faith.

We must also know the religious vision and story being told and lived out in our surrounding "secular" culture. People are embedded in this culture, and its vision shapes their way of seeing the world and addressing their deepest needs. How has our humanist culture tried to answer or to satisfy the deepest religious longings of life? Why has it failed? How can the gospel meet these longings in a more satisfying way?

But perhaps more powerful than the exact words we speak or approach we take is our disposition and posture. True humility, respect, compassion, kindness, sympathy, and solidarity adorn the gospel. Remember what Paul says in 1 Corinthians 13:1: "If I could speak with all human eloquence—*or even angelic!*—but speak without love, I would be of no more use than a clanging gong" (paraphrased). We need to learn to be at once both *bold* and *humble* in what we say. Jesus Christ *is* the truth and the life; this needs to be said without reservation, because it is simply true! Yet if those words lack humility, and instead convey mere self-righteousness, we will not be heard. And in all of this we must remember that conversion is a work of the Spirit. Our words and disposition will never be enough. In our weakness we merely point to Jesus, and the Spirit works in power.

DOING

We point to new life in Christ with our deeds. Few things speak more clearly of the truth of the gospel than a church deeply involved in the needs of their neighbors, pursuing justice, mercy, and peace. We have for too long tolerated a dualism that separates our deeds from our words and says, "Just preach the gospel." But if our words are not connected to deeds that authenticate them, they will sound—indeed, they will *be*—hollow. The power of the ancient church's witness and its dramatic growth in its first few centuries came because the church invested itself deeply and sacrificially in deeds of love, mercy, justice, and compassion for each other *and* for those outside the church. Julian the Apostate, a fourth-century emperor who sought to turn Rome back to paganism, was irritated by the growth of the church and commented that the real power of the Christian message was a community that took care of its own poor *and* those of Rome!

Often, we recognize the importance of good deeds but are blind to the opportunities for *doing* good that are all around us. Or we lack the imagination for taking the next steps. We need to find the needs in our own backyards through demographic studies, through conversations with those who are already caring for people in our cities, by seeking information from government offices, and (in all of this) by engaging in thoughtful, purposeful listening. Few things "speak" more powerfully than sacrificial love in action: caring for the poor, welcoming the orphaned, loving the marginalized, seeking justice for the foreigner, loving the enemy. Who are these people among our neighbors? And what can we do?

SENDING

God has given each congregation the task not only of making known the good news in its own place but also of establishing a witness to the gospel in places where there is none. We must ask, "Where in the world are there places and peoples that have no opportunity to see and hear the good news?" And we will find that there are many.

It is true that the church is growing fast in many parts of the world. Over half of the world's Christians today live in Africa and Latin America. Nevertheless, many peoples around the world do not yet have a witness to Christ's love and life. There are many ways to identify this need; for example, some organizations highlight unreached people groups.[8] One of the problems is that our past colonial view of "mission" has set us down a wrong path. We consider that to witness to Christ anywhere outside of North America or Europe (anywhere "overseas") is mission. This has sometimes led us to send significant financial and human resources to places where the witness to Jesus Christ is already strong. Over 90 percent of the money and people we allocate to overseas "mission" aids areas of the world where the church is stronger than it is in North America! Certainly, there is a place for interchurch aid, and we need to partner with the global church in every place. But in doing so it is important to discover which places or peoples in the world still have no or little opportunity to hear and see the good news. And then, as a global church in partnership, with each local congregation playing its part, we need to help establish a vital witness in these places and among these peoples.

With the growing concern for reaching those in our own neighborhoods, our interest in the lost elsewhere in the world has sometimes subsided. This needs to change. We need to recover a sense of God's loving desire to gather in all nations to the ends of the earth.

CHAPTER 14

A Missional People Today, Part 2

Gathered Life

Sunday's worship is unto Monday's work. Worship, which opens the door to a new week, is not a retreat from reality, but a rallying-point, a launching-pad, a spring-board which sends believers forth upon their way as "living letters known and read of all men." The preaching and teaching ministries of the church must shape and mold the Christian community to challenge the "principalities and powers" of this world as it carries out its reconciling mission in society.

—Reformed Ecumenical Synod, "The Church and Its Social Calling"

A PARALLEL CULTURE

In the late 1980s the world witnessed a series of revolutions: the tearing down of the Berlin Wall and the collapse of communism in eastern Europe. Václav Havel, a dissident playwright and philosopher, was a leader in the "Velvet Revolution" in Czechoslovakia. In the years leading up to the fall of communism in his country, he wrote many essays in which he outlined a strategy for dissidents. These essays were later gathered into the book

Living in Truth.[1] Havel explores there how people who live within a culture based on a fundamental lie that dominates every aspect of people's lives could yet in their *own* lives live out the truth. The lie Havel opposed presented a comprehensive story and worldview, an all-embracing ideology. In Czechoslovakia it functioned as a secularized religion, combining a communist dictatorship with a consumer culture. This false vision had for many years, since the close of the Second World War, shaped the culture and dominated the lives, thoughts, and imaginations of the Czechoslovakian people. Havel's essays sought first to expose that lie for what it was and then to ask, "How can we live in the truth?"

Havel proposed that the dissidents should create "parallel cultures," living a different kind of communal life alongside their neighbors, demonstrating what human life could and should be: *a life lived in the truth*. In Havel's model, the truth is lived out by its adherents adopting a different approach to art, education, science, the economy, and politics. The parallel society he envisioned would not seek to retreat into a ghetto or isolate from Czechoslovakian culture in a selfish escape. Rather, it would take a real part in the public life of society, seeking the common good, picturing what life should be, and bearing the brunt of an encounter with the lie of the state.

To sustain that kind of parallel life amid the powerful lies of the dominant culture, it is necessary to create spaces where you can gather with those who believe as you do, to speak the truth to one another, to nurture your common identity. There you perform your plays, sing your songs, read your novels, recite your poetry, discuss your philosophy. Engaging in these cultural practices together frees your reason and imagination from the prison of the dominant cultural mindset. This is what Havel hoped would break the communist system: a new vision of truth, nourished within a parallel culture, forming a people tasked to live out the truth in public life and not be conformed to the lies of the dominant culture.

The "gathered" life of the church similarly nourishes and equips the church to be the new humanity as its members are scattered throughout the week. The church is a parallel society that lives out of the truth, which tells a very different story from the one told by our own dominant culture. Truth is lived out in public life, not by a community that withdraws or isolates itself but by one that participates in culture for the common good. But the lives of Christians in the church must be shaped by the truth of the gospel and not by the destructive lies informing their culture. To sustain life in the truth, against the powerful formative pressures of the surrounding culture, it is necessary to gather and nourish ourselves with an alternative vision. We must create a space where we can live out the truth as it is narrated by Scripture, yet without withdrawing from the "real" world. We dwell in the biblical story of the world rather than in the very different story on which our dominant culture is based. We sing our songs, read our Scriptures, enact our story with water, bread, and wine; we offer our prayers, confess our sin, teach new ways of life, all to strengthen our grasp of truth. Thus, as we go out to live in the surrounding humanist culture, we can say to its lies, "we don't believe you anymore."

One of the differences between Havel's vision for his parallel society and the Christian vision is that the church's truth has been *revealed by and accomplished by God*. Not only is God present to us in Scripture—God's own Word—to tell us the truth about the world, but he is also present in power by his Spirit among his gathered people to make that new world a living reality. The resurrected Christ is personally present amid his gathered people, and (through the communal practices he instituted) he gives his very life to them. The biblical truth that stands against the cultural lie is more than an alternative story, more than the image of a different world; it is also the Person who has embodied that story fully, who was raised from the dead into that new world, and who now empowers us to live the truth by giving us his very life.

How can our gathered life nourish us to be faithful in our vocation? We'll touch on four areas—worship, prayer, formation, and fellowship (see fig. 14.1)—before we conclude this chapter with some comments on the importance of leadership.

Figure 14.1. **The Gathered Life of the Church**

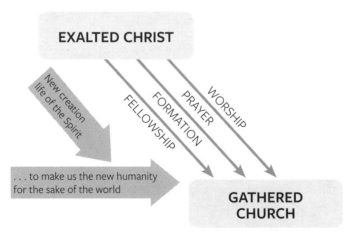

WORSHIP

Gathering for worship each Sunday is the most important thing Christians do. Our communal worship is not a mere means to an end, a way to be equipped for mission, but an end in itself. For we were made for worship, which immerses us in the glorious splendor of the true King of the cosmos. Worship, though, can ready us for our vocation, and there is much to learn about it from the book of Revelation. That book is full of worship and was written specifically to equip God's people to be faithful in their mission amid the powerful idolatry of the Roman Empire.

The book opens with the risen Son of Man exhorting the seven churches living in the Roman Empire to be "victorious" amid their differing circumstances (Rev. 2:7, 11, 17, 26; 3:5, 12, 21). "Victory" (Greek *nike*) is a key word throughout the book and refers to the faithfulness of the church as it shares in the victory of the Lamb. To be victorious here means to *align* oneself with God's kingdom in the cosmic battle, to faithfully *witness* to God's reign in life and word, and to *resist* the idolatry of the Roman Empire so that the nations might be converted and enter the new creation.

Allegiance to God and to the Lamb is expressed in terms of worship. The word "gospel" appears once in Revelation, and its content is spelled out here: "Fear God and give him the glory, because the hour of his judgment has come. Worship him who made the heavens, the earth, the sea and the springs of water" (Rev. 14:7). "Worship" here clearly means more than corporate acts of praise; it is absolute allegiance to God and the Lamb, an allegiance that suffuses the whole of life. The alternative to worshiping God is to "worship the beast and its image" (14:9; cf. 13:4, 8, 12). There are only two options: true worship or false worship, the true God or the false "gods." True worship allows no room for the political, social, and economic idolatry of Rome.

The crucial chapters of Revelation depict the throne room of God, symbol of God's present and coming rule over the world through the Lamb (Rev. 4–5). God sits on the throne, which he shares with the Lamb. The glory of God moves the whole creation, including the people of God, to sing and shout his praise (4:8, 11). The victory of the Lamb at the cross to achieve God's purpose likewise brings forth a chorus of worship (5:9–10, 12, 13). These chapters graphically picture the true nature of the real world, which is imbued with the glory of God and made to respond in worship. And all who hear the words of Revelation are invited into this worship.

Praise erupts in song at every important stage in the coming of the kingdom as it is described throughout the book. The *life* of worship is sustained by the *activity* of worship, which includes songs, words of praise, prayers, and hearing the prophetic words of the risen Christ.

There is much to learn about worship by attending to the way Revelation shows how it sustains God's people in the midst of the Roman Empire. I will briefly note four things.

First, worship is an invitation to come and dwell in the *real world*. The praises of God's people reflect a very different world than what is seen in the Roman Empire, where Caesar is lord. Worship is not an escape from the real world, but an accurate portrayal of the real world, where God alone reigns. Imagine the small and fragile churches of Asia Minor, set in the midst of the most powerful empire ever known, trying to be faithful to the one true God. Roman propaganda constantly reinforced the image of an all-powerful Rome and her "gods," and all her citizens were pressured to conform to this vision.

But John's words in Revelation invite God's people into a very different world. Rome is not the beautiful woman she claims to be, but a harlot about to be destroyed. God's kingdom will endure; the Roman Empire will fall. It is God and the Lamb who rule history, not Caesar. Rome will not triumph by her tremendous military power; the Lamb will triumph through his own crucifixion. For the churches addressed in Revelation, as for ourselves, worship is not a mere therapeutic activity designed to help us cope with the real world, or even a safe haven from it. Worship is our entrance into the real world. From there, we embody that real world amid the falsely narrated world of our culture.

It is worth asking if the worship we actually experience in our churches now does bring us into the world that is narrated in Scripture. Or does our worship instead serve to reflect the story of the surrounding secular culture? In "A Call to an Ancient-Evangelical Future," signed by hundreds of evangelical leaders almost two decades ago, the prologue says, "Today, as in the ancient era, the Church is confronted by a host of master narratives that contradict and compete with the gospel. The pressing question is: who gets to narrate the world?" That is, *Which story* will shape God's people? The paragraph on worship urges "public worship that sings, preaches and enacts God's story," contrasting that with styles of worship that reflect the story of idolatrous secular culture: "lecture-oriented, music-driven, performance-centered and program-controlled models that do not adequately proclaim God's cosmic redemption." If "God's story [is to] shape the mission of the Church to bear witness to God's Kingdom," worship that faithfully reflects the biblical narrative is essential.[2]

The world to which true worship admits us is deeply *theocentric*, saturated with the splendor and majesty of God. We live in a world created, ruled, and being renewed by God, a world drenched in his presence, radiant with his glory, full of the grandeur of God. The entire creation and all peoples *must* worship him as their eyes are opened to his glory. We are to fear God and give him the *glory* (Rev. 14:7; 15:3–4). The word "glory" in Scripture is meant to suggest the substance, the *weightiness*, of God's holy character as it is revealed in his mighty deeds, a presence that demands our recognition and appropriate response. In a world characterized by a profound lightness of being, does our worship help us to see and feel the weightiness of God? In Revelation, the real splendor and glory of God (14:7; 15:4; 18:1) is set in contrast against the superficial splendor and glory of Rome (18:7, 14). Which is capturing the hearts of God's people today: the shallow glamour of a consumer society or the weighty glory of the living God?

Worship should give us a clearer vision of our transcendent and glorious God so that we will be inspired to worship him in our whole lives. We need to see a God on Sunday who is infinitely greater, more majestic, more glorious, and more compelling than the cultural idols that call to us throughout the week. Richard Bauckham says that "only a purified vision of the transcendence of God . . . can effectively resist the human tendency to idolatry. . . . The worship of the true God is the power of resistance to the deification of military and political power . . . and economic prosperity."[3] So it is today!

Is our worship saturated with the glory of God? Does the weight of God's character permeate it? Is the God of our praise, music, sermons, and prayers the God revealed in Scripture—far greater than the idols of our culture and performing deeds far more powerful than our technological "gods" can achieve? Do we need to hear again the famous words of J. B. Phillips: "Your God is too small"?[4]

Revelation further reminds us that when we worship, we are in the *presence of the Spirit,* characterized there as *the sevenfold Spirit* (Rev. 1:4) and *the Spirit of prophecy* (19:10). The first image suggests that the Spirit works as the one who carries out God's purposes (already accomplished in the Lamb) *in the world*, through the mission of the church (4:5; 5:6). The sphere of operation here is the whole world. The second image reminds us that it is the Spirit who brings the words and life of the risen Christ *to his church* through the ministry of human beings. The sphere of ministry here is the gathered church.

In the early chapters, the risen Christ walks among the churches and speaks to them as they gather on the Lord's Day. Each exhortation closes with the words "whoever has ears, let them hear what the Spirit says to the churches" (Rev. 2:7, 11, 17, 29; 3:16, 13, 22).

Do we have a sense that the risen Christ is present among us by the Spirit to speak, empower, and bless? As we hear God's Word read and preached, do we recognize that it is the living Christ who comes to us clothed in the words of Scripture? As we witness baptisms and partake of the Lord's Supper, do we see the Spirit coming to us clothed in water, bread, and wine? As we sing and pray the Word of God, are we aware of the Spirit's presence and power at work? As we gather, do we know that we are meeting with the living Christ who by his Spirit will give us his very life? Do we see the Son of Man walking in our midst on Sunday morning?

Finally, our worship must orient us to the horizon of God's redemptive work and our missional vocation. The church sings, "Great and marvelous are your deeds, Lord God Almighty. Just and true are your ways, King of the nations. Who will not fear you, Lord, and bring glory to your name? For you alone are holy. *All nations will come and worship before you*, for your righteous acts have been revealed" (Rev. 15:3–4, emphasis added). Does our worship do more than simply nourish us with new life? Does it orient us to our calling, to make this life known amid *all nations*?

Our worship matters! As we learn to worship the true and living God revealed and present with us in the risen Christ by the Spirit, we will be equipped to live out lives of full six-day worship in every corner of creation.

PRAYER

If we are to be faithful congregations, we must be committed to corporate prayer. The strong language of "devotion" to prayer expresses how New Testament authors viewed its importance (Acts 2:42; Col. 4:2). This describes the sacrificial, all-consuming devotion of Olympic athletes to their training regimen. Reflecting that importance, the Heidelberg Catechism gives us this fine statement on prayer (Q & A 116):

Q. Why do Christians need to pray?

A. Because prayer is the most important part of the thankfulness God requires of us. And also because God gives his grace and Holy Spirit only to those who pray continually and groan inwardly, asking God for these gifts and thanking God for them.[5]

The strength of this statement may be founded on John Calvin's teaching in *Institutes*, where he compares prayer to a shovel that digs up those treasures in the gospel that would otherwise lie buried.[6] Our participation in communities of prayer, in the church "gathered," is essential if we are to be faithful in our scattered lives. Most exhortations to prayer in the New Testament are *plural* imperatives and refer to communal prayer. "*You all* must devote yourselves to prayer" would be a good way to read them (Col. 4:2; cf. Rom. 12:12). This is our challenge: to weave more prayer into the existing fabric of our congregational lives, whether in our corporate worship or in smaller groups. But it may also inspire us to find other creative ways of keeping prayer central to the ministry of the church. To use but one example, Charles Spurgeon's practice was always to have a team of people praying in a room in the church basement while he was preaching in the sanctuary above. This functioned as the power pipeline of his church.

FORMATION

"Non-discipleship is the elephant in the church," says Dallas Willard. "The fundamental negative reality among Christian believers now is their failure to be constantly learning how to live their lives in The Kingdom Among Us. And this is an *accepted* reality."[7] We need to recover this dimension of our gathered life, "constantly learning how to live." In some traditions, this is called "discipleship" (reflecting the Jewish imagery of the Gospels; cf. Matt. 28:18–20); others describe it as "catechesis" (from other places in the New Testament that emphasize teaching; e.g., Luke 1:4). More recently, the word "formation" has been used to remind us that these practices that "teach us how to live" are there to *form* us into the image of Jesus. Whatever the process may be called, I join with those who are deeply concerned about the harm being done to the church's witness when we neglect rigorous discipleship.

Discipleship begins with the gospel and the biblical story, the core of the Christian faith. It continues as we come to understand our role as God's people in the story and learn to navigate a way of *faithfulness in all areas of life*, amid our idolatrous culture. Such learning continues for a lifetime but begins with parents who pass on to their children what they have received in their own rigorous discipleship, forming their young lives in the faith with humility, intentionality, and love. Training parents for this task must be a priority for the local congregation.

Discipleship continues as we struggle with what it means to be faithful in our work, where most of us spend most of our lives, and where the public truth of the gospel most clearly challenges the "private" faith to which culture would keep us bound. Faithful believers equipped to take up key roles in the surrounding culture will contribute significantly to the common good.

In all of this we need to be *formed* so as to faithfully embody the story of Scripture. If we are not on guard, even discipleship (like worship) can be shaped more by our cultural narrative than it is by the biblical one. As the "Call to an Ancient-Evangelical Future" points out, "Spirituality, made independent from God's story, is often characterized by legalism, mere intellectual knowledge, an overly therapeutic culture, New Age Gnosticism, a dualistic rejection of this world and a narcissistic preoccupation with one's own experience."[8] Consideration of each of these dangers would be worthy of discussion.

In my early years it was intellectualism and legalism that most threatened true discipleship. It was easy then to make discipleship a matter of mastering biblical knowledge, learning certain devotional practices (especially praying and reading Scripture), and of personal ethical formation. Much of this sort of discipleship was good, but it was too narrow, too focused on the individual. Today we have recovered much that can widen and deepen our formation practices: We've been reminded of the grand story of Scripture; we've been shown a broader understanding of mission; we've seen renewed emphasis on the importance of spiritual disciplines, of training for vocation, of faithful life in the public square.

The danger of reacting against a reductionist intellectualism (in the spiritual formation models of the past) is that too often it leads us to embrace an *anti*-intellectual spirit that betrays us by neglecting the strong scriptural emphasis on teaching. In the Gospels, Jesus *teaches* his disciples; in the epistles, Paul *teaches* his young churches, leading them to better knowledge of the truth. The Colossian church is urged to equip themselves against the spiritual powers, the gods and idols of the Roman Empire, through spiritual disciplines (including prayer: cf. Col. 1:9–14; 4:2, 12), so that the church might be rooted in Christ and strengthened in faith for their spiritual battle. But in this context of spiritual powers, Paul's stress on *teaching* and *knowledge* is striking (cf. 1:9, 28; 2:2–3, 6–7; 3:16). "In reflecting on how the church can best resist succumbing to today's alternative lordships that compete for adherence, we would do well to consider again the way in which [Col. 2:6–7] assigns particular importance to the role of . . . catechesis in the process of appropriating the reality of Christ's lordship. Colossians assumes that, if there is to be effective demonstration of that lordship, believers will continually avail themselves of the resources of Christian teaching about their roots and foundation in order to nourish and support their active allegiance to Christ as Lord."[9]

FELLOWSHIP

The New Testament word for fellowship (*koinonia*) means a sharing together in the life of the Spirit. It is more than simply the church's social dimension; it is a shared life of the new creation in communion with Christ (1 Cor. 1:9) and in the Spirit (2 Cor. 13:14). The Spirit works in worship on Sunday morning through the Scriptures, the Lord's Supper, baptism, prayer, and other communal practices to give us more of the life of the new creation, so that we might live it out as we are scattered in our various vocations throughout the week. But more is needed.

Two prominent themes in the New Testament characterize the fellowship of God's people. The first is the "one another" refrain. The reciprocal pronoun usually translated "one another" is found in the New Testament more than a hundred times, about two-thirds of which teach us how we must live together. This reveals something central to what it means to be the church. We are challenged to live together such that we embody the attractive life of the new humanity. Loving one another deeply from the heart (1 Pet. 1:22), honoring one another (Rom. 12:10), living at peace with one another (1 Thess. 5:13), submitting to one another (Eph. 5:21), being patient and bearing with one another in love (Eph. 4:2), being kind and compassionate to one another (Eph. 4:32)—all these express something of how God intended humankind to live in community. Living in this way will certainly present an attractive alternative to our culture's way of living.

These exhortations also reveal channels of communal life the Spirit uses to bring the life of the new creation to us also *for the sake of the world*. This missional orientation in the "one another" passages is often neglected. We are enjoined to spur one another on to love and good deeds as together we seek to be faithful in an idolatrous culture (Heb. 10:24). We are to instruct one another on how to be obedient in our vocations (Rom. 15:14). We are to bear one another's burdens as our encounters with "the powers" of our culture prove burdensome (Gal. 6:2). We are to confess our sins to one another as we pursue faithfulness amid powerful idols (James 5:16). We are to encourage one another in the struggle to be faithful in public life (1 Thess. 5:11). And we are to do what is good for one another in those times of special need or temptation that come to us in our scattered lives (1 Thess. 5:15). All these commands have clear implications for our faithfulness in the world. We need to be more intentional in creating a "one-anothering" kind of life, especially in a culture that places such a high value on privacy and individual autonomy as ours does.

The second characteristic of authentic Christian fellowship is in the gifts that God has given for the upbuilding of God's people. Paul affirms that we are *members* of one another (using the imagery of the human body; cf. 1 Cor. 12; Rom. 12). Each member has different gifts to contribute to the body. But the missional implications of the gifts—how they are meant to equip the church for its mission in the public life of culture—are often overlooked. Of the four lists of these gifts in the New Testament, the one given us by Peter in his first epistle emphasizes their purpose to *equip* the church for its engagement with the broader culture (1 Pet. 4:10–11).

Peter's first letter addresses the complex issue of how to live under Christ's lordship in the public life of society, within the idolatrous institutions of pagan Rome. In his letter's opening, he lays the foundation by establishing who the believers are: Their *true* identity is in the coming resurrection life of the kingdom; they are therefore strangers and foreigners within the Roman Empire (1 Pet. 1:1–2:10). This leads to the problem of how they are to live holy lives within pagan structures and institutions (2:11–4:11). In the last section of his letter, he warns that suffering is the unavoidable result of faithful discipleship in such a setting (4:12–5:11). The discussion of gifts comes at the end of the letter's middle section (4:7–11). Thus, the whole context of the list of gifts suggests that they are part of the equipment given to the community for faithful and responsible participation in the life of society, especially as their obedience brings suffering to them. For Peter, the gifts are for more than simply building up the internal communal life of the church. Can we too develop a more missional orientation for the use of the spiritual gifts God has given?

Many church members now gather only on Sunday mornings. Is it even possible to live the one-anothering life, or to use the gifts for mutual benefit as reflected in the New Testament, or to make formation itself a reality today, when we spend so little time together and when mutual accountability in community is so rare? Surely this teaching demands a greater effort within congregations to develop small groups where such a life is possible. But it may also show us that our love of autonomy and individualism—which we have adopted from secular culture—can hinder the formation of that deep and bracing community the church needs to carry out its mission faithfully.

LEADERSHIP

The importance of leadership in building up faithful missional congregations is evident throughout the New Testament. It is striking that at the end of Peter's discussion of suffering amid the idolatry of the Roman Empire, he immediately appeals to the elders to shepherd the flock through these circumstances (1 Pet. 5:1–4).

Leaders empower God's people for faithfulness first by modeling Christ in their own lives. "Remember your leaders," the author of Hebrews says near the close of his letter, where he exhorts the church not to drift from the gospel as they face cultural pressure. "Consider the outcome of their way of life and imitate their faith" (Heb. 13:7). Paul can say to the Corinthian church, "Follow my example, as I follow the example of Christ" (1 Cor. 11:1), and he expected leaders within churches to be able to say the same.

Leaders also equip God's people for missional obedience through their teaching. Writing to the Ephesian church, Paul highlights the leadership gifts that primarily involve teaching, which equips God's people for their mission to embody the fullness of Christ amid the world (Eph. 4:11–12). Through the teaching ministry of these leaders, God's people will take the Word of God on board so as not to be blown about by the idolatrous winds of culture. Instead, they will grow in maturity and exhibit the life of Christ in their vocations (Eph. 4:13–16).

And finally, leaders build up God's people for their calling by praying for them. Paul is himself the best example of this, reminding the church at Colossae, for example, that he and his colleagues "have not stopped praying for" them (Col. 1:9), and then offering up his prayer (1:9–14). He describes Epaphras as the model of a faithful leader, "always wrestling in prayer for you, that you may stand firm in the will of God, mature and fully assured" (4:12).

Leading in the church is more than the work of a pastor. The professional model of pastoral leadership in our congregations has placed too much weight on the role of paid ministers, with detrimental results both for pastors (and their families) and congregations. There is a need for more attention to lay leadership training within local congregations; and in general churches must pursue the kind of training for both professional clergy and lay ministers that will equip them to lead their congregations in missional faithfulness.

GATHERED AND SCATTERED AGAIN

For many centuries the church was primarily turned inward, preoccupied with its own institutional and communal life. Worship, prayer, teaching, discipleship, fellowship, and leadership were often focused exclusively on caring for the needs of the church's own members, with little thought given to the world outside. Because Christendom (where everyone was nominally Christian) gave the illusion that the church ministered within a Christian society, it seemed that the church could safely concentrate on its own needs. But today, as we become more aware that our missional vocation is lived out in a culture increasingly hostile to the gospel, many have embraced mission in a way that now neglects the gathered life of the church. Though this attitude is understandable, it is an overreaction to the former selfish introversion of the institutional church. Both parts of the life of the church—gathered and scattered—are essential to its faithfulness. The more rigorous our missional engagement with culture, the more evident it will become how much we need those gathered spaces, those God-given communal practices, to continually receive the new life of the kingdom—not for ourselves only, but for the sake of the world.

PART 4

A MISSIONARY ENCOUNTER WITH CULTURE

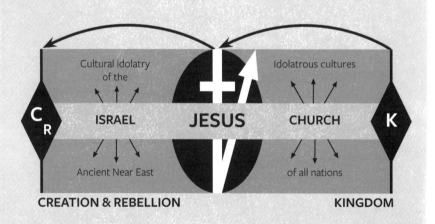

Cultural idolatry of the

ISRAEL

Ancient Near East

JESUS

Idolatrous cultures

CHURCH

of all nations

C
R

K

CREATION & REBELLION

KINGDOM

CHAPTER 15

A Missionary Encounter with Western Culture Today

To the extent that Christian churches ignore their relationship to the dominant culture and leave their members without guidance or reflection on being Christian in relation to it, Christians will be torn between the two poles of sectarian withdrawal and assimilation. What is needed is for the Christian community to develop as a counter-cultural alternative to the dominant culture . . . in critical solidarity with all that is good in dominant society and in prophetic critique of all that is corrupting and destructive.

—*Richard Bauckham,* James: The Wisdom of James, Disciple of Jesus the Sage

In C. S. Lewis's *The Silver Chair*, Prince Rilian of Narnia is held prisoner by the enchantments of the evil queen of Underland. Aslan, the great lion of Narnia (and Christ-figure of that imagined world), sends two children of our world on a mission to rescue Rilian. They too (along with their companion, a marsh-wiggle named Puddleglum) fall under the sorceress's spell. With hypnotic words and music, and stupefying fumes from a brazier, she comes near to persuading the would-be rescuers that her Underland is the only *real* world. There is no Narnia, no Aslan. Struggling heroically against this spell, Puddleglum declares his allegiance to Aslan (whose existence

173

the queen has caused them to doubt) and stamps out much of the sweetly drugged fire with his bare foot. Their heads now clear again, they slay the evil queen (who reveals her true form as a serpent), make good their escape, and triumphantly return to Narnia.

Lewis's story illustrates vividly the New Testament's account of humanity in bondage to the powers. The book of Revelation warns that the church is in peril from the delusion (Rev. 19:20), deception (13:14), seduction (18:3), intoxication (17:2), and the *magic spell* (18:23) of Roman idolatry. In the imagery of Revelation, it is the dragon (Satan) and the beast (Rome) who seek to hold Christians in bondage to the powerful idolatry of the empire.

The costly self-sacrificial act of Puddleglum is Lewis's allusion to Christ's own sacrifice, who by his death on the cross freed his people from the enchantments of idolatry. This emancipation is pictured in Revelation as a new exodus by which God's people are delivered from their former slavery to the powers of the empire (Rev. 5:9–10; 15:1–4). The goal of the book of Revelation is to challenge God's people to seize their freedom from the enchantment of Roman idolatry so that they can carry out their mission and inherit the new creation.

How can we be liberated from the idolatry of our culture, escaping the seductive power and enchantment of the gods that rule it? The sober truth is that Christian churches in the West often have not paid sufficient attention to the relationship of the church to the surrounding secular humanist culture, and this leaves us vulnerable to its powerful "magic."

NEED FOR MISSIONARY ENCOUNTER

Throughout the biblical story, God's people are called to be a distinctive people, revealing God's creational design for human life in their lives. We are to offer a distinctive and attractive alternative to the dominant culture around us that is in bondage to dehumanizing idolatry. In the Old Testament, the gods of their pagan neighbors presented a constant threat to Israel, for it had been called to be a different sort of nation. Israel had been liberated from bondage to pagan idolatry (Exod. 1–15; cf. 12:12) and called by God to be a priestly kingdom and a holy nation for the sake of the world (19:3–6). They had been given the Torah to form them as the true humanity (chaps. 20–23).

But Israel was repeatedly seduced and enchanted by the gods of the nations. So it was that Isaiah promised a second exodus that would accomplish what the first had not done: It would deliver them once and for all from pagan idolatry. Hundreds of years on, the promise of this new exodus was accomplished in the death of Jesus. Thereafter, God's people have been sent to live not as one nation but as many smaller, scattered communities among all the nations of the earth.

This new situation in redemptive history presents an acute problem. How can God's people serve the true and living God while living amid those who serve other gods? How can Christians live as a distinctive people, in enclaves of the new creation, outposts of the kingdom, as a counter-cultural alternative to the idolatrous dominant culture, *while still living within that culture*?

The two constant dangers are *assimilation*, on the one hand (whereby the Christian community takes on the idolatry of the surrounding pagan culture and thus loses its distinctiveness), and *withdrawal*, on the other (fearing assimilation, Christians attempt to retreat from the culture that surrounds them). Succumbing to either would mean forsaking the vocation God has given us.

The language of "missionary encounter" is widely used today to describe the proper approach that God's people must take in relation to the dominant culture. We have been taught this language by missionaries whose cross-cultural experience has taught them well the difficulty of relating the gospel to an idolatrous culture.

WHAT IS A MISSIONARY ENCOUNTER?

It is first of all an *encounter*. All cultures, including our own Western culture, have a comprehensive religious vision that shapes every aspect of life. We can see this quite readily in a Muslim culture where faith forms and unifies the entire culture. Our own Western culture is no less religious. Here too a dominant faith shapes every part of our lives together and demands our conformity. However, the gospel makes an equally radical and comprehensive claim on our lives. Christ reminds us that "no one can serve two masters" (Matt. 6:24). So we live between two religious stories—each demands our total allegiance; each lays claim to our whole lives.

This should produce a *painful tension* at the very heart of the church's life. Too often we have avoided the problem by trimming the gospel to fit within our culture's story. Yet Hendrik Kraemer, a longtime missionary in Indonesia, stresses that such a tension is necessary if we are to be faithful to Christ: "The deeper the consciousness of the tension and the urge to take this yoke upon itself are felt, the healthier the Church is. The more oblivious of this tension the Church is, the more well established and at home in this world it feels, the more it is in deadly danger of being the salt that has lost its savor."[1]

This encounter must be a *missionary* encounter, for a missionary is one who brings good news. A missionary encounter is not coercive; we do not compel others to follow Christ. The cross stands at the center of the Christian faith as a vivid reminder that Jesus himself, when faced with violent resistance, meekly suffered and died rather than coercing belief in anyone. The power of the gospel is the power of suffering love.

A missionary encounter does not seek to displace the dominant culture. Instead, the gospel seeks to renew all cultures from within, embracing all that is good but rejecting their idolatry. The Christian faith is by its nature *multicultural*—cultural expressions of the gospel come in many forms, differing from one another yet rooted faithfully in the gospel.

A missionary encounter leads believers not to withdraw from culture but to engage it, in solidarity with their neighbors. A genuine missionary encounter acknowledges that for us to be part of human culture is good, reflecting the way God created human life to be. We are called to love our culture while hating its idolatry, which is destructive and dehumanizing. We participate in the historical development of our culture, always seeking the common good. God loved—and loves—the world, and so must we.

A missionary encounter is not adversarial, contentious, belligerent, or self-righteous, but loving, respectful, humble, and kind. The gospel can become discredited if we stand for the truth of the gospel in unattractive ways.

DISCERNMENT AND EMBODIMENT

When it comes to relating to our cultural context in terms of a faithful missionary encounter, we can learn much from cross-cultural missionaries who struggle to understand how to be both *at home in* and *at odds with* their new cultural settings—loving the culture and hating its dehumanizing idolatry.

Faithfulness involves both discernment and embodiment. Paul had precisely this goal in mind for all the churches he planted and nourished, recognizing their cultural setting within the Roman Empire. For example, in his letter to the young church at Colossae, Paul begins, "We continually ask God to fill you with the knowledge of his will through all the wisdom and understanding that the Spirit gives [*discernment*], *so that* you may live a life worthy of the Lord and please him in every way [*embodiment*]" (Col. 1:9–10, emphasis added).

In every cultural institution, practice, or custom, there is both a good underlying creational structure (given by God in creation) and an idolatrous twisting element (shaped by sinful idolatry). The gospel is the power of God to renew and heal all aspects of our culture. Thus, discernment involves recognizing and affirming creational structures and insights, while recognizing and rejecting the idolatrous twisting.

A good example of this is found in Paul's teaching concerning the household (e.g., Eph. 5:21–33), the fundamental social unit of the Roman Empire, which indiscriminately merged marital, family, economic, and political relationships. Since it had largely been shaped by the idolatry of *power* that lay at the core of the empire, the *oikos* (home) was often an oppressive institution, where the authority of the head (*paterfamilias*) was virtually unrestricted, often extending to the power of life and death.

How does Paul engage creatively such a disfigured and corrupt institution? He does not simply reject it out of hand. His instructions to the church assume that the Ephesian believers will remain within the *oikos*. Nor does he simply accept it, since he understands well how oppressive the *oikos* is. Paul recognizes the tension between the differing ways in which the gospel on the one hand and the Roman Empire on the other seek to shape the household, and he shows his readers how to be faithful to their calling within that tension.

Paul discerns the good creational relationships in the structure of the Roman household—husband and wife, parent and child, employer and worker. But he uproots those relationships from Roman paganism and replants them in the soil of the gospel. Thus, Paul exhorts husbands to love their wives sacrificially, to nurture their children gently, and to treat their slaves with respect—and these admonitions are vastly more radical and revolutionary than we may realize! The gospel gives dignity and agency to women, children, and slaves, and calls them to *submit themselves voluntarily* for the sake of the Lord.

The relationships within the *oikos* became transformed by the gospel. Insofar as the early church heeded Paul's words, its members instituted a very different sort of household than had ever been seen by their pagan neighbors. In their distinctiveness, those Christian households became very attractive. The *oikos* remained recognizable to those who were living in Roman culture, but the new-cast relationships within Christian households witnessed to the renewing and life-giving power of the good news. The *paterfamilias* had become a servant. Wives, children, and slaves had been raised to a new level of dignity. We can only imagine how attractive this must have looked amid the oppressive culture of Rome.

We would do well to follow the pattern Paul establishes in his own cultural setting. He starts with the social institutions and practices of his day, discerning the wholesome creational relationships embedded there as well as the idolatry that had deformed them. He then challenges the church to embody an attractive alternative to cultural norms that would embrace the good while rejecting the distortion. What would that look like in businesses characterized by the idolatry of profit motive or universities shaped by consumerism?

FAITHFULNESS AT THE CROSSROADS OF TWO STORIES

As a Christian community we live at the intersection of two comprehensive stories (fig. 15.1). From our births we have been socialized into the cultural story that both forms the neopagan culture surrounding us and urges us to conform to it. But as believers we are being discipled into the very different story of our world that God sets out in the Bible. How can we be faithful at this crossroads?

Figure 15.1. **Living at the Crossroads**

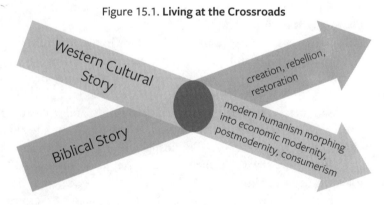

First, we must be unreservedly committed to Jesus Christ, determined to live within and be shaped by the story of the Bible. This must be our unwavering ultimate allegiance, for it is the Bible that tells the true story of the world and what it means to be truly human. It is from within *this* story that we must interpret and engage our culture.

This will lead, secondly, to an ongoing dialogue with our culture to discern the creational good and idolatrous deformity within it. It will be first of all a *personal* dialogue as we discern how these two different stories seek to shape our lives. But it cannot remain merely personal; it must also become *communal*. We need each other, and we especially need our Christian brothers and sisters from other parts of the world, so that together we may discover faithful paths amid our neopagan cultures.

If such a dialogue is to take place it will require us to understand how the gospel calls us to live faithfully in every part of our lives: in our use of technology, our political commitments, our educational choices. And equally, such a dialogue will require us to understand well the story being told in our culture—and how that seeks to shape technology, politics, and education.

AN ADVANCED CASE OF SYNCRETISM

On the eve of the Second World War, T. S. Eliot expressed concern that most Christians were not conscious of being formed by cultural practices inimical to the Christian faith and thus were being de-Christianized:

> The problem of leading a Christian life in a non-Christian society is now very present to us. . . . It is not merely the problem of a minority in a society of *individuals* holding an alien belief. It is the problem constituted by *our implication in a network of institutions from which we cannot dissociate ourselves: institutions the operation of which appears no longer neutral, but non-Christian*; and as for the Christian who is not conscious of his dilemma—and he is in the majority—he is becoming more and more de-Christianized by all sorts of unconscious pressures.[2]

Years later Lesslie Newbigin also expressed concern about the way the Christian church was being "de-Christianized." He puts it this way: The Western church "is an advanced case of syncretism."[3] This is a startling charge!

To explain what he means by religious syncretism, Newbigin takes his readers to the great hall of a Ramakrishna temple, which holds a gallery of all the gods and great religious figures of humankind. Among them is a portrait of Jesus. Each year on Christmas Day, Hindus offer their worship and devotion up to Jesus as one among these figures. Newbigin comments that it was obvious to him that "this was an example of syncretism. Jesus had simply been co-opted into the Hindu worldview." He continues, "It was only slowly that I began to see that my own Christianity had this syncretistic character, that I too had—in a measure—co-opted Jesus into the worldview of my culture."[4] Newbigin believes that Jesus has, for many Christians, been accommodated to the modern Western worldview along-side its many "gods."

None of us naturally has critical distance from our own culture. A proverb says, "If you want to know about water, don't ask a fish." We are always swimming in our own cultural water and so are hardly aware of its existence. The culture we are immersed in tells us this is just the way things are.

But the problem of our being unaware of our culture's deepest religious beliefs is further complicated by two myths peculiar to the Western church. The first is the myth of a "Christian culture." By assuming that our culture retains a Christian ethos, we can be lulled into thinking that it is friendly to our faith, its vision neatly aligning with the gospel. Others assume that our culture is at least religiously *neutral* because we have become a genuinely pluralistic society, allowing *all* religious visions to flourish in a neutral space, or that our culture is neutral because we have built it on science. In either case, we can be fooled into believing that the neutrality of our culture does not pose any challenge to what we believe.

And there are yet other reasons for our slide into syncretism. Western culture is deeply individualistic. We have often unwittingly adopted this individualism in our understanding of the Christian faith, both in our view of salvation and in our view of sin. We often don't have eyes to see the structural or systemic dimensions of idolatry taught in Scripture. And thus "Christian individualism would run the risk of cultural assimilation."[5]

The cultural story of the West insists that religion remain a *private* matter. When scientific reason becomes accepted as the fundamental public doctrine and arbiter of truth, all other claims to truth (those that cannot be verified by scientific method) are no longer considered to be *public* truth (see fig. 15.2). In this view, all religions, including the Christian faith, are mere matters of private values, subjective opinion, individual preference, or personal taste. Thus, religion has no place in shaping the public life of culture.

Figure 15.2. **Privatized Religion**

Fact-Value Dichotomy

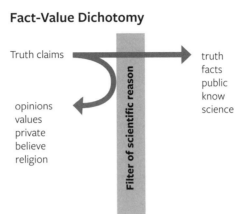

This understanding of religion is peculiar to the modern West and utterly incomprehensible to anyone who has not been shaped by our culture. In fact, the "greatest change" that the growing and vital non-Western churches may bring to the Western church is a challenge to the notion that "religion should be segregated into a separate sphere of life, distinct from everyday reality."[6] An African brother expresses this clearly: "In African culture, religion and culture are inextricably bound up. Religion derives its profound meaning to the African from the fact that it touches him in the totality of his culture. Religion touches every aspect of life. . . . Life is religion and religion is life; and religion is not restricted to certain areas of life but pervades all of life."[7]

WHAT IS RELIGION?

Often when we hear the word "religion" in modern parlance, it refers narrowly to practices and beliefs regarding a transcendent being—that area of life concerned with such things as worship, prayer, holy books, an ethical system, and beliefs about the afterlife and the spiritual realm. These are classified as "spiritual" and kept quite separate from the rest of life. This is not at all how Scripture itself would define religion.

"Religion" properly understood refers to our most deeply held convictions, our fundamental beliefs, which give shape and coherence to all other aspects of our lives. Religion comprises our core beliefs about the world, what it means to be human, and what will offer us true and lasting fulfillment. It implicitly answers the question, What is the chief end of human life?—and all human cultures are built around *a communal answer to this very question* (see fig. 15.3).

Figure 15.3. **Religion and Culture**

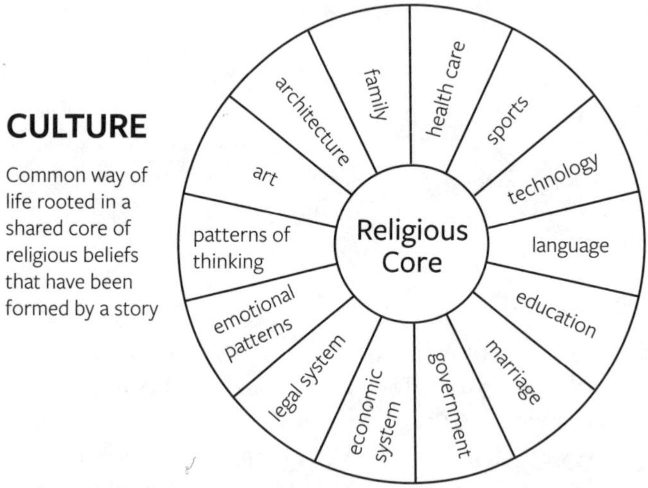

CULTURE

Common way of life rooted in a shared core of religious beliefs that have been formed by a story

Wheel labels, outer ring clockwise: architecture, family, health care, sports, technology, language, education, marriage, government, economic system, legal system, emotional patterns, patterns of thinking, art

Center: Religious Core

We were created as God's image, meant to mirror him and to carry out our whole lives in allegiance to him. We were created also to live in community with one another, to know and serve God together, forming cultures to reflect his glory into the world. When our first parents rebelled, human beings retained their nature as serving and worshiping creatures. But we transferred our religious loyalty from him to one or another of the things he had created, in a vain attempt to find life elsewhere (Rom. 1:18–23). This was and is the primal sin: to turn from God to some part of the creation in our efforts to find life. This is what the Bible calls idolatry. Idolatry shapes the whole of human life, including our cultural life together. In Western culture, for example, we have turned to economic growth as our god, convinced that consumer goods and experiences can make us happy.

Since God has put so much life into his creation, and because all the gifts of his world were created to bless humanity, we *will* find evidence of his goodness in created things. If we serve the gods of economic growth and consumption, there may well be much enjoyment of the creation to be had. But to elevate a created thing to the status of the Creator is to twist the good gift of God into an idol that can never satisfy those who worship and serve it. This leads cultures ultimately to injustice, immorality, and death. God gives us over to our idols and we reap the consequences (Rom. 1:24–32).

Modern Western culture is every bit as religious as the Islamic culture of Saudi Arabia or the Hindu culture of India. It is because we have allowed an erroneous definition of religion to prevail in the West that we don't see this, and thus we have become vulnerable to syncretism. This betrays the vocation God has given us to be the new humanity, to live distinctively, and to refuse to conform to the idolatrous patterns of our culture.

WE MUST BECOME GODS

If we are to liberate the church from its captivity to Western culture, we must understand the religious beliefs of that culture, "probe behind the unquestioned assumptions of modernity and uncover the *hidden credo* which supports them."[8] The Latin word *credo* means simply, "I believe," and a creed expresses our foundational beliefs. There is in every society an implicit creed that often lies unnoticed but, like the foundation of a house, supports all the visible aspects of human culture built on it (see fig. 15.4).

Figure 15.4. **Hidden Creed**

CULTURE

(Patterns of life together)

family economics politics education media sports entertainment
art architecture technology legal health care language customs

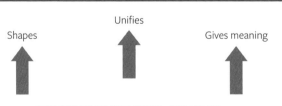

Unifies

Shapes   Gives meaning

RELIGIOUS BELIEFS (CREDO)

[Religion as a *directional power*]

What is the implicit creed of Western society? We can begin with Friedrich Nietzsche's famous parable of the madman.[9] A madman lights a lantern and runs into the marketplace, crying out, "I seek God! I seek God!" Because the people who hear him don't believe in God, they are amused and ask him if God has become lost or strayed away like a child. But the question is serious: "Whither is God?" he asks, and then responds, "I will tell you. *We have killed him*—you and I. All of us are his murderers." Then begins a chilling soliloquy, probing the momentous consequences of murdering God. What have we done? We have wiped out the horizon of history so that there is no meaning to human life. How can the world hold together? Is not life meaningless? Is not the world now colder and darker? God is dead and we have killed him. The enormity of the act poses the ultimate question: "Must we ourselves not become gods simply to appear worthy of it?"

Then the madman falls silent, as do his listeners. He throws his lantern to the ground and says, "I have come too soon." God is dead, but his killers hardly seem able to take in the significance of what they have done. When lightning strikes, Nietzsche writes, it is some time before the thunder is heard. So it is with the death of God; the thunderous consequences have not yet reached his murderers.

Nietzsche's parable is both brilliant and utterly chilling. And it opens the very heart of the religious creed of Western culture. The murder of God, for Nietzsche, took place during the eighteenth-century Enlightenment, about a century and a half before he wrote his parable, when "the light" of a new religion had come on for Europe—the light of human autonomy and reason. God and the Christian faith had been virtually banished from the public square and relegated to the private realm. God had been "murdered." We had wiped out the horizon of history—there was no longer any goal to universal history, and thus no true story to give meaning to human life.

Most sobering is Nietzsche's contention that, having murdered God, we must now become gods. If there is no God, no Creator to give meaning to life or set down standards of right and wrong, good and evil, true and false, we ourselves must become the Creator and assume his task. If there is no God, no Ruler to give meaning to history, we must create our own meaning and guide human history toward some goal of our own devising. If there is no God, no Savior to deliver us from evil, we must become our own saviors. This is Nietzsche's brilliant analysis of the implications of the confessional humanism that broke in on Europe in the eighteenth century: If God is dead, we must become gods.

In the late nineteenth century, confidence in the Enlightenment vision reached its zenith. That is why the madman's audience cannot hear him. And the parable has a poignant autobiographical edge to it, since Nietzsche was calling attention to the ominous implications of the Enlightenment vision, but (along with a few other philosophers and artists) he was a lonely and largely unregarded figure amid a nearly universal consensus of confident optimism. Sadly, Nietzsche himself at last went mad. Today, long after his death, he has come to be regarded as a prophet of postmodernism because he saw clearly what removing God from the public square would ultimately mean.

The very term "Enlightenment" is a religious image. It proclaims in faith that a light—the light of scientific reason—has dawned in the darkness and that all the rest of reality can be seen and truly understood only by this light. In the Christian faith, it is Jesus who is the light of the world. In Buddhism, Siddhartha Gautama became the Buddha, meaning the enlightened one, who proclaims the Four Noble Truths. In Islam, Allah's revealed will in the Qur'an is "the light"; and in Hinduism, Brahman is *the* light from which all others derive. The Enlightenment in eighteenth-century Europe was a breathtaking, monumental religious conversion to *a new light*, the key to human happiness.

But, as Nietzsche observes, with the death of God the world grows darker. Today there are many people who believe that the light of the eighteenth-century Enlightenment has dimmed, that the humanist gods have failed to deliver on their promises.

CONFESSIONAL HUMANISM

The deepest religious faith of the secular West is *confessional* or *secular humanism*, the conviction that humanity is *autonomous* (from two Greek words meaning "self" and "law"): there is no god, no rule or order that is above humanity. As autonomous beings, people can define and give meaning to the world, can decide right from wrong. We have become the Creator. And we believe (or used to) that we can solve the problems of our world, especially through science and technology, and thus bring about by our own efforts a new world of freedom and material prosperity for all. We have become our own saviors; there is a new goal to universal history, bringing new meaning to human life. The notion of *progress* replaces *providence*, for it is humankind, not God, that now controls history and is leading it toward a paradise crafted by human hands. So in the Enlightenment project we can discern a full-blown religious narrative claiming to encompass all of life and promising ultimate fulfillment.

The question arises, What makes it possible for humankind to do such godlike things? The answer given in the eighteenth century was, simply, human reason under the discipline of the scientific method. This was the new path to salvation. Scientific rationality would enable human beings first to *understand* and then to *control* the nonhuman world through technology. Moreover, we could also bring order to the human world if we grasped the natural laws of economics, politics, education, and law and then rationally organized society on those bases. Together, the natural and social sciences would open up a new world of freedom and material prosperity. It is perhaps not too surprising that eighteenth-century descriptions of this anticipated "new world" dramatically mirror Scripture's own portrayals of the new creation. Scientific reason had explicitly taken on the role of messiah.

THE EMERGENCE OF THE MODERN WEST

Before the triumph of confessional humanism in the eighteenth century, *Christendom* had dominated Europe for at least a thousand years. In Christendom three religious visions flowed together into one cultural stream: the classical Greco-Roman, the tribal Germanic, and the Christian faith. Thus, even though somewhat compromised by being mingled with these two streams of pagan thought, the gospel retained a significant role in shaping Western culture. When Europe ultimately converted to confessional humanism in the eighteenth century, there followed a cultural revolution that continues to this day. Western nations unleashed the creational power of God's gifts through science and technology, making truly remarkable progress and achieving unprecedented human control over the world, as well as reaching a level of material prosperity hitherto unknown even to royalty.

The Hungarian scientist and philosopher Michael Polanyi offers us a vivid image to describe this remarkable development.[10] He describes the Enlightenment as an explosion in Western culture. Modifying his image somewhat, we can see the combustion of the flame of humanism in the oxygen of the Christian faith. So much that is good in Western culture had come from the centuries-long process of working the gospel into the fabric of European culture. Yet it seems that it is only a matter of time before the flame will burn away the oxygen.

What has happened to the Enlightenment's religious vision today? We can discern three powerful currents. The first is a postmodern spirit—the increasingly comprehensive and widespread loss of confidence in the modern faith because it has failed to deliver on its promises. Yet an economic version of the modern faith, a second powerful current, has survived and is now becoming a global religious vision. The fruit of these two currents is consumerism—a culture organized around the human goal of the consumption of goods and experiences.

This religious vision did not drop out of the sky; it is the product of a long story. So, to understand confessional humanism, we *must* tell the story. That is the only way to get a perspective on where we are today.

CHAPTER 16

The Story of the West

To get straight where we are, we have to go back and tell the story properly. Our past is sedimented in our present, and we are doomed to misidentify ourselves, as long as we can't do justice to where we came from. That is why the narrative is not an optional extra, why I believe that I have to tell a story here.

—Charles Taylor, The Secular Age

Once, when I was still a teenager in a small Canadian town, I was hanging out in a hockey arena with my friends, and we were seriously misbehaving. We didn't know we were being watched from a short distance by the chief of police until he called out, "Hey Goheen, you don't have the faith of your father, do you?" I fell silent, cut to the heart by what he'd said. I knew my dad had worked hard to be a faithful witness to Christ where we lived, and now here I was, undoing all that he had done. It wasn't the Christian faith that I cared so much about then; but I did love my dad, and I was suddenly ashamed of the way I was tearing down what he had built up. This memory has remained vivid across the years for two reasons: First, I bore my dad's name, and what I was doing had brought dishonor to it and to him. Second, I'd been unthinkingly conforming myself to the patterns of my peer group.

We bear Christ's name before the world. Our way of life will bring either honor or disgrace to his name. If we are conformed to the patterns of our culture, we will fail to commend Christ to our neighbors.

The Old Testament prophet Ezekiel addresses Israel as "the LORD's people," those who bear his unique name to show his holiness among the nations. But by imitating the pagan nations around them, Israel had become defiled by idolatry and had profaned the Lord's name among the nations (Ezek. 36:16–23). As Christians we bear the name of Christ, and if our lifestyle is shaped more by the idolatry of our unbelieving neighbors than it is by the gospel, we too are guilty of profaning the name of the Lord.

Paul says, in the memorable translation of J. B. Phillips, "Don't let the world around you squeeze you into its own mould, but let God re-mould your minds from within" (Rom. 12:1–2). By "world" here, Paul means the "present evil age" as it is manifested in "cultural idolatry"; for the early church in particular, that meant the idolatrous structures of the Roman Empire. He calls the church to resist being squeezed into the idolatry of the dominant culture. Instead, they are to be transformed by the gospel, which brings the power of "the age to come."

To resist being conformed to "the world," we must know our culture, understand its idolatry and the patterns of life that flow from it. But that's not as easy as it sounds. If the surrounding culture's way of life is the only environment we know, the patterns and spirit of that culture will seem normal to us, even when those patterns and that spirit are idolatrous.

Probably one of the best things we can do is listen to Christians who stand outside our own cultural setting, who have some distance from our way of life. But another helpful way for us to come to understand our surrounding culture's true nature is to learn its *story*. Our culture and its implicit religious beliefs did not drop out of the sky. There is a story behind their development, and by learning that story we can begin to discern the patterns of our culture and the religious beliefs that lie beneath.

THE TRIUMPH OF ENLIGHTENMENT HUMANISM

The humanism of our present Western culture is rooted in ancient Roman culture; they inherited it from the Greeks before them, as Alexander the Great had spread the vision of his mentor Aristotle from one end of the then-known world to the other. The good news of Jesus suddenly brought a new religious vision into this world, a vision that clashed utterly with the pagan Greco-Roman culture of his day. But in the medieval period these two worldviews—Christian and pagan humanist—had become merged together in an uneasy, syncretistic way. And as the "barbarians" took over the Roman Empire, the Germanic vision was also grafted in, forming what came to be called "Christendom." This hybrid worldview endured for many centuries, and so came to shape the spiritual center of Europe.

During the fifteenth-century Renaissance, especially in northern Italy, the humanist strand in Christendom was "born again" to gradually become by the eighteenth century the dominant cultural vision of the West. The genuinely Christian element within culture retained much of its formative power until the scientific revolution in the sixteenth and seventeenth centuries. That revolution opened the way for a new ascent and ultimate triumph of humanism in the next century—not because of a clash between real science and the Christian faith of Scripture (as many observers falsely assume), but chiefly because of two historical events occurring at that time.

The first was the response of the church (both Catholic and Protestant) to the new science of Galileo, Kepler, and others. The church used mistaken interpretations of Scripture to denigrate the insights of the new science. In this mistaken view, the psalmist's words, "He sets the earth on its foundations; it can never be moved" (Ps. 104:5), meant that the new scientific view (that the earth both rotates on its axis and orbits the sun) must be simply wrong and thus heretical. Martin Luther quoted Joshua's words—"O sun, stand still"—to mock Galileo, arguing that only if the sun had been revolving around the earth would Joshua command it to stand still (Josh. 10:12). Similarly the poetic image from Ecclesiastes—"The earth remains forever. The sun rises and the sun sets, and hurries back to where it rises"—was taken to mean that it is the sun that revolves around the earth—rising, moving across the sky, setting, and returning to the place where it rises again (Eccles. 1:4–5).

The new science certainly challenged the traditional world picture of the medieval church. But instead of reflecting on their faith in this new setting, the church leaders clung to a dogmatic conservatism and sought to impose their beliefs (and retain their cultural power) by intimidation, excommunication, persecution, and anathema. The church's reactionary response to the scientific revolution would prove devastating for subsequent Western history. As more and more people became convinced of the truths revealed by the new science, the conviction spread that the church and the Christian faith were simply outdated (see fig. 16.1). Science had wrongly been pitted against faith, and the obvious choice for the thinking person was that science held the better answers.

Figure 16.1. **Opposition to the New Science**

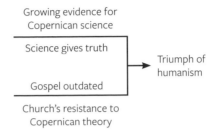

The second historical influence leading to the ultimate victory of humanism in the Enlightenment was the disastrous religious wars of the sixteenth century, when the church was split into warring factions following the Reformation. At that time, the church still held political, social, economic, and military power, and the Catholic, Lutheran, and Calvinist states of Europe each sought to gain control as the true inheritor of Christendom's legacy. Europe became soaked with the blood of Christians killing one another.

This senseless violence shocked and sickened more and more people. Voltaire came to despise the Christian faith because of it. Descartes, who lived most of his life through one of the worst religious wars in Europe, searched for a new foundation in human reason, *apart from the Christian faith*, upon which to build culture. While the new science was gaining victory after victory in explaining the world and uniting people in agreement to its truth, the Christian faith was, it seemed, tearing Europe to pieces (see fig. 16.2). Many Europeans drew the obvious conclusion that science might bring them together while the Christian faith could only drive them apart.

Figure 16.2. **Religious Wars**

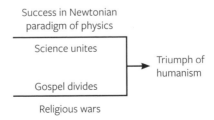

Thus the genuine advances of science and the deplorable violence of so-called Christian states in Europe combined to prepare for the triumph of scientific humanism as the *religious* vision of the Enlightenment world. Science would no longer be constrained within its proper creational bounds as a valuable method by which to understand the regularities of our world. Instead, science would assume the status of a messiah, an idol, a god, the light of the world. In his impish paraphrase of Genesis 1:3 and John 1:4–9, titled "Epigram on Sir Isaac Newton," Alexander Pope (himself a Catholic) captures the spirit of the age: "Nature and nature's laws lay hid in night; / God said, 'Let Newton be! and all was light.'"

THE FAITH OF ENLIGHTENMENT HUMANISM (EIGHTEENTH CENTURY)

"The West had 'lost its faith'—and found a new one, in science and in man."[1] True—but it is vital to recognize that Europe was never truly Christian. What it had lost was *Christendom*: that syncretistic amalgam of *three* faiths had at last come apart. Yet this was a pivotal religious conversion in Europe (see fig. 16.3). Confusion between the *Christian* faith and the syncretistic beliefs of *Christendom* had at last led to a rejection of the gospel itself as a legitimate influence in the new Europe. The new faith was in the ability of autonomous humanity to employ science to build a better world.

Figure 16.3. **Conversion of Europe in the Eighteenth Century**

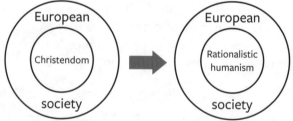

The Enlightenment faith offered its adherents a comprehensive story with a new goal for universal history. It spoke of progress toward a world of human perfection and peace, happiness and justice, freedom and prosperity, equality and harmony with nature. There was deep faith in humankind's ability to progress toward this kind of world. According to the older

Augustinian vision of history (which had guided the West for a thousand years), God was leading all of human history toward the establishing of his kingdom: Augustine's *City of God* was the most widely read book throughout the medieval period. Now Augustine's story and city were being reimagined; *humanity* would now lead history toward a perfect city built by scientific reason. The old language of "providence" (which had referred to history governed by God) was replaced by the concept of "progress" with the rebirth of humanism.

One important Enlightenment figure was Adam Smith. His vision was to bring material prosperity to Europe by harnessing science and technology to production, and by ordering society around an economic vision. The goal of human life was material abundance. Similarly, French philosopher and economist Pierre-Paul Mercier de la Rivière writes, "The greatest happiness possible for us consists *in the greatest possible abundance of objects suitable for our gratification and in the greatest freedom to profit by them.*"[2]

Enlightenment figures believed that human reason, disciplined by the scientific method, could propel history toward a better world. Science played a messianic role. It enabled humanity to discern the natural laws of the nonhuman creation, which they would then translate into technology to dominate the world. The same scientific method was to be employed in the organization of society. The task of the social sciences was to probe the laws of politics, the judicial system, economics, and education so that all of society could be organized upon a firm rational foundation.

Progress would come by the application of scientific reason to both technological and social issues. Thus, John Locke sketched a rational vision of politics, Adam Smith discerned an "invisible hand" ordering economics, Hugo Grotius sought to set law on a rational foundation, and a host of people championed a more "rational" educational process. All of these visions for a rational society were "liberal" in the traditional sense that they were based on the sovereign freedom of the individual. Politics and law were based on the fundamental rights of individuals, economics was devoted to harmonizing the economic self-interests of individuals in the marketplace, and education was constructed around the needs of individual learners. Such liberal individualism was baked into the Enlightenment vision from the beginning. They imagined a better world shaped by human effort with the tools of science. Human society could be free, prosperous, just, and at peace. The light of science shone brightly for believing humanity. A new world was coming.

And meanwhile, what had happened to the Christian faith? The first step away from the biblical Christian faith had been the slide into deism, by which God was banished from active involvement in the world to a distant heaven as an onlooker. He had perhaps been needed at the beginning of things to make the world and set it going, but (like the builder of any machine) had become redundant once that machine began to work.

Further, all religion was increasingly considered to be a merely private matter. As scientific reason became the public doctrine shaping the West, those truth claims that could not be substantiated by the scientific method were set aside. Since the gospel is not open to scientific analysis, it was relegated to the private realm of values, tastes, and preferences, which may be strongly believed by any of us but can play no role in the shaping of public life. Thus, at the center of Western culture, a divide opened up between fact, truth, and knowledge on the one hand, and values, opinions, and faith on the other (see fig. 15.2 above). Only those elements in the first group were credited with the right to shape the public life of culture. And sadly, it was not only the avowed humanists who believed this; many Christians allowed *their* faith to be tailored to fit into this new, overarching faith commitment. They settled for a privatized gospel concerned only with future, individual, and spiritual immortality—and thus irrelevant to the public life of culture.

The Bible conveys a comprehensive vision of sin and salvation that includes all of life. It was always God's mission to redeem the whole of his creation—including every endeavor of humankind—from the pernicious creation-wide effects of sin. This vision had been recovered during the sixteenth-century Reformation, but under the withering power of the Enlightenment faith, belief in the biblical story of *cosmic* rescue and renewal was abandoned by many, until all that was left was a personal relationship between the individual and God. More and more of life was interpreted now according to the "true light" of scientific humanism, *even by Christians*.

The Christian faith did continue to exercise a formative influence, and it bequeathed many gifts to Western culture: Christian ethics and views of justice; a high estimation of reason; a sense of an intelligible, ordered world; a calling for humankind to exercise dominion; an understanding of our intrinsic dignity and inalienable rights; the moral responsibility of the individual; the moral imperative to care for the helpless and less fortunate; a sense of the importance of history; and an orientation toward the future in historical development—all these derive ultimately from a biblical view of the world and have remained part of the Western legacy.

THE ENLIGHTENMENT FAITH IN THE NINETEENTH AND TWENTIETH CENTURIES

True faith in anything can never be confined to our inner lives only; it will always seek to engage and reshape the world outside ourselves. Thus, *faith* in progress begets a *program* for progress. The *dream* of a better world brought about through science and technology becomes a *blueprint* for rebuilding that society. According to the Enlightenment vision, it was Christendom's social structures and institutions that thwarted humanity's efforts to build the new world. Since science and technology would indeed create heaven on earth, we had an ethical imperative to travel that path. If there had to be revolutions to overturn institutions and customs blocking our way to this new world, so be it!

So it was that the eighteenth-century revolution of thought in the Enlightenment was followed by many *other* revolutions—political, social, economic—in the nineteenth and early twentieth centuries, each intended to bring society into conformity with the Enlightenment faith. Although they vary considerably from one another, the American Revolution, the French Revolution, the Industrial Revolution, the democratic revolutions in continental Europe, and the Russian Revolution all share the vision of a future of progress brought about by uprooting old social institutions and structures and planting new ones in their place.

The slogan of the French Revolution, "*liberté, égalité, fraternité*" (freedom, equality, brotherhood), was not intended as mere aspiration; it was a demand for social and political revolution to change the structures of French society and bring them into conformity with the new faith. The revolutionaries sought educational reform, a new political system based on individual rights and the sovereignty of the people, and a new social order that would remove guilds, priests, and clergy—all remnants of the old order, which they felt was blocking the way to a new world. The French Enlightenment philosopher Denis Diderot reportedly wrote that he longed to "strangle the last king with the guts of the last priest."

Just how *religious* this revolution was can be seen by the action of the French revolutionaries to create a new way of marking time. To mark the advent of a new age, they replaced the Christian calendar with their own secular calendar. Year one was no longer the incarnation of Christ but 1792, the year of the founding of the French Republic. A new age had dawned, a new era was being born—a world characterized by reason, science, and freedom.

The focus of the Industrial Revolution of the nineteenth century was primarily economic and technological. The new industrialists sought to implement the Enlightenment vision of progress toward economic prosperity. Progress would come through technological innovation and the rational organization of production. Science and technology (which had to this point been two separate enterprises) came together to produce a science-based technology, and this did indeed usher in a period of tremendous technological innovation. Human labor was organized to maximize output and profit, many jobs became specialized and mechanized, and the result was a remarkable boost in productivity. And the sudden great rise in wealth in the industrialized nations of the West certainly seemed to validate the Enlightenment worldview.

These nineteenth-century revolutions changed the shape of Western nations. The humanist faith became embodied in the political, economic, educational, juridical, and educational structures of culture. Much of creation's potential was developed in positive ways, for the betterment of humankind. Science, technology, social institutions, freedom, and economic development are all gifts given to us by a loving God to bless us. But when these good things are elevated to the role of the highest good, they become idols. We begin to imagine that *they* give meaning to life and will bring ultimate happiness and fulfillment.

Thus, some Enlightenment figures in France came to speak of *bonheur* (happiness) as the true political, economic, and social goal for the whole life of humankind. Ultimate happiness, they said, would come to individuals and society as people satisfied their desires, when the rights and freedoms of individuals were protected by the state, when economic development provided material prosperity, when education equipped the population with the scientific knowledge to build this world.

The ideals of the revolutions were one thing, the reality another. The enduring symbol of the French Revolution is not the flag of universal liberty and brotherhood; it is the guillotine. Charles Dickens and Karl Marx (among many others) laid bare the horrifying poverty and injustice that flowed to the common people from the Industrial Revolution—along with the enormous profits that flowed to wealthy industrialists. Thus, the story of progress by scientific reason faced some serious skepticism in the wake of the revolutions it had inspired.

Two significant efforts to reconcile the rosy promises of the Enlightenment progress with some of its less savory results were made, the first by those who continued to advocate *liberalism* in a new setting, and the second by those who embraced *Marxism*. Both of these philosophies maintained the Enlightenment faith in progress and attempted to explain human suffering as part of their story. Liberalism maintained the vision of a new society rooted in the freedom of the individual in economic affairs, and in the rights of individuals in politics. It defended the freedom of the market (despite the suffering it often brought about) either by explaining away such suffering as the unfortunate but inevitable consequence of the social evolutionary process or by reflecting on how government might mitigate it. Karl Marx, on the other hand, recognized the injustice systemic within liberal individualism, and he preached that progress would come through a series of class revolutions to overturn these structures, ultimately leading to equality, justice, and the equitable distribution of wealth. These twin daughters of humanism—liberalism and Marxism—squabbled as most sisters do. Their competing visions of progress would in the twentieth century migrate from their European home to dominate the world, with Marxism (the basis of communism) centered in Moscow and liberalism (which evolved into democratic capitalism) centered in Washington, DC.

We might characterize the development of the Enlightenment faith in the twentieth century as one of *both* progress and breakdown. On the one hand, in our own day we've seen tremendous scientific, technological, and economic progress. The beneficial potential of these creational powers *was* developed, and human life has been enriched because of it. But on the other hand, the Enlightenment vision had already shown signs of strain as early as the nineteenth century—signs of collapse beneath the weight of its own idolatry. Thereafter, and throughout the twentieth century, there was growing uneasiness about the limitations of the Enlightenment religious vision, and this would ultimately lead to the emergence of the postmodern spirit of the late twentieth century, which rejects the entire Enlightenment worldview.

A PANTHEON OF MODERN GODS

The United States was formed as a nation in 1776 at the peak of the Enlightenment. It is thus not surprising to see the Enlightenment faith celebrated in the fresco *Apotheosis of Washington* that is painted on the domed ceiling of the US Capitol. Apotheosis can mean the highest point in development or the elevation of someone to divine status. In this painting, George Washington is exalted to the heavens, flanked by the Greek goddesses Freedom and Triumph. These three form part of a circle along with thirteen maidens (representing the original colonies). This inner circle is surrounded by six tableaux of Greek gods, which depict the Enlightenment faith upon which the country was founded: the goddess Freedom, armed to cast down tyranny; Minerva, the goddess of science; Vulcan, the god of technology; Neptune, the god of marine technology; Ceres, the goddess of agricultural technology; and Mercury, the god of commerce and wealth. These are the gods of the Enlightenment religious vision.

Many would simply see here a harmless representation of "secular" ideals using symbolism from Greek mythology. But to accept that is to be deceived by the myth of secular neutrality. "The truth is that in those areas of our human living which do not submit to the rule of Christ . . . we fall under another power. We become, in Pauline language, slaves to the 'principalities and powers,' to the 'elemental spirits of the universe' (Gal. 4:3)."[3] We may smile condescendingly at the "primitive" worldview that includes belief in such "powers." But the "only significant difference between us and our pagan ancestors appears to be that they recognized the situation and gave the forces vivid names, while we hide them behind the grey obscurity of vague words."[4] There *are* demonic powers, who use the good gifts of creation—in this case the gifts of science, technology, social organization, freedom, and material prosperity—to hold us in bondage to them, as we make them our idols.

The Capitol fresco portrays the modern "gods" that have played such an enormous role in shaping our Western world. Here we list those gods (with reference to John Dewey, one of humanism's premier twentieth-century spokesmen, and the father of modern education).[5]

- *The god of human autonomy*: Human beings are free, and there is no authority above them. As Dewey puts it, "There is the gradual decay of authority"—the authority of God, of Scripture, and of the church on human life. Humanity alone can determine the meaning of life, what is right and wrong, good and bad, true and false. We are capable of guiding history toward the goal of our choosing. We can save ourselves from the misery of a fallen world.
- *The god of rationalism*: Reason is the human capacity that enables humanity to achieve this goal as rationality is disciplined by

scientific method. Dewey expresses a "growing belief in the power of individual minds, guided by methods of observation, experiment and reflection . . . *to attain the truths needed for the guidance of life."*

- *The god of scientism*: Science enables us to attain the truths that will guide our whole lives and enable us to live well. But science also has the power to transform our culture. Indeed, "knowledge is power." We can control the nonhuman world and bend it to our use through technology. We can discern the laws of economics, politics, education, law, and society and form a society based on science. This will usher in a new world of flourishing.

- *The god of progress*: Western humanity puts "great store . . . upon the idea of progress. The future rather than the past dominates the imagination. The Golden Age lies ahead of us not behind us. Everywhere new possibilities beckon and arouse courage and effort." We are capable if we "will but exercise the required courage, intelligence and effort, of shaping [our] own fate. Physical conditions offer no insurmountable barriers."

- *The god of technicism*: Technology will play a major role in ushering in this new world. The "patient and experimental study of nature, bearing fruit in inventions which control nature and subdue her forces to social uses is the method by which progress is made."

- *The god of material prosperity*: The primary characteristic of the dawning golden age will increasingly become material prosperity. Creating and consuming wealth defines the central meaning of human life. Science and technology give us the resources to create the wealth, a rational economic system enables us to produce and distribute that wealth, and freedom protected by a rational government allows us to enjoy the consumption of it.

Each of these good gifts of creation has power. When they are forged into a religious vision as part of a story that encompasses the whole of human life and is offered as the way to happiness, the powers enslave us, and we become victims of our own idolatry. But when they find their rightful place in the symphony of God's creation, they have the power to bless humanity and the world. The song "Turn Your Eyes upon Jesus" points us in the right direction (if we change the third line to be more biblical).

Turn your eyes upon Jesus;
look full in his wonderful face.
And the things of earth take their rightful place
in the light of his glory and grace.

This is a recipe for human flourishing. We find life when the good gifts of human agency and freedom, reason and science, technology and material prosperity, cultural development and historical progress are centered in the Creator. As the people of God who bear the name of Jesus, we are summoned to offer this way of life as a distinctive alternative to our surrounding culture's idolatry: to serve Christ and delight in all his good gifts in creation. Only then will these good gifts—and we ourselves—reflect his glory as we ought.

CHAPTER 17

The Spirit of Postmodernity

The real question is: What is God doing in these tremendous events of *our time? How are we to understand them and interpret them to others, so that we and they may play our part in them as co-workers with God? . . . We are required, in the situation in which God places us, to understand the signs of the times in the light of the reality of God's present and coming kingdom, and to give our witness faithfully about the purpose of God for all people.*

—Lesslie Newbigin, "Rapid Social Change and Evangelism"

STAND FIRM

In 480 BC, Xerxes, King of Persia, brought one of the largest armies in ancient times to conquer Greece. A much smaller contingent of Greek forces, led by Leonidas the Spartan with three hundred of his own men, waited at the narrow pass of Thermopylae to stop the advancing Persian army. On the first day of battle the Greek strategy worked well, with few casualties on their side and many of their enemies dead. But that night, the Persians sent a contingent across the mountains, outflanking the Greeks. Leonidas, knowing defeat was now inevitable, sent all the Greeks home except for his three hundred Spartans and another thousand Greek soldiers who elected to stay on till the end.

In Hollywood's fanciful 2006 portrayal of the battle, titled *300*, Leonidas exhorts his soldiers on the morning of the third day: "No retreat. No surrender. That is Spartan law. And by Spartan law we will stand and fight." *Stand firm.* Director Zack Snyder has the camera zoom in on the feet of the Greek soldiers as they dig in to stand against the Persian hordes.

This image of standing firm in battle captures the apostle Paul's imagination. In Ephesians 6, he implores the church to be strong in the Lord and "take their stand" against powerful spiritual forces arrayed against them. It is only through their use of the "armor" God supplies that they will "be able to stand [their] ground, and after [they] have done everything, to stand." He ends the passage with one last reminder that their task is to "stand firm" (Eph. 6:11–14).

God's people are engaged in a cosmic battle. Like the brave Spartans at Thermopylae, the church is to hold its ground against the powers and spirits of our culture. But Paul also reminds his readers that, unlike Leonidas's doomed three hundred, the church is assured already of victory.

THREE CULTURAL SPIRITS TODAY

The spiritual forces at work in our culture today, against which we must take our stand, are the remnants of the powerful spirit of Enlightenment humanism that transformed Western nations:

- *The postmodern spirit*: an increasingly comprehensive and widespread challenge to the Enlightenment faith
- *The spirit of economic modernity*: the survival and global spread of a narrowly economic form of the Enlightenment faith that shapes society around the goal of material prosperity
- *The spirit of consumerism*: a culture formed upon the conviction that consumption is the chief end of human life, the fruit of the first two developments

We will consider each of these in turn in this and the following chapters, beginning with postmodernity.

A COMPREHENSIVE CULTURAL SPIRIT

Confidence in the Enlightenment story of progress reached its pinnacle at the end of the nineteenth century and gradually declined throughout the twentieth. David Harvey neatly sums it up: "The twentieth century—with its death camps and death squads, its militarism and two world wars, its threat of nuclear annihilation and its experience of Hiroshima and Nagasaki—has certainly shattered [our earlier] optimism."[1] The atrocities of Hitler's Germany and Stalin's Russia undermined faith and hope in the modern "gods" as the world saw what frightening forces had been unleashed by the modern faith.

Postmodernity has often been narrowly defined and confined to academic discussions in the university. But we need to understand that postmodernity is a pervasive cultural spirit at work today throughout Western culture. Indeed, the two political ideologies presently tearing the United States apart are animated to some degree by the same postmodern spirit. Conservative nationalism and "woke" progressivism have both arisen in recent times because of the perceived failures of the Enlightenment liberal story of progress and the failure of liberal institutions. Western culture is increasingly animated by the postmodern spirit.

At its heart, postmodernity is a comprehensive challenge to the modernist vision. There have been numerous such reactions and protests against the reductions and failures of modernity, from nineteenth-century Romanticism to the countercultural movement of the 1960s. But what sets postmodernity apart is precisely the scope of its challenge, now observed in every aspect of modern Western culture.

THE GRAND STORIES OF PROGRESS HAVE FAILED

Quite simply, postmodernity is disillusioned with the Enlightenment story and dismisses its grand *narratives of progress*—for which we use the handy shorthand terms "modernism" or "modernity"—as not having lived up to its own promises.

Modernity had promised material prosperity for all but delivered a widening gap between rich and poor. Modernity promised freedom but delivered bondage to media, education, big business, government, and technology. Modernity promised truth but delivered a bewildering relativism and pluralism. Modernity promised justice and peace but delivered oppression, violence, and injustice. Modernity promised happiness but delivered dissatisfaction, psychological pain, and growing rates of suicide. Modernity promised equality and justice but delivered injustice to many groups.

Postmodern skepticism is founded on modernism's failures. Here are a few:

- *Poverty*: The gap between the richest billion in the world and the poorest has grown from 30 times in 1960 to more than 120 times today.
- *Ecological crisis*: If the whole world lived at the level of consumption enjoyed by the average North American, the world's resources would last only another decade.
- *Militarization*: There are now approximately twelve thousand nuclear warheads in the world, capable of destroying it many times over.
- *Psychological and social problems*: Modernity has produced a dramatic rise in psychological maladies and social evils that affect our overall well-being.
- *Failure of cultural institutions*: Withering criticism of governments, economic leaders, the press, the courts, and the police has become commonplace as these entities have demonstrated an inability to attain the truth, justice, equality, and freedom once promised.

The optimistic spirit of the eighteenth century is gone. Few believe in the promise of paradise; many believe that in the name of human flourishing we must abandon our Enlightenment path.

It was inevitable that the idols of Enlightenment modernism would fail their worshipers, and in our own day we are witnessing the dynamic of idolatry and judgment that Ezekiel warned of: "You shall suffer the penalty . . . and bear the consequences of your sinful idolatry" (Ezek. 23:49).

HUMANITY IS MORE THAN RATIONAL CAPACITY

Postmodernity at its best does recover something of what modernism suppressed. Postmoderns rightly believe, for example, that there is more to humanity than mere reason. God created humankind with *many* gifts and abilities, intending us to use them all in service to God and other people. But when we turn away from serving God, we will inevitably turn to one or another of the capacities he has given, using *that* to define what it means to be human. Modernity had reduced humanity to its rational ability alone, denying the fullness of what God made us to be: his image. The tyranny of reason caused us to undervalue God's *other* gifts in us: emotions, passions, sensuality, creativity, imagination, the body, and sexuality.

But God is faithful to the harmony of his diverse creation. Trying to suppress any part of our humanity is like pushing down a tightly coiled spring; it will force its way back. When the creational powers of these suppressed aspects of our humanity are at last released, they can enrich our lives. But of course when they are misused and given undue attention in their turn, they can become the new idols of the next era (see fig. 17.1).

Figure 17.1. **Humanity: Religious Center and Diverse Aspects**

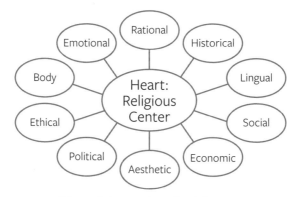

"Above all else, guard your heart, for everything you do flows from it." (Prov. 4:23)

In the postmodern assault on modernism, reason has been devalued, and other aspects of our humanity have been elevated to new—often idolatrous—prominence. Among these are the current obsession with the human body and sexuality, confidence in emotions and instincts to give authentic truth, addiction to sensual stimulation, the quest to satisfy our desires and passions at any cost, and the longing for "spiritual" fulfillment. There is also a renewed sense of the importance of spontaneity, instinct, and intuition; recovery of the aesthetic dimensions of experience; and an interest in probing the deep psychological influences of our past. These aspects of humanity recovered in the turn to postmodernity have shown the good creational power latent in them but long suppressed by modernism. But the obsessions noted above have been exalted to the status of new postmodern idols that their acolytes believe should now define our humanity.

What is God doing in our time? Human rationality is a good gift, but it was never meant to be our messiah. Nor can it fully define the human person. And simply to put another idol in reason's place—such as emotion, imagination, or sensuality—is to repeat the mistake in a different key. No *one* of God's gifts defines us. Believers have an opportunity to demonstrate what it is to be truly human, as creatures whose whole lives are an answer to God's call.

THE PURSUIT OF OBJECTIVE KNOWLEDGE IS MISLEADING AND DANGEROUS

Enlightenment humanity was confident that its rigorous use of the scientific method would allow it access to a neutral standpoint above subjectivity and the relativities of history, from which it would at last be able to see the objective world of fact as it truly exists "out there." This knowledge, again, would grant the power to shape the world into what *humanity* determined it should be.

Postmodern thinkers reject the dream of achieving "objective" knowledge. It has become increasingly clear that we cannot escape the many subjective factors—the historical "situatedness"—that have given shape to what we know. Human knowledge is always contextual and is shaped and conditioned by our traditions, the communities we inhabit, the languages we speak, the cultures that form us, and the faith commitments we have. What we "know" is also influenced by our feelings, imagination, and subconscious, and by our gender, class, and race—all these personal factors color our understanding. The rediscovery of these truths has made postmoderns highly sensitive to the way context shapes all knowledge, to the point where it is now common to hear the very concept of objective knowledge being dismissed as the myth of Enlightenment humanity. There is no truth, the postmodernist assumes, only our experience of the world as it has been shaped by our contexts and identities. There are many versions of reality and no way to judge which is true—if, indeed, any of them are. We are plunged into a world of pluralism and relativism.

But a postmodern critique of the modernist elevation of reason goes deeper still. It is not just that our knowledge is shaped by our context; knowledge is seen by many as just another instrument of oppression and domination. We do not *discover* order and truth in the world "out there"; we *construct* it. The socially constructed world that shapes the dominant culture has been created by the powerful, solely to further their own interests. The "powerful" modernists, according to many postmoderns, are white heterosexual men whose constructed world allows them to maintain power. They appeal to their own vision as objectively *true* only in their attempt to mask its tyrannical function.

What is God doing? Postmodernity offers the church an opportunity to recover the truth that "the fear of the LORD is the beginning of wisdom" (Prov. 9:10). Postmoderns have seen truly that human reason always functions in *some* light. But the "light" of scientistic idolatry has failed indeed to disclose liberating knowledge—instead, it has shown the way to further uncertainty and oppression. But the postmodern option of relativism—rejecting the very notion of truth—only makes the problem worse. Only by the light of the gospel will we find our way to the life-giving order of God's creation. Knowledge is a positive gift of God when it is employed in the service of God and other people. But when we bow down to it as a god, it brings only injustice, tyranny, and death.

MODERNITY HAS BROUGHT MANY INJUSTICES

Postmoderns protest the injustices arising from the modernist story, and this protesting sensibility has moved to the center of our culture today. For postmoderns, our colonialist legacy has led to the oppression of third world nations for our own advantage. The wealth of the West was built upon the slavery of Black people. Many other minorities have been marginalized and oppressed, including women, the poor, people who are gay, transgender persons, First Nations peoples and other people of color, and adherents of non-Christian religions. The environment too has become a victim of our lust for domination and consumption. The postmodern spirit identifies with victims of the oppressive modernist story and seeks justice for them, especially through critical theory and identity politics. The growing dominance of these two features of the progressive agenda is further evidence of the failure of the modernist liberal vision to bring the justice it promised. But new kinds of discrimination and injustice inevitably attend those seeking to root out the old ones.

What is God doing? Christians have a fresh opportunity to rethink their view of justice from a sound biblical foundation. Scriptural justice will differ from both left-wing critical social justice (based on neomarxist postmodern assumptions) and right-wing liberal social justice (based on individualistic assumptions). Biblical justice is based on a clear view of God's order of creation. It requires social space for all people to express themselves as God's image in various tasks and areas of life, and for all human institutions to function according to God's Word. It requires just and fair access to resources to allow us all to fulfill our calling. Seeking justice aims to set things right according to God's order in creation so that every creature may flourish in the role God has given it. Only a wide view of God's creation, order, and justice can embrace the good insights—*and* correct the deficiencies—of humanistic views of justice, whether "progressive" or "conservative."

MODERN STRUCTURES AND INSTITUTIONS HAVE FAILED

Postmoderns distrust the structures and institutions created from within the modernist story. The heirs of the Enlightenment believed that if our social, economic, educational, and political institutions were built on the solid foundation of science, they would be neutral and good and would allow truth, peace, and justice to flourish. "Woke" progressives, on the whole, believe these structures to be radically unjust and of benefit only to the "powerful," who are often caricatured as white, male, heterosexual, wealthy—and Christian. Such distrust of social, political, economic, and legal institutions is by now not confined to those who identify as progressives; it is pervasive across the whole ideological spectrum. The press, the judicial system (including the Supreme Court), public schools, the university, the electoral system, the FBI, the CIA, the government, and even the Constitution itself are currently viewed with deep suspicion by many. As I write, the headlines are dominated by allegations of "fake news," the bias of Republican appointees to the courts, and "stolen elections." It seems that all institutions are now judged to be deeply compromised, unjust instruments of one political ideology or the other.

What is God doing? The light of science could not lead society to create neutral and beneficial institutions. As believers, our challenge is to recover the biblical understanding of wisdom: the wise discernment of God's creational order for all societal institutions, pursued in the fear of the Lord by the light of the gospel.

HUMAN NATURE IS NOT UNIVERSAL

The modernist view of human beings was that we are autonomous rational individuals able to master the creation by applying our scientific reason. This identity was believed to be fixed and universal; there is but one nature common to all humanity. But postmoderns offer new answers to the question of what it means to be human.

Postmoderns no longer believe the story of progress that provided the narrative context for this shared human identity. Moreover, they contend that belief in that story, based on the rational individual, has produced much injustice—and this sense of injustice has bred widespread disillusionment. Postmoderns consider that this concept of a universally shared human identity was itself socially constructed during the Enlightenment. And what is *constructed* can of course be *deconstructed*—and *rejected*, if it is deemed to be oppressive.

And so, we find postmodern humanity adrift, asking the urgent existential question, Who are we? The postmodern answer is that there is no abiding core, no basic humanity. Rather, we construct our own identity and can change it if we so desire. Our humanness is like soft clay to be shaped into whoever or whatever we choose. The devotion to *personal autonomy* espoused in humanism reaches its pinnacle here—there are no limits to our freedom, not even our given biological makeup or the constraints of nature. It is the right of individuals to define themselves and their own ultimate good as they please.

Throughout history, human identity has been forged by participating in a community with a shared story. In the West, our shared cultural story is failing, and our communities are fragmenting. Postmoderns are in search of identity. Those aspects of being human that they believe to have been suppressed in the modernist story are often now seized upon as the clues to discovering authentic identity, including race, ethnicity, gender, and sexuality.

What is God doing? This new missionary setting offers the church the opportunity to recover and celebrate the true human identity. The new identity markers favored by postmoderns are just as reductionist as the old modernist ones. But true human identity rests in our creation and restoration by God as told in the biblical story: We are his image, restored to him in the likeness of Jesus Christ by the Spirit to live together as part of a new humanity. Only when we live into *this* identity can we find the true life all human beings long for.

ENTERING A NEW MISSIONARY SITUATION

So how are Christians to respond to the new postmodern spirit of our time? As a believing community, we are entering a new missionary situation. We need to sympathetically understand the postmodern spirit at work among our neighbors—and among us!—and not react in knee-jerk fashion. Fleeing from modernist idols into the arms of new postmodern ones is not an option. Nor is adopting an ignorant fear of postmodernity that leads us to hanker after the "good old days" of modernity.

As we take our stand on the gospel, we must engage in dialogue from within the biblical story to discern the spirits of our culture, to see both its genuine insights and its distortions. As we dialogue with postmodernity, we will see more clearly how the modernist worldview has been shaping our culture for centuries and be able to identify the modernist idols that have brought death. But we must discern also where modernism's true insights into creation have brought life. We must then go on to identify similar idols—and insights—in postmodernity. It has recovered many life-giving dimensions of the creation long suppressed by modernity but has also unleashed new destructive spirits. The present mix of modern and postmodern waters is our own cultural environment. In it, we must struggle for discernment together, in community and in the light of the gospel. Our call is to embrace the life-giving currents and reject the death-dealing spirits of both modernity and postmodernity.

A DISTINCTIVE COMMUNITY TODAY

Our postmodern world worships autonomous freedom. In the areas of gender and sexuality, we are convinced that we are free to construct ourselves in whatever way we choose. Yet God has created humanity in his own image as male and female and has ordered creation for a man to be joined to a woman in the bond of marriage: this defines the bounds of human sexuality. And it must be stated clearly: This does not constrain human freedom but is the very ground for the good and flourishing of humanity. As believers we need to affirm and to conform to God's creational order for gender and sexuality. But we must meanwhile acknowledge that we too are sexually damaged to some degree and that sexual brokenness comes in many forms. *All* of us share in that brokenness. Humility, love, and sympathy should characterize our interactions with our gay and transgender neighbors.

Our postmodern world is one of uncertain relativism and bewildering pluralism and has concluded that *there is no true story*. We have, as Nietzsche put it, wiped away the horizon of history with a sponge. In this context we must be committed to the truth that is in Jesus Christ, and to Scripture itself as the true story of the world. This commitment should be bold in the face of the overwhelming tides of relativism that threaten us, yet that boldness must be tempered by love and humility. Jesus Christ *is* the truth—there is no room for wavering here. But as fallible and erring followers of Jesus, we don't always see or live the truth clearly. And it is evident that our misunderstandings (willful or otherwise) through history *have* brought oppression and pain where we should have brought freedom and healing. We would do well to recognize that in our own yet-sinful state, we too are often guilty of acting unjustly and without love. We must remain open to correction in the light of Scripture. Moreover, we need to be kind, gentle, and respectful with those who disagree with us. They are our neighbors. And they could be right.

Our postmodern world is fixated on achieving justice for those who have historically been mistreated through the modernist story. Concern for social, economic, racial, and ecological justice is more evident and more public today than perhaps at any time in history. This is partially the fruit of the Christian faith. We need to be a people of mercy and justice, carefully distinguishing a truly biblical understanding of justice from both critical justice and classical liberal justice. Biblical justice is that mighty source of human flourishing that the prophet Amos longed to see: "Let justice roll on like a river, righteousness like an ever-flowing stream" (Amos 5:24). It came at last to fruition in the life, death, and resurrection of Jesus. And we follow Jesus in seeking first the justice of the kingdom for the sake of the world (Matt. 6:33).

CHAPTER 18

The Spirit of Economic Modernity

The reality of our world is not the end of grand narratives, but the increasing dominance of the narrative of economic globalization. . . . Globalization as an ideology has grown out of the older idea of progress but differs in that it reduces progress to economic growth, which is supposed to bring all other goods in its train. . . . It entails a worldview, a notion of the human good.

—*Richard Bauckham*, Bible and Mission: Christian Witness in a Postmodern World

LA DOLCE VITA

In 1960, Federico Fellini released one of the greatest movies of all time, *La Dolce Vita* (*The Sweet Life*). It is set in Rome during Italy's postwar "economic miracle," when industry was growing rapidly, a consumer society was emerging, and the Roman Catholic Church was in decline. The new fruits of material abundance were very much on display in the glamorous lives of the rich and famous. In the film, Marcello Rubini, a tabloid journalist, yearns for the sweet life he sees among these movie stars, aristocrats, artists, and intellectuals. He is seduced by the wealth and fame, the sex and lust for pleasure, on display in the Via Veneto. The story is set out in seven nonlinear scenes that together paint a picture of Marcello's fruitless search to find happiness and contentment—the good life. *La dolce vita* cannot be found in the hedonistic lifestyles Marcello so envies.

Fellini's film struggles with a perennial human question: What *is* the good life? What brings true happiness, fulfillment, meaning, and purpose? The story of economic modernity and the consumer culture offers one answer: Material prosperity is the good life. But Fellini's film says that it is not so.

Modern Enlightenment humanism is collapsing into postmodernity under the weight of its own idolatry. But one central aspect of the modern story survives, flourishes, and continues to shape the way we live. It is the *economic* vision for society embedded in modernism, and it is no longer simply the story of the West but now part of a *global* story that has spread to all the nations of the earth.

THE CHIEF END OF HUMAN LIFE

Q 1: What is the chief end of human life?

A: To know God by whom we have been created.

Q 2: Why do you say this?

A: Because God has created us, and placed us in this world in order that he should be glorified in us. And indeed, it is right that since he is the author of our life we should return it to his glory.

Q 3: What is the supreme good of human life?

A: It is the same thing.[1]

All human beings want the sweet life, or, as Jesus puts it, "life to the full" (John 10:10). The apostle Paul calls it "life that is truly life" (1 Tim. 6:19). As John Calvin's catechism makes clear, that life is found in knowing God, serving him in creation, and reflecting his glory in the world. He is himself our chief end and supreme good. Serving him brings ultimate satisfaction, joy, fulfillment—life that is truly life. As we serve God, we become more fully human, formed more and more into his image and likeness. And we form a society that reflects the God we serve.

When humanity turned from God in rebellion, this calling from God did not simply vanish. We continued to be serving creatures (after the fall) but transferred our worship and allegiance to created things. We looked for satisfaction, fulfillment, and true life in some other aspect of creation and developed our cultures to pursue these "gods." For every culture is formed upon its people's answer to the fundamental religious question: What is the chief end of human life?

In the West, we serve the "gods" of economic growth and material prosperity, thinking that there we'll discover our chief end, our supreme good, our true life. As the Enlightenment economists might have answered the question, the supreme good according to this vision lies in amassing the greatest possible abundance of objects suitable for our gratification and securing the greatest freedom to enjoy them.

This "supreme good" has been at the core of Western culture since the eighteenth century, unifying and shaping it. All other parts of our culture—including education, technology, and government—play their role in relation to that single organizing core. In this chapter I will briefly trace the "making of an economic society," which is the goal around which our society is unified, with the creation of wealth as its gravitational center.

ROOTS OF ECONOMIC MODERNITY

The West was converted to a new religious vision in the eighteenth century; at its core was a deep and unwavering belief in progress. Human beings could guide human history to a place where justice, peace, happiness, and (especially) material prosperity would cover the earth as the waters cover the sea. Scientific reason, technology, and the rational organization of society would help humankind to achieve this goal.

A key figure was Adam Smith, whose expression of the Enlightenment faith would become dominant the world over. He was a moral philosopher (since economics was not yet its own discipline but was a part of ethics) who lived in a time of deprivation and abject poverty in much of Europe. "No society can surely be flourishing and happy," he said, if "by far the greater part of the numbers are poor and miserable."[2] His goal was noble: to increase the amount of material goods available and so to improve the living conditions of the poor.

But, since he was a typical Enlightenment thinker, Smith turned to the new humanist faith to help accomplish that goal. As a deist he believed there were mechanical natural laws built right into the world that must (he thought) be obeyed to guide human society to a better future. Like the

214

law of gravity, the natural laws of economic life, especially manifest in the "invisible hand" of the market, must be discerned and obeyed. Scientific rationality, natural law, technology, progress, the mechanism of cause and effect—these were the tenets of Smith's Enlightenment faith.

For Smith, the goal of the progress story was material abundance. The rational and technological organization of economic life, production, and distribution would lead to this goal. Through the accumulation of capital, the business owner could acquire better technology and mechanize labor. By specializing and mechanizing labor, the country would dramatically increase the output of goods.

At the root of all economic activity, Smith believed, was selfishness and greed—individuals acting in accordance with their own rational self-interest. But the invisible hand of the market would harmonize these conflicting self-interests, producing great wealth and prosperity for all. Gradually, this growing wealth would trickle down to benefit even the poorest in society.

The idolatry of Smith's vision emerges at two levels. First, Smith isolates one social goal—economic growth and prosperity—as the chief end of human life. "For what purpose," he asks, "is all the toil and bustle of this world?" His answer? The pursuit of wealth for all.[3] This, he believed, was what would make humanity truly happy. And secondly, he identifies certain social means to enable us to achieve this end: innovative technology and the free market. For Smith, the processes of production, distribution, and consumption are no longer embedded in the broader social and political life of the culture. Rather, he offers a comprehensive vision that functions as "a blueprint for a whole new mode of social organization" built around the production, flow, and consumption of goods and services.[4] He seizes on but one aspect of human life as the key to forming a society in which we might find our supreme good. The economic dimension of social life is extracted from the rest. And Smith's work was soon to reshape all of Western society in its image.

For Smith and other classical economists, this vision for society was just a dream. In the next century, the Industrial Revolution turned vision into reality and set the trajectory for Western society to the present day. The symbol of this new industrial era was the factory, a rationally organized economic institution that could dramatically increase production by specializing, dividing, and mechanizing labor. The result of these innovations was tremendous economic growth in those countries that industrialized.

From 1840 to 1900, Britain's gross national product tripled from $300 to over $900 per capita. (By contrast, Portugal did not industrialize, and its GNP grew from $250 to just $260 in the same period.) In the United States between 1859 and 1899, the number of factories increased from 140,000 to 512,000, and the value of manufactured goods rose from $1.9 billion to an astonishing $13 billion.

THE CREATION OF AN ECONOMIC SOCIETY

The word "capitalism" describes this new form of society, organized around economic production and growth. Capitalism "reorganized the social structure for the purpose of manufacturing, production, and consumption," and in so doing "changed the shape of our world."[5] The growth of capitalism continued through the twentieth century. What remained constant through the various stages of that growth was the totalitarian influence of economics on the formation of Western culture.

During the medieval period, the authority of the institutional church played a totalitarian role, and often it usurped the authority proper to the state, family, educational institutions, and other elements of society. In communist systems, the state similarly takes on a totalitarian role, and frequently encroaches on other spheres of life. Today in the West, the tyrannical authority of economic life distorts many aspects of our cultural and social life, usurping the role of other legitimate social spheres and institutions.

Consider what can happen to marriage when household income becomes its primary concern. How is the family affected when planning for children is based on how they may affect the financial bottom line? What happens to education when it is focused primarily on forming the next generation to contribute to a growing economy? What happens to politics when its primary concern is to protect the individual rights of consumers or the rights of wealthy corporations? What happens to sports when corporations and the media turn professional teams into businesses and inject large amounts of money into them? What happens to human sexuality when it is used primarily as a merchandising tool—or bought and sold as just another commodity?

Every area of social and cultural life in the West has been affected by economic considerations, with their creational integrity thereby deformed. God's blessing for humanity comes when each area of human life remains in the rightful place, plays the proper role, and functions in the way God intended.

Of course, much good has come to humankind through economic progress. Industrialized nations have done much to discover and release the economic potentials latent in creation, bringing increasing wealth and prosperity in keeping with God's intention for humanity to enjoy and delight in his creation. But this singular power and potential now drives the whole of society. We have made of this good part of human life the *supreme* good and our chief end: the center of human culture. Economic progress is the idol to which we have sacrificed virtually everything else. We have formed an idolatrous society in our vain search for the sweet life.

ECONOMIC MODERNITY AND THE PROGRESS STORY

What has happened to the optimistic progress story of the eighteenth century? The twentieth-century postmodern backlash that continues to this day is evidence of modernism's collapse. The idols of the Enlightenment failed to deliver the peace, happiness, justice, and equality they had promised. But because modernism *did* deliver on the *one* promise of material prosperity—at least for some—the economic version of the progress story has managed to survive the assault of postmodernism in the twentieth century and remains the dominant cultural force today.

Throughout the past century, the world in general saw a steady rise of comfort, especially in the West. But one further step was necessary to complete the capitalist revolution—to extend it to *all* the nations of the earth. They too needed to share in this religious vision, to partake of the "good life" of material prosperity. If one could create a global market, the good news of material prosperity might indeed go to the ends of the earth.

At the beginning of the twentieth century, when optimism and confidence in progress toward material prosperity was at its height, the wealthy Scottish American industrialist Andrew Carnegie wrote an essay entitled *The Gospel of Wealth*. His tone in the book is positively evangelistic. He proclaims the "good news" that industrial capitalism will bring bounty, material development, and progress to the human race, reaching to all peoples and solving the problem of world poverty. In words reminiscent of the angels' good news concerning the birth of Jesus (Luke 2:10–14), Carnegie proclaims "the true gospel concerning wealth, obedience to which is destined some day to solve the problem of the rich and the poor, and to bring 'Peace on earth, among men good will.'"[6]

And by the late twentieth century, economic modernity had indeed taken this next step. The good news of material wealth had begun its spread to the ends of the earth. Economic modernity had become a *global* culture.

ECONOMIC MODERNITY AS A GLOBAL CULTURE

Sometimes globalization is thought of as merely the formation of a world-wide economic system, a market that connects all national economies and makes them one. This process is facilitated by relaxing or eliminating trade barriers and by the rise of communication and information technology, air travel, the proliferation of multinational and transnational corporations, and the development of financial capital.

But true globalization is about much more. It is the global spread of secular humanism's economic faith, which seeks to shape the public ethos and the whole structure of culture. This vestige of late modern humanism is a worldview driven by a deeply idolatrous economic spirit. The same comprehensive religious vision that formed Europe over many centuries has now become a global worldview. Because of its pervasive influence, Western approaches to education, politics, popular culture and the arts, knowledge and law, technology, and social relationships are all expanding across the globe. But this new globalism remains rooted in economic idolatry.

Assessments of how economic modernity has impacted the cultures of the world vary dramatically. Those in the *celebration* camp laud the economic opportunities and wealth created by the global spread of capitalism and the creation of a global market. Theirs is the old motto, "A rising tide lifts all boats." Indeed, most countries are wealthier, and the economic lot of many people worldwide has improved as a result of more liberal global trade. And with the increased material prosperity, many other modern blessings of the West have begun to be shared worldwide, in such areas as medical care and education, for example.

On the other side of the argument are those in the *crisis* camp, who bring heavy criticisms against the sometimes devastating results of globalization driven by economic forces, including environmental destruction, a growing gap between rich and poor both globally and within nations, the displacement of peoples, the unjust and oppressive business practices of large global corporations, cultural imperialism, and the impoverishment of the dispossessed and marginalized peoples of the world.

The problem we face in assessing these two very different evaluations has to do with the nature of idolatry itself. On the one hand, even idolatry can release much of the life-giving potential of many areas of creation as they are discovered and developed. There is no question that the gifts of economic modernity are now possessed by many beyond the West: advancements in science and technology; insights into political, economic, and educational life; and material wealth have improved the quality of life of *many* peoples, and that is something to be celebrated. On the other hand, idolatry inevitably also brings distortions and injustices that dehumanize. "Precisely because the culture of economism is a quasi-religion," says Cambridge economist Jane Collier, "with the pretense of encompassing the totality of life and of bringing happiness and fulfillment, we find ourselves obliged from a Christian point of view to denounce it as a dehumanizing idolatry."[7] The injustices of our economic practices have been devastating and dehumanizing.

Take, for example, the global market, which, if it were truly free and just, could benefit all peoples. But we can see that it does not do so in practice. Wealthy countries have the power to shape the market to their advantage, to control the currencies that are used in it and the global institutions that regulate it. They can force smaller countries to open their markets to Western exports while protecting their own from imports. Corporations dominate the global market and make decisions in the interests of their Western investors. Cheap labor and the control of resources channel goods from poor countries to the rich West. The reality is that an unjust global market has produced a massive imbalance of wealth and crippling debt for many "third world" countries, especially in Africa.

N. T. Wright speaks of the "massive economic imbalance of the world" as "the major task that faces us in our generation" and the primary moral issue of our time. "The present system of global debt is the real immoral scandal, the dirty little secret—or rather the dirty enormous secret—of glitzy, glossy Western capitalism. Whatever it takes, we must change this situation or stand condemned by subsequent history alongside those who supported slavery two centuries ago and those who supported the Nazis seventy years ago. It is that serious."[8]

This is not meant to demonize globalization per se, or the global market, economic growth, or Western culture. A global market *can* be structured in a just and stewardly way. Responsible and sustainable economic growth *is* a legitimate part of cultural endeavor *when it is kept in its rightful place*. And Western culture, like every other culture, has many good gifts to share with the world. If Christians are to be faithful in this global context for the good of all people and all creatures, we must understand the idolatrous vision that has led to the injustices. God calls us to be a healing presence, to be agents of compassion, mercy, and justice. He calls us to be, together, a glimpse of the new humanity that will inhabit the new creation. What does this look like in our globalized, economic, modern world? To answer that question more fully we need to turn to look at the flip side of an economic society: a consumer culture.

CHAPTER 19

The Spirit of Consumerism

In a nation that was proud of hard work, strong families, close-knit communities, and our faith in God, too many of us now tend to worship self-indulgence and consumption. . . . But we've discovered that owning things and consuming things does not satisfy our longing for meaning. We've learned that piling up material goods cannot fill the emptiness of lives which have no confidence or purpose.

—Jimmy Carter, "Crisis of Confidence"

In 1965, the song "(I Can't Get No) Satisfaction" topped music charts on both sides of the Atlantic, and the Rolling Stones were second in worldwide popularity next to the Beatles. Today, "Satisfaction" remains one of the most popular songs ever recorded.

The song begins quietly, with a single wistful voice ("I can't get no—satisfaction"), building in intensity and volume as the band joins in on the vocals ("'cause I try and I try and I try and I try") until Mick Jagger wails, "I can't get no—satisfaction!" The verses catalog the singer's disappointments and frustrations. It seems that all the toys, the fame, the "sex, drugs, and rock and roll" that come your way when you finally become a rock star in the world's second most popular band just aren't enough. Today, some sixty years on, that song continues to express the heart-cry of a consumer society; there is an emptiness there that neither goods nor experiences can fill.

In the heart of every human being is a thirst for life that we attempt to satisfy with material goods (houses, cars, technological "toys," clothes, food, and drink) and with experiences (travel, gaming, sports, entertainment, music, social media, sex). These things are all aspects of the good creation given to us by God to be enjoyed, but when we seek life itself from them, and when we begin to shape society around pursuing them, they will always fail to satisfy.

The prophet Jeremiah offers a vivid picture of this futile quest when he quotes God as saying, "My people have forsaken me, the spring of living water, and have dug their own cisterns, broken cisterns that cannot hold water" (Jer. 2:13). The people of ancient Israel, like us, were looking for life in all the wrong places, putting created things above the Creator. The Bible calls that idolatry. And idols will never fail to fail.

> Looking for life without God, we find only death . . .
> pursuing pleasure, we lose the gift of joy.[1]

EIGHTEENTH- AND NINETEENTH-CENTURY ROOTS

Consumerism is a *religious* spirit that dominates the waking lives of many twenty-first-century people. But it wasn't inevitable: Our consumer society did not just happen; we created it. It may be helpful to briefly trace its history here so that we can gain some critical distance from a cultural phenomenon that is so near to us that we find it difficult to see.

Consumer society is rooted in the religious vision of the Enlightenment, where faith in progress toward a better world was often depicted in images of paradise or the new creation, images borrowed from Scripture. Scientific reason, technological innovation, and the rational organization of society were supposed to lead us to this paradise of material abundance, along with the leisure time to enjoy it all. This vision was implemented in the nineteenth-century Industrial Revolution and was wildly successful in producing economic growth.

THE GAP BETWEEN PRODUCTION AND CONSUMPTION

The late nineteenth century witnessed unprecedented growth in wealth and the production of goods; in fact, more goods were produced than could be consumed. While the American population grew 3 percent from 1860 to 1920, industrial production increased 12 percent. In 1927, US textile mills could produce in six months all the cloth needed annually. Fourteen percent of the shoe factories could produce enough shoes for everyone, and a single cigarette factory could make *in one day* more cigarettes than all Americans could smoke in a year. Production so far outstripped demand that by the early twentieth century, the United States was suffering from consumptive satiation.

Faced with the prospect of a complete halt to economic growth, the country's leaders had but two options. The first—advocated by many scholars, and religious and labor leaders—was to stabilize production to meet current demands, reduce working hours to make sure everyone had work, and increase free time, allowing workers to develop other areas of their lives. In 1930, Kellogg's cereal company was one of the few businesses to choose this option, reducing their work week to thirty hours and raising wages to partially compensate for the reduced hours of labor. Kellogg's employees, though now earning slightly less than before, were in favor of these changes, revealing in subsequent interviews that their reduced working hours had increased their time with family, fostered the growth of various hobbies, led to more reading and the cultivation of the mind, and contributed to the public life of communities, among other benefits. When new owners of the company later offered those employees more money for longer hours of work, they were turned down. Kellogg's experiment lasted until 1985.

BOOSTING CONSUMPTION

But another option was available to United States leaders dealing with overproduction in the early 1900s, and that was to pump up consumption. This was the *consumer* solution: Persuade people to spend more money, raise levels of demand to meet the supply, expand the markets, increase consumption, and keep the economy growing. This was the choice of most economists and manufacturers. They were committed to selling it to the masses and influencing public policy to promote it, and their choice won the day.

The primary way they found to boost consumption was to stir up dissatisfaction with then-current levels of consumption. In 1927, an industrial consultant preached the new economic *gospel of consumption*, which was to form workers in the lifestyle of consuming. A 1929 presidential committee report enthusiastically predicted a rosy economic future in which "we have a boundless field before us. . . . There are new wants which will make way endlessly for newer wants, as fast as they are satisfied."[2] That year, the director of General Motors Research published an essay entitled "Keep the Consumer Dissatisfied," arguing that the key to economic prosperity is to create organized dissatisfaction. GM had begun to make annual model changes, and their strategy was to employ sophisticated advertising techniques to make consumers unhappy with the cars they already owned. People had to be convinced that, no matter how much they had, it still wasn't enough.

The merchandisers did not always find it easy to mold the consumer imagination and root out old, settled habits. For example, the Protestant Christian tradition had long taught the virtues of frugality and thrift and warned against the dangers of riches. This heritage was embedded in much of the American psyche. So too was a lack of trust in mass-produced goods marketed by strangers: Americans were accustomed to dealing with skilled artisans and trading face-to-face. There was a need for a training process.

TEACHING A CONSUMER WAY OF LIFE

How could people be indoctrinated into the "benefits" of a consumer way of life? They had to be taught. A consumer society had to be constructed. A variety of incentives to lavish spending were introduced, including money-back guarantees and time payment options. Advertisers worked to link certain brands and items with images of status and upward social mobility, and to associate consumerism with American patriotism. Popular articles on the public good of consumerism were published in newspapers and magazines. Films, magazines, and books encouraging consumption were placed in libraries and schools. Corporate lobbyists pressed elected officials to reshape government policy to reflect manufacturers' interests.

All of these methods became common practice in the United States, but *advertising* came to be the engine that would drive consumer culture. Heavy resources were invested into probing its potential. The insights of psychology were scoured to learn the art of manipulation, to disciple a culture into the new, consuming way of life.

Advertising can create *new wants*. The famous and influential Thompson Red Book of Advertising (1901) promoted advertising as an educational

224

power that could teach and train people that they had wants they didn't know they had.

Advertising can sell the vision of the *good life*. People buy goods only if they see in them the possibility of satisfying a need, gratifying a dream, generating the thrill of a new experience. People buy goods not simply to possess them but to enjoy what they bring with them. It is not just the new car that you are after; you want the thrill that comes in driving it or the social status it brings. You buy a certain brand of beer not necessarily for how it tastes but for the image that advertisers have linked to it. Advertising was remarkably successful in capturing consumers' imaginations with such glimpses of the good life.

Advertising can help make people *dissatisfied* with what they have and the lives they live. "Can't get no satisfaction"? Mission accomplished.

A SECOND WAVE OF CONSUMPTION

The first wave of consumerism ended abruptly with the Great Depression of the 1930s. A war economy soon followed, and mass consumption was put on pause for a time, though it never strayed far from the social imagination. A second wave of consumerism began just after the Second World War, in perhaps the greatest era of economic expansion and production in the history of the world, which carries on to our own day.

In 1952, President Harry Truman established a commission to survey the postwar potential for economic development. The report of that commission enthusiastically endorsed "economic Growth" as "sacrosanct," based on an ever-increasing output of consumer goods and "ever more luxurious standards of consumption." Economist John Kenneth Galbraith points to the report's spelling of "Growth" with a capital G, indicating that a "certain divinity is associated with the word."[3]

The new strategy to promote consumption was expressed vividly by one economist and retail analyst of the time: "Our enormously productive economy . . . demands that we make consumption a way of life, that we convert the buying and use of goods to rituals, that we seek our spiritual satisfaction, our ego satisfaction, in consumption."[4] The biblical notion of cultural idolatry could hardly be expressed more clearly.

Other approaches to stimulate consumption were generated, including planned obsolescence—intentionally producing inferior products that would not last but would be discarded and replaced. Accompanying this, and building on psychology's insights, was the use of advertising to manipulate buyers by fostering perceived obsolescence. The goal was that consumers would feel the need to own something newer or better than what they had—or could be persuaded to replace it sooner than necessary. During the 1920s, radio was a powerful advertising tool, reaching into the homes and imaginations of the masses. But when the even more potent technology of television became available, powerful visual images began fomenting dissatisfaction with old things and old ways, stirring up new desires in order to sell the "good life."

OUR CONSUMER WORLD

All of these strategies adopted by producers, marketers, and advertisers are familiar to us today. New technology in communications and ever more sophisticated psychological techniques to manipulate consumer behavior have boosted the power and extended the reach of their messaging.

Our consumer world continues to fan the flame of desire for goods, but perhaps even more so today it has turned to an expanding array of *experiences*. While the negative results of consumerism are somewhat better known today and have encouraged some of us to adopt "simple living" and "minimalist" lifestyles, these remain on the margins. Consumer culture still dominates.

When you form a culture in the image of your god, inevitably, it turns to form *you* into *its* image. We have allowed more and more of our lives to become mere *experiences* to be consumed. Our attitudes toward sex, marriage, relationships, sports, music, and many other good things in our lives have been deeply conditioned by the cultural attitudes of consumerism: *If it no longer suits or satisfies me, or if something better, brighter, shinier, or simply newer is available, I should cheerfully discard what I had and take up something else in its place.* Sadly, this has invaded even the congregation, as sometimes we have allowed it to become a mere vendor of religious goods and services. Our musical praise, preaching, children's and youth ministries, "mission" trips, and spirituality itself have too often become mere commodities for "religious" consumption.

How are we as Christians to live faithfully in the consumer story of our culture?

ANALYZING OUR CONSUMER CULTURE

In his incomparable goodness, God invested the world with many powers and potentials to be discovered and developed, to bless humanity with a rich and abundant life. As these gifts find their rightful place within God's world, humanity flourishes. Idolatry is the human turn to trust in any one of these powers to give us the good life, and then to trust other creational powers or potentials to achieve it for us. It may bring real benefits, at least for a time—who doesn't rejoice in the comforts of abundance we enjoy today?—but ultimately idolatry brings injustice and dissatisfaction.

Cultural idolatry, perhaps the most common way of speaking of sin in the Old Testament, is the organization of the whole of our cultural life around some good creational power that promises the abundant life and seeks creational paths to achieve it. A consumer culture orders society around the ultimate good of consuming goods and experiences.

Romans 1:18–32 offers us a pattern by which to understand our culture. There Paul describes the pagan world of the Roman Empire and offers an analysis of it that is in keeping with both the Old Testament and other Jewish writings of his own day. God's wrath, Paul says, is being visited upon the Roman Empire because of its turning from God to idolatry. The Romans did not glorify God nor give him thanks but exchanged the truth of God for a lie and worshiped and served created things rather than the Creator. God's wrath is expressed in simply giving humanity what it wants: He "gives them over"—the phrase is repeated three times—to the natural consequences of their idolatry. Their worship of created things rather than the Creator ends only in widespread misery.

What are the rotten fruits of a consumer society? Let me briefly mention four things.

The first two are well-known. On the one hand, the few consume much more than they need, while the many often lack even the basic necessities. In North America and much of the West, the wealth gap between richer and poorer households continues to widen. But globally, the inequality is much worse: a small percentage of the world's richest peoples account for the majority of global consumption while the poorest peoples account for very little. And Americans consume close to a third of the world's resources while representing just over 4 percent of the global population. On the other hand, excessive consumption also threatens the environment. One-third of the earth's resources have already been consumed, while close to two-thirds of what remains has been degraded in some way by overconsumption.

Consumerism harms not only the poor and the environment but also (ironically) those who *seem* to profit most from it. We eat too much, drink too much, play too much, work too much—and pay the price. Consumerism has not produced human flourishing. We were promised that our technology-based consumer culture would give us more free time, yet we seem to have *less* time for family, friendships, sustained leisure, exercise, and volunteer activities. For Christians in particular, there seems to be less time for prayer, for savoring Scripture, and for deep fellowship.

And consumerism has brought other harmful effects to society. The costs of the service sectors of culture, like education and health care, continue to climb as those "industries" try to keep pace with the profits-based business sector. Debt—and the anxiety that comes with it—has grown dramatically. Doctors lay the blame for many of our physical health problems at the door of our orientation as consumers. But perhaps the most pervasive damage to our well-being, as psychologists are increasingly warning us, is the toll on psychological health. Rather than happiness, a consumer lifestyle brings depression, isolation, angst, anger, and dissatisfaction. The more a person pursues as part of a consuming lifestyle, the poorer their quality of life. God has "given us over," it seems, to become victims of our idols.

Finally, there is also an explicit link between consumerism and ungodly behavior. It is true that a consumer society seeks to shape us in subtle ways that do not honor God. But it goes deeper: *The very existence of consumer society depends on the cultivation of ungodly character.* Insatiability, greed, and envy are *required* to keep a consumer economy running; contentment is its enemy. The restless desire for instant gratification boosts the economy; patience and self-control do not. Consumers must remain dissatisfied—never content, never thankful. Selfishness, narcissism, and entitlement advance a consumer culture; self-giving love does not. A wasteful person is a much better consumer than a stewardly person will ever be.

And what is true of us is true also of our children, targeted early as consumers by those with something to sell. "When it comes to targeting kid consumers, we at General Mills," says one of their executives, "follow the Procter & Gamble model of 'cradle to grave.' We believe in getting them early and having them for life."[5] Studies show that children who are indoctrinated early into a consumer lifestyle by advertising become more narcissistic, entitled, impatient, angry, and dissatisfied. Sadly, they come to resemble their consuming parents.

HOW SHOULD WE THEN LIVE?

To receive—and to consume—the good gifts of creation is a blessing, a matter of delighting in God's good creation as we were meant to do. We've been blessed with innumerable gifts: "God . . . richly provides us with everything for our enjoyment" (1 Tim. 6:17). An ascetic spirituality that diminishes the goodness of those good gifts is seriously misguided. The problem comes when the pursuit of these gifts becomes for us *the way to achieve the abundant life*, when our societies are built in homage to the gods of economics and material abundance, and when this produces injustice for the poor and the environment.

As we seek a remedy to the sinful excesses of consumerism, Rabbi Tsvi Blanchard's language of "sacred consumption" and "consecrated consumption" is a great place to begin.[6] Sacred consumption begins by delighting in God's good creation and is characterized by four virtues.

The first is *gratitude*. Paul warns Timothy against deceiving spirits and demonic teaching in false teachers who were trying to get believers to abstain from marriage and from eating certain foods. Paul's response was that "God created [these things] to be received with thanksgiving by those who believe and who know the truth. For everything God created is good, and nothing is to be rejected if it is received with thanksgiving, because it is consecrated by the word of God and prayer" (1 Tim. 4:3–5). Radical gratitude reminds us from whom these gifts come and is an antidote to a grasping acquisitiveness.

The second virtue is *generosity*. In the same letter, Paul addresses those who are wealthy, urging their pastor Timothy to "command them to do good, to be rich in good deeds, and to be generous and willing to share . . . that they may take hold of the life that is truly life" (1 Tim. 6:18–19). Paul commends the (financially struggling) Macedonian church for the fact that "their extreme poverty welled up in rich generosity." He then urges the wealthier Corinthian church to "excel in this grace of giving," imitating the self-giving generosity of Jesus (2 Cor. 8:1–9).

Third, our lives in a consumer society should be characterized by *contentment*. Paul warns against the dangers ahead for those who want to get rich, who will be plunged into ruin and destruction. But for Paul, "godliness

229

with contentment is great gain. . . . If we have food and clothing, we will be content with that" (1 Tim. 6:6–10). The author of Hebrews offers similar instruction: "Keep your lives free from the love of money and be content with what you have" (Heb. 13:5). Contentment is living with an attitude of "enough" in a culture of "never enough."

The final virtue is *stewardship*. A basic assumption of the biblical story is that the world belongs to God and that we have been entrusted with some of it for his glory, to care for ourselves and to serve other people. Stewardship means being entrusted with something that ultimately does not belong to us and being accountable for the way we use it.

Developing such virtues demands that we reflect on and exercise the spiritual practices, rhythms, and habits that will form us for an alternative way of life while we live in the midst of a consumer society, subject to its powerful shaping influence. If we make the deliberate, principled choice to pause in our work to honor the Sabbath (in a work-and-spend culture), periodically exercise self-denial, regularly examine ourselves and repent for our own complicity in the excesses of consumer culture, and habitually give generously, anonymously, and sacrificially, we will be formed into a different pattern of life, one that

- displays contentment and generosity in a world of insatiable desire,
- expresses gratitude in a world of dissatisfaction,
- exhibits sacrificial self-giving love in a culture of self-interest and entitlement,
- manifests joy in a world dominated by a frantic pursuit of consumer experiences,
- shows patience and self-control in a world of instant gratification, and
- embodies stewardship in a world of waste.

CHAPTER 20

A Closing Appeal

Therefore, I urge you, brothers and sisters, in view of God's mercy, to offer your bodies as a living sacrifice, holy and pleasing to God—this is your true and proper worship. Do not conform to the pattern of this world, but be transformed by the renewing of your mind. Then you will be able to test and approve what God's will is—his good, pleasing and perfect will.

—Romans 12:1–2

The Roman Empire of the first century AD was no easy place in which to maintain a faithful Christian witness. Thus, when Paul writes to the young church at Rome—the epicenter of imperial hostility to the faith—his letter is filled with both compassion for their situation along with foundational teaching and admonishment to equip *and* challenge them to be clear about who they are and what their calling before God looks like. Paul spends eleven chapters of the epistle in a careful exposition of the pagan culture that surrounds his readers, the gospel foundation that undergirds them, and the way of life to which God is calling them in this most uncongenial of mission fields.

The church at Rome was set in the midst of a thoroughly pagan culture devoted to the many gods of the classical pantheon. But the clearest and most potent opposition to the worship of the one true God in Rome was its cult of emperor worship. Caesar was commonly referred to as god or god's son, god made manifest, lord or lord of the whole world, and savior. The "Lord's Day" was, for Romans, dedicated to the worship of Caesar. Statues, monuments, architecture, and inscriptions multiplied the claims of Caesar's lordship; processions, festivals, sacrifices, hymns, and poetry honoring him filled the public life of the city; and every person in Rome was compelled to be part of it all. Together, this made for a sophisticated propaganda program designed to mold each citizen into a loyal servant of Caesar in every moment and every arena of life's activities. Those who worshiped and served another lord would have no easy time of it.

Paul offers his readers a double counterweight to the formidable molding force of Roman culture. First, he urges the young church to *understand* Roman idolatry for what it is—at heart, a simple mutiny against the God who made them, expressed in the worship of created things instead of the Creator. The whole cult and culture of Rome and her emperor is based, Paul says, on idolatry, and idolatry is always dehumanizing and leads to injustice, immorality, and death. Second, Paul presents the alternative: the bedrock truth of God's work in Jesus Christ, anticipated in his long and patient history with Israel and revealed at last in truth and power by the life, death, resurrection, and triumph of God's only Son. Christ alone is the Lord to whom all mortal leaders must ultimately bow, the founder of the one, true, everlasting kingdom.

All of this, Paul says, is evidence of God's *mercy*. In the face of the worst examples of human rebellion and depravity, God remains faithful to his covenant. The very existence of the believers in Rome is an emblem of that faithfulness, that mercy.

This is the context of Paul's stirring challenge in the first verses of Romans 12. He urges the believers to give themselves in *total commitment* not to Caesar but to God, as living sacrifices, honoring him in every moment and with every inch of their lives. They are to resist the empire's pressure to *conform* to its own idolatrous image and are instead to submit themselves to the transforming power of Christ at work in their hearts and minds by the presence of his Holy Spirit, the instruction of his Word, the pattern of Jesus's life, and the encouragement and example of his faithful witnesses. Paul understands very well that this is a long, difficult, and costly process of formation, but the alternative is to submit to the conforming pressures of pagan culture. Only through this transformation will the church be able to discern between the good, creational elements of culture and the idolatrous distortions that have wrenched it from God's good purposes.

The challenges faced by the church in twenty-first-century Western culture are no less dangerous, no less hostile to faithful Christian witness, than those faced by the early church in Rome. The idols' names and faces may appear different, but we are still being pressed on every side to conform to our own culture's model of what human life should be. Our culture too has been shaped by systemic idolatry, which assaults us in television, movies, social media, popular music, and the news—urging us relentlessly to be conformed to its image. We should be grateful that, even as one idolatrous empire falls and another rises in its place, God's mercies in Christ Jesus remain constant. Paul's word to us is what it was to his brothers and sisters in first-century Rome: Be as living sacrifices before God, not conforming to the surrounding culture of death, but being transformed by the power of the gospel into what God has always intended us to be. In this new life we are to be a constant demonstration of God's good, pleasing, perfect plan for human flourishing to the world.

The task is not easy, Paul warns us, and we must therefore be committed to it, allow ourselves to be consumed by it, be transformed by it, and stand firm in it. May it be so of us.

NOTES

Chapter 1 An Opening Appeal

1. Jeffery M. Jones, "U.S. Church Membership Falls Below Majority for First Time," *Gallup News*, March 29, 2021, https://news.gallup.com/poll/341963/church-membership-falls-below-majority-first-time.aspx.

2. James Ernest, quoted in Peter Wehner, "The Evangelical Church Is Breaking Apart: Christians Must Reclaim Jesus from His Church," *Atlantic*, October 24, 2021, https://www.theatlantic.com/ideas/archive/2021/10/evangelical-trump-christians-politics/620469/. Ernest is vice president and editor in chief at Eerdmans Publishing.

3. Dallas Willard, *The Great Omission: Rediscovering Jesus's Essential Teachings on Discipleship* (HarperCollins, 2006), xiii.

4. Alan Kreider, *Worship and Evangelism in Pre-Christendom* (Gorgias Press, 2010), 23.

5. Everett Ferguson, *The Early Church at Work and Worship*, vol. 2, *Catechesis, Baptism, Eschatology, and Martyrdom* (James Clarke, 2014), 16.

6. Kreider, *Worship and Evangelism*, 24.

7. Kreider, *Worship and Evangelism*, 10.

8. *The Canons of Hippolytus*, par. 19, trans. Carol Bebawi (Gorgias Press, 2010), 25.

Chapter 2 Reading the Bible as Jesus Did

1. This portrait can be viewed at https://www.nationalgallery.org.uk/paintings/hans-holbein-the-younger-the-ambassadors.

2. Hans Conzelmann, *Die Mitte der Zeit: Studien zur Theolgie des Lukas* [*The Middle of Time: Studies in Luke's Theology*] (Mohr, 1954; Mohr Siebeck, 1993).

3. Ben Witheringon, *The Acts of the Apostles: A Socio-Rhetorical Commentary* (Eerdmans, 1998), 439.

Chapter 4 The True Context of the Gospel

1. Irenaeus, *On the Apostolic Preaching*, trans. John Behr (St. Vladimir's Seminary Press, 2002).

2. Gordon J. Spykman, *Reformational Theology: A New Paradigm for Doing Dogmatics* (Eerdmans, 1992), 176.

3. Abraham Kuyper, *On the Church*, ed. John Halsey Wood Jr. and Andrew M. McGinnis (Lexham, 2016), 51.

4. G. C. Berkouwer, *Sin*, trans. Philip C. Holtrop (Eerdmans, 1971), 240.

5. I owe this diagram to my former colleague Mariano Avila at Calvin Theological Seminary, who used it in the 2013 Opening Convocation. I gratefully use it with his permission.

6. Berkouwer, *Sin*, 235, 239–241, 259–265.

7. Herman Bavinck, *Reformed Dogmatics*, vol. 3, *Sin and Salvation in Christ*, ed. John Bolt, trans. John Vriend (Baker, 2006), 145.

Chapter 5 The Whole Truth of the Gospel

1. C. René Padilla, *Mission Between the Times*, rev. ed. (Langham Monographs, 2010), 63 (emphasis added).
2. C. René Padilla, foreword to John Driver, *Understanding the Atonement for the Mission of the Church* (Herald, 1986), 9–10.
3. N. T. Wright, *Colossians and Philemon*, Tyndale New Testament Commentaries (IVP Academic, 2008), 77.
4. N. T. Wright, *Following Jesus: Biblical Reflections on Discipleship* (Eerdmans, 1994), 19.
5. Herman Bavinck, *The Wonderful Works of God*, trans. Henry Zylstra (Westminster Seminary Press, 2019), 382–83.
6. Bavinck, *Wonderful Works*, 382.
7. Dallas Willard, *The Great Omission: Reclaiming Jesus's Essential Teachings on Discipleship* (HarperOne, 2006), 61.

Chapter 6 Continuing in the Gospel

1. James Boswell, *The Life of Samuel Johnson, LLD*, vol. 3 (1791; University of Chicago Press, 1952), 351.
2. Anthony C. Thiselton, *I Corinthians: A Shorter Exegetical and Pastoral Commentary* (Eerdmans, 2006), 160 (emphasis original).
3. John Calvin, *Institutes of the Christian Religion*, bk. 3, trans. Ford Lewis Battles, ed. John T. McNeill (Westminster, 1960), 548.
4. Martin Luther, *The Large Catechism* 4:65, in *The Book of Concord: The Confessions of the Evangelical Lutheran Church*, ed. Robert Kolb and Timothy J. Wenger (Fortress, 2000), 464.

Chapter 7 Israel's Story, Part 1: The Book of Moses

1. This summarizes a conversation often recorded in Lesslie Newbigin's writings, e.g., *A Walk through the Bible* (Regent College Publishing, 2005), 4. I learned more about this discussion in a conversation with Newbigin in 1995.
2. Craig G. Bartholomew and Michael W. Goheen, *The Drama of Scripture: Finding Our Place in the Biblical Story*, 3rd ed. (Baker, 2024); Craig G. Bartholomew and Michael W. Goheen, *The True Story of the Whole World: Finding Your Place in the Biblical Drama* (Baker, 2020).
3. Mark 12:26 speaks in the singular as "the Book of Moses" (cf. Ezra 6:18; Neh. 13:1) because the first five books of Moses were seen as a single literary unit, meant to be read together as one story.
4. This is a revised version of the diagram in Christopher Wright, *Old Testament Ethics for the People of God* (IVP Academic, 2004), 196.

Chapter 8 Israel's Story, Part 2: Life in the Land

1. Erich Auerbach, *Mimesis: The Representation of Reality in Western Literature*, trans. Willard R. Track (1953; repr., Princeton University Press, 2013), 14–16.

Chapter 11 The Urgency of Reading the Bible as One Story

1. Jeremy Olimb, "Which Stream Will It Be?" Redemption Church Gilbert website, December 4, 2020, accessed May 31, 2024, https://gilbert.redemptionaz.com/articles/which-stream-will-it-be. Olimb is lead pastor of Redemption Church in Gilbert, AZ.
2. Lesslie Newbigin, "Biblical Authority" (unpublished paper, 1997), 2 (emphasis added).

3. N. T. Wright, *Jesus and the Victory of God* (SPCK, 1996), 198.

4. School Act, preamble, accessed August 7, 2024, https://www.bclaws.gov.bc.ca/civix/document/id/consol9/consol9/96412_01.

5. This is a slightly revised version of N. T. Wright's analogy in *The New Testament and the People of God* (SPCK, 1992), 140–43.

6. Christian Reformed Church, *Our World Belongs to God: A Contemporary Testimony* (CRC Publications, 1987), 32, 44–45, accessed August 15, 2023, https://missionworldview.com/wp-content/uploads/2020/06/ea8a85_f0ae5e48aa344ebfb43e88d5d37cb0b7.pdf.

7. Wright, *New Testament and the People of God*, 132.

8. Lesslie Newbigin, *The Other Side of 1984: Questions for the Churches* (WCC Publications, 1983), 23.

9. Lesslie Newbigin, *Gospel in a Pluralist Society* (Eerdmans, 1989), 15.

10. Richard Bauckham, *Bible and Mission: Christian Witness in a Postmodern World* (Baker, 2003), 87.

11. John Carroll, *The Existential Jesus* (Scribe Publications, 2011), 7.

Chapter 12 The Missional Vocation of God's People

1. "Imagine All the People Living Life in Peace," John Lennon (website), accessed June 10, 2024, https://www.johnlennon.com/news/imagine-all-the-people-living-life-in-peace/.

2. "Yoko Ono Net Worth," Celebrity Net Worth (website), accessed June 10, 2024, https://www.celebritynetworth.com/richest-celebrities/yoko-ono-net-worth/.

3. Here I follow the three narrative trajectories sketched by Richard Bauckham in his brilliant little book *Bible and Mission: Christian Witness in a Postmodern World* (Baker, 2003), 27–49.

Chapter 13 A Missional People Today, Part 1: Scattered Life

1. PBS, "Secret State of North Korea," *Frontline* documentary, 2014 season, episode 2.

2. Friedrich Nietzsche, *Thus Spoke Zarathustra: A Book for None and All*, trans. Walter Kaufman (1883; Penguin Books, 1978), 92.

3. Lesslie Newbigin, "The Work of the Holy Spirit in the Life of the Asian Churches," in *A Decisive Hour for the Christian World Mission*, ed. Norman Goodall et al. (SCM, 1960), 28.

4. Abraham Kuyper, "Sphere Sovereignty," in *Abraham Kuyper: A Centennial Reader*, ed. James D. Bratt (Eerdmans, 1998), 461 (emphasis original).

5. C. S. Lewis, *Christian Reflections* (Eerdmans, 1967), 33 (emphasis added).

6. N. T. Wright, *Spiritual and Religious: The Gospel in an Age of Paganism* (1992; repr., SPCK, 2017), 117 (emphasis added).

7. Wright, *Spiritual and Religious*, 117.

8. See, for example, https://joshuaproject.net/ and http://www.operationworld.org/.

Chapter 14 A Missional People Today, Part 2: Gathered Life

1. Václav Havel, *Living in Truth*, ed. Jon Vladislav (Faber & Faber, 1989).

2. Robert E. Webber, "A Call to an Ancient Evangelical Future," Institute for Worship Studies, accessed August 1, 2024, https://iws.edu/wp-content/uploads/2012/07/Call-to-An-Ancient-Evangelical-Future.pdf.

3. Richard Bauckham, *The Theology of the Book of Revelation* (Cambridge University Press, 1996), 160.

4. J. B. Phillips, *Your God Is Too Small: A Guide for Believers and Skeptics Alike* (Touchstone Books, 2004). Originally published in 1952, this book has many newer editions.

5. The Heidelberg Catechism can be viewed online in many places, including https://www.heidelberg-catechism.com/pdf/lords-days/Heidelberg-Catechism.pdf.

6. John Calvin, *Institutes of the Christian Religion 3.20.1–2*, ed. John T. McNeill (Westminster, 1960), 2:850–51.

7. Dallas Willard, *The Divine Conspiracy: Recovering Our Hidden Life in God* (HarperCollins, 1997), 301 (emphasis original).

8. Webber, "Call to an Ancient Evangelical Future," par. 5.

9. Andrew T. Lincoln, *The Letter to the Colossians: Introduction, Commentary, and Reflections*, in *The New Interpreter's Bible*, vol. 11 (Abingdon, 2000), 621.

Chapter 15 A Missionary Encounter with Western Culture Today

1. Hendrik Kraemer, *The Communication of the Christian Faith* (Westminster, 1956), 36.

2. T. S. Eliot, *The Idea of a Christian Society* (Faber & Faber, 1940), 22 (emphasis added, although "individuals" was emphasized in the original).

3. Lesslie Newbigin, *The Other Side of 1984: Questions for the Churches* (WCC, 1983), 23.

4. Lesslie Newbigin, *A Word in Season: Perspectives on Christian World Missions* (Eerdmans, 1994), 99.

5. Richard Bauckham, *James: The Wisdom of James, Disciple of Jesus the Sage* (Routledge, 1999), 174.

6. Philip Jenkins, *The Next Christendom: The Coming of Global Christianity* (Oxford University Press, 2002), 141.

7. Kofi Asare Opoku, "The Relevance of African Culture to Christianity," in *Mid-Stream* 13, nos. 3–4 (Spring-Summer 1974): 156.

8. Lesslie Newbigin, "Gospel and Culture—But Which Culture?," *Missionalia* 17, no. 3 (November 1989): 214.

9. Friedrich Nietzsche, *The Gay Science*, trans. Walter Kaufmann (1882; Vintage, 1974), 181–82.

10. Michael Polanyi, *Personal Knowledge: Toward a Post-Critical Philosophy* (University of Chicago Press, 1958), 265–66. I have modified the image. Polanyi speaks of the "combustion of the Christian heritage in the oxygen of Greek rationalism."

Chapter 16 The Story of the West

1. Richard Tarnas, *The Passion of the Western Mind: Understanding the Ideas That Have Shaped Our World View* (Ballantine, 1991), 320.

2. Pierre-Paul Mercier de la Rivière, *L'Ordre Naturel et Essentiele des Sociétés Politiques*, ed. Edgard Depitre (Paris: Librairie Paul Deuthner, 1910 [1767]), 20 (my translation; emphasis original).

3. Lesslie Newbigin, *The Other Side of 1984: Questions for the Churches* (WCC, 1983), 39.

4. N. T. Wright, *Following Jesus: Biblical Reflections on Discipleship* (SPCK, 1994), 13.

5. John Dewey, *Reconstruction in Philosophy* (Beacon, 1957). All following quotes come from pages 48–49 (emphasis added).

Chapter 17 The Spirit of Postmodernity

1. David Harvey, *The Postmodern Condition: An Inquiry into the Origins of Cultural Change* (Blackwell, 1990), 13.

Chapter 18 The Spirit of Economic Modernity

1. This is my translation of the first portion of the Geneva Catechism.

2. Robert L. Heilbroner, *The Worldly Philosophers: The Lives, Times and Ideas of the Great Economic Thinkers*, rev. 7th ed. (Simon & Schuster, 1999), 48.

3. Heilbroner, *Worldly Philosophers*, 58.

4. Heilbroner, *Worldly Philosophers*, 42.

5. David Wells, *God in the Wasteland: The Reality of Truth in a World of Fading Dreams* (Eerdmans, 1994), 8.

6. Andrew Carnegie, *The Gospel of Wealth and Other Timely Essays* (Century Co., 1900), 19.

7. Jane Collier, "Contemporary Culture and the Role of Economics," in *The Gospel and Contemporary Culture*, ed. Hugh Montefiore (Mowbray, 1992), 122.

8. N. T. Wright, *Surprised by Hope: Rethinking Heaven, the Resurrection, and the Mission of the Church* (HarperCollins, 2008), 216–17.

Chapter 19 The Spirit of Consumerism

1. Christian Reformed Church, *Our World Belongs to God: A Contemporary Testimony* (CRC Publications, 1987), par. 15, accessed July 31, 2024, https://missionworldview.com/wp-content /uploads/2020/06/ea8a85_f0ae5e48aa344ebfb43e88d5d37cb0b7.pdf.

2. "Report of the Committee on Recent Economic Changes of the President's Conference on Unemployment," 1929, xviii, accessed August 12, 2024, https://www.nber.org/system/files/chapters /c4950/c4950.pdf.

3. John Kenneth Galbraith, "How Much Should a Country Consume?" in *Perspectives on Conservation: Essays on America's Natural Resources*, ed. Henry Jarrett (Johns Hopkins Press, 1958), 93, 95.

4. Victor Lebow, "Price Competition in 1955," *Journal of Retailing* (Spring 1955), accessed July 31, 2024, https://100goals.org/wp-content/uploads/2009/05/journal-of-retailing.pdf.

5. Quoted in Roberto De Vogli, *Progress or Collapse: The Crises of Market Greed* (Routledge, 2013), 47.

6. Rodney Clapp, ed., *The Consuming Passion: Christianity and the Consumer Culture* (IVP, 1998), 92, 169.

MICHAEL GOHEEN is professor of missional theology at Calvin Theological Seminary. He is also the director and professor of missional theology at the Missional Training Center in Phoenix, Arizona. He is the author or coauthor of numerous books, including *The True Story of the Whole World*, *The Drama of Scripture*, *Living at the Cross-roads*, *A Light to the Nations*, and *The Church and Its Vocation*. He splits his time between Vancouver, British Columbia, and Phoenix, Arizona.